Organizations and the Bioeconomy

Routledge Studies in Management, Organizations, and Society

This series presents innovative work grounded in new realities, addressing issues crucial to an understanding of the contemporary world. This is the world of organised societies, where boundaries between formal and informal, public and private, local and global organizations have been displaced or have vanished, along with other nineteenth century dichotomies and oppositions. Management, apart from becoming a specialized profession for a growing number of people, is an everyday activity for most members of modern societies.

Similarly, at the level of enquiry, culture and technology, and literature and economics, can no longer be conceived as isolated intellectual fields; conventional canons and established mainstreams are contested. **Management, Organization and Society** addresses these contemporary dynamics of transformation in a manner that transcends disciplinary boundaries, with books that will appeal to researchers, student and practitioners alike.

Organizations and the Bioeconomy

The Management and Commodification of the Life Sciences

Alexander Styhre

Routledge
Taylor & Francis Group
New York London

First published 2012
by Routledge
711 Third Avenue, New York, NY 10017

Simultaneously published in the UK
by Routledge
2 Park Square, Milton Park, Abingdon, Oxon OX14 4RN

First issued in paperback 2017

*Routledge is an imprint of the Taylor & Francis Group,
an informa business*

Library of Congress Cataloging-in-Publication Data
Styhre, Alexander.
 Organizations and the bioeconomy : the management and
commodification of the life sciences / by Alexander Styhre. — 1st ed.
  p. ; cm. — (Routledge studies in management, organizations, and
society ; 18)
 Includes bibliographical references and index.
 1. Biotechnology—Economic aspects. 2. Life sciences—
Economic aspects. 3. Biotechnology industries. 4. Medical
economics. I. Title. II. Series: Management, organizations and society
(London, England) ; v. 18.
 HD9999.B442S79 2012
 338.4'76606—dc23
 2011048805

ISBN 13: 978-1-138-10734-2 (pbk)
ISBN 13: 978-0-415-52926-6 (hbk)

Typeset in Sabon
by IBT Global.

Contents

Preface and Acknowledgments

This book aims to present a reasonably integrated yet complex view of how the life sciences are becoming increasingly subject to economic interests and venturing, not only being produced in laboratories and only slowly and eventually pouring into, e.g., the health care practices in the forms of practices, policies, and recommendations, but also taking the form of goods and services in their own right. The social sciences and the economic sciences at times suffer from an inferiority complex vis-à-vis the sciences and medicine, which are capable of presenting robust data and clinical evidence, in many cases leading to far-reaching social and humanitarian consequences (think, e.g., of the vaccine and what it has meant to life expectancy), while the social sciences can only provide relatively porous empirical evidence, always at the peril of being overturned by new conditions and social preferences and beliefs. However, despite their apparent social merits and implications, even the life sciences—the subset of the sciences examined in this volume—and all the authority and finance invested in their pursuits of revealing the secrets of life, are in need of being transformed into goods and services, practices and routines, obeying the same mechanisms of supply and demand as any other commodity. The commercialization of the life sciences is, however, not exactly the same thing as occurs in other business ventures as there are significant regulatory controls, ethical standards, legislations, and other forms of social regulation and monitoring of the life sciences. At the same time, in the era characterized by neoliberal doctrines promoting and encouraging enterprising and entrepreneurial activities, the life sciences, once a domain of primarily academic interests, by and large separated from short-sighted economic interests and financial considerations and firmly embedded in the academic system, are gradually becoming a major resource to be tapped by innovative and creative social actors. The emergence of heterogeneous practices such as assisted fertilization, cosmetic surgery, new drug development, and biomaterials innovation has its own idiosyncratic developmental paths and histories, but these practices share their roots in the academic life sciences. While some of these life-science based practices and activities are highly legitimate and respected, even admired, others are subject to more debates and discussions (e.g., cosmetic surgery and gestational surrogacy), in many ways instituting a new form of fear of where the life sciences are capable of taking us as well as a skepticism regarding the value and legitimacy of the sciences at large. In other words, the commercialization of the life sciences is not of necessity an unproblematic and socially insignificant transit from the laboratory to the market but rather demands scholarly attention to be properly understood and theorized. Especially in the setting of the business school—a complex and in many ways contradictory institutional milieu operating in the intersection between scholarly pursuits and traditions and practical, managerial interests (readers may consult Khurana's [2007] intriguing account to get an overview of this discussion)—the commercialization of the life sciences needs to be recognized and acquire scholarly attention. As has been emphasized by, e.g., the reviewers of this book proposal and the early drafts of this volume, this is a topic that to date is relatively little explored in the business school setting. Still, this marginal interest for the life sciences and the venturing activities they enable and induce is arguably to be found in the institutional arrangement of the business school and its emphasis on the continuation of research within entrenched domains of expertise rather than being a matter of the social significance of the life sciences per se. This volume is thus an attempt to connect the transdisciplinary domain of research in the life sciences and organization theory and management studies. Even though this volume reviews an extensive literature, the literature is a far from exhausted, and it is thus my hope that more organization theorists and students of management practice will dedicate more time and efforts to the life sciences in the future.

* * *

This work has been written during a transitional period when I have been standing with one foot in one domain and one in another. First, I would like to thank a number of persons I have been collaborating with in research work pertaining to the topics addressed in this volume: Mats Sundgren with whom I have conducted a bit of research over the years, and Rebecka Arman whom I have started to collaborate with recently. In addition, I would like to thank the editor at Routledge, Laura Stearns, for contracting the volume and the anonymous reviewers offering insightful and helpful comments in early drafts of the text. Finally, I would like to thank the Bank of Sweden's Tercentenary Fund for the research grant that enabled some of the empirical and theoretical work demanded to produce the text. In general, I would like to thank my colleagues at the department of Business Administration and Gothenburg Research Institute, School of Business, Economics, and Law, University of Gothenburg, for creative discussions over the years.

Introduction

In the *SCUM Manifesto*, Valerie Solanas (1996: 1) famously portray men (i.e., humans of male gender) as a "biological accident":

> The male is a biological accident; the Y (male) gene is an incomplete X (female) gene, that is, has an incomplete set of chromosomes, In other words, the male is an incomplete female, a walking abortion, aborted at the gene stage. To be male is to be deficient, emotionally limited; maleness is a deficiency disease and males are emotional cripples. (Solanas, 1996: 1)

Solanas lived an adventurous and unhappy life and died alone in a sordid hotel room in the Tenderloin district in San Francisco after being *inter alia* a scientist, play writer, prostitute, and convict (after shooting Andy Warhol in 1968, turning Solanas into a peculiar kind of celebrity). Solanas's disappointment with life and men in general was channeled into the minor classic the *SCUM Manifesto*. Solanas here claims that maleness is a product of genetic deficiency—the male is biologically incomplete and damaged. She has the nerve to accuse nature of being incomplete and causing "biological accidents"; nature and biological systems are thus expected to be understood or even explained on the basis of the aesthetic ideals of symmetry and harmony, in themselves bourgeoisie virtues (McClary, 1987: 58). Solanas might not be wrong in drawing conclusions regarding her experiences with men but *en passant* she unnecessarily brings in nature and places it on the bench of the accused. A complementary view invites us to think of humans in terms of what is emergent and inherently fluid and changeable rather than what may be easily predicted on the basis of algorithms, universal scientific laws, or mere inspections of genetic symmetries. Such romantic views of humanity, thoroughly rooted in commonsense thinking—people don't like to think of themselves as a automata of flesh and blood—are actually contested by a range of advancement of the life sciences, which have made progress based on the very idea that the human body is in fact a form of machinery that operates on the basis of biological pathways and systems. However, unlike the Cartesian view of the body as a framework that may be relatively easily mapped and that more or less functions as a clockwork, the more recent enactments of the body recognize its immense complexity. The human body demonstrates many non-linear and self-regulating mechanisms, both on the level of organs and biological systems and on the microbiological, cellular level. The human "biomachine" is then not what we can expect to fully map and understand in the next decades, but maintaining the idea of the body as a self-regulating yet emerging system helps provide a framework for further joint collaborations.

This book is not intended to present a biophilosophical view of the body, an ontological and epistemological framework for a variety of activities and operations within what is here, after Rose (2007), referred to as the bioeconomy,[1] a handy phrase first used in an OECD report capturing the sense that contemporary capitalism is increasingly based on the capacity to in various ways explore and commercially exploit biological resources (for a particularly celebratory account regarding the future of the life sciences, see Carlson, 2010). "Medical neoliberalism" (Fischer (2009) and "biomediated capitalism" (Pitts-Taylor, 2010) are two other such concepts proposed, but the concept of bioeconomy, in my mind, more effectively connects the two Greek terms *bios*, life, and *oikonomia*, householding, i.e., "economy" at large (see Aristotle, *Politics*, 1255b21). The bioeconomy is then the translating of *bios* into the sphere of economic activity. Rather than seeking to present one single and unified image of the body, this volume draws on what Mol (2002) speaks of as the *body multiple*, Hogle (2009) calls *pragmatic objectivity*, and Cambrosio, Keating, Schlich, and Weisz (2006) refer to as *regulatory objectivity*. Mol (2002) studied the organization of a Dutch hospital and found that different medial disciplines enact their own individual and idiosyncratic—at times even mutually excluding—images of the human body and its organs. The patient is then passed across the boundaries between epistemic cultures or communities, each maintaining its own professional enactment of the human body. For Mol (2002), in the eyes of the medical professions, the body is never whole and unified but emerges as a patchwork of processes and mechanisms each with its own domains of expertise, know-how, and medical practice. Hogle (2009) suggests that when there are no firm standards for what counts as being "objectively true," truth becomes enacted as what is practically possible to accomplish on the basis of such a standard. Objectivity is thus not given by standards outside the core discipline but is rather one of the accomplishments of joint work in a field of expertise (see also Throsby, 2009; Jonvallen, 2006).[2] Both Mol (2002) and Hogle (2009) suggest that biological organisms, just like other natural and social entities or processes, are not "discovered" in the conventional sense of the term but are enacted, agreed upon on the basis of technoscientific evidence, professional ideologies and doctrines, economic possibilities, and public interests. The term *regulatory objectivity* advocated by Cambrosio, Keating, Schlich, and Weisz (2006) here denotes a form of pragmatic objectivity "based on the systematic recourse to the collective production of evidence." That is, what is objectively true is a matter of the procedures used in, e.g., clinical testing, that is, objectivity is what is enacted as the outcome of procedural uses of specific arrangements of resources (humans, objects, technologies, practices). Cambrosio, Keating, Schlich, and Weisz (2006) here contrast "mechanical objectivity" (see Megill, 1994; Daston and Galison, 2007) and "regulatory objectivity":

> [W]hereas mechanical objectivity displaces the bearer of objectivity from the human expert to the object, regulatory objectivity turn the focus away from objects towards collective forms of expertise combining people (clinicians, researchers, administrators, patients, etc.) and objects (entities, instruments, tools, techniques, etc.) connected by specific coordination regiments. Depending on the domain under consideration, these human and non-human elements are attributed to differential weight. (Cambrosio, Keating, Schlich, and Weisz, 2006: 194)

In this view, objectivity is not a matter of revealing innate qualities and conditions of the object of study, but of complying with collectively and professionally enacted procedures for using adequate resources. Furthermore, the regulatory objectivity does not present one single image of the body but operates on a continually changing operative model wherein new data and information are constantly accommodated by the regulatory procedures: "Regulation generates results, raises questions and produces phenomena whose significance feeds into the practices that are the subject of regulatory activities," state Cambrosio, Keating, Schlich and Weisz (2006: 195). Regulatory objectivity is thus related to what Timmermans (2008: 170) speaks of as *disciplinary objectivity*, a form of objectivity "associated with the valuation of tacit knowledge, with the artful application of insight that comes only with learned experience among peers, and with a disdain for standard solutions to complex problems." In this new, "post-mechanical" view of objectivity, the body is what professional expertise and technoscientific instrumentation make it to be. The body becomes multiple, distributed over various technoscientific, experimental systems.

In the bioeconomy, the socio-economic and politico-cultural framework being sketched in this volume, such enactments of both biological systems and their deviations give rise to economic possibilities. That is, in the bioeconomy, biological systems are enacted not strictly on basis of life science data and doctrines and theories, but also in terms of the economic possibilities derived from such enactments. Instead of discussing what the human body *is* in some kind of objectivist or foundationalist sense of the term, the principal interest is what may be accomplished by different enactments. In the bioeconomy, pragmatist (Hogle, 2009), regulatory (Cambrosio, Keating, Schlich, and Weisz, 2006), or disciplinary (i.e., professional) objectivity (Timmermans, 2008) dominates. In a certain sense of the term, the body is what it may accomplish outside the very surface or interior of the body per se; enactment is not strictly located in the body but in the wider framework where theories, technologies, therapies, etc., may be effectively developed and brought to the market. Expressed differently, the key interest in this setting is not the issue of the biological per se (what are biological systems, etc.) but the role of the biological in the socio-economic context of the bioeconomy (how various ideas of the biological systems may lead to social activities and eventually to marketable products or services).

Books published recently with titles such as *Body Shopping: The Economy Fuelled by Flesh and Blood* (Dickenson, 2008), *Human Bazaar: The Market for Human Tissue in the Biotechnology Age* (Andrews and Nelkin, 2001), *Biology Is Technology: The Promise, Peril and New Business of Engineering Life* (Carlson, 2010), *The Baby Business: How Money, Science, and Politics Drive the Commerce of Conception* (Spar, 2006), and Harvard Business Review articles talking about the "life science revolution" (Enriques and Goldberg, 2000) are indicative of the intersection between economic interests and rationales and the possibilities opened up by the life sciences. These titles are apparently supposed to serve as eye-catchers in the constant flow of books and papers being published, and one may get the impression that the authors represent a skeptical attitude toward the economization of human bodies, tissues, and organs. Still, they are capable of capturing something rather fundamental in the late modern period that this volume addresses in an organization theory setting: for perhaps the first time in human history, the full potential of the life sciences is opened up for commercial interests. These titles are thus indicative of what institutional theorists refer to as "shifting institutional logics" (Thornton and Ocasio, 2008; Suddaby and Greenwood, 2005; Lounsbury, 2001; Oakes, Townley, and Cooper, 1998), that is, "taken-for-granted rules guiding behavior of first-level actors" (Reay and Hinings, 2009: 629). In our case, the shift in focus is from thinking of the life sciences as being of primarily scientific interest and being regulated and controlled within the confined professional domain of the sciences to increasingly thinking of the sciences as a public stock of resources from which a variety of goods and services can be produced and marketed.

Instrumental enactments of the human body—surrogacy is a strictly economic relationship, organ donation is a matter of using biological resources wisely, available drugs are defining the illnesses and not the other way around, and so forth—may be debated, but they commonly help humans overcome ethnical and existential concerns and *aporias* and help to advance the possibilities for how to influence and shape life, in turn leading to reconciliations and new issues to debate. This does not suggest that the technosciences and the life sciences more specifically are developed ahead of society at large and that social and cultural beliefs are lagging behind or are even dragged behind the motors of technoscience. Instead, there is a complex and recursive relationship between such beliefs and the technoscientific possibilities; the one would not subsist without the other.

This volume is thus an attempt to point out the intersection between the life sciences, the economy, and the social institutions and beliefs regarding the commodification of life-science products and services. It is not precisely concerned with ontological and epistemological questions, but such issues remain irreducible elements in any theoretical framework addressing technoscience. The key interest here is how life science know-how may be translated into marketable goods or services.

AN ORGANIZATION THEORY PERSPECTIVE
ON THE BIOECONOMY

Zald and Lounsbury (2010: 964) declare that the field of organization studies is no longer making contributions to "policy and public debates": "[O]ur discipline as a whole had become a fragmented set of inward gazing communities, unnecessarily impotent as a critical voice of contemporary societal institutions and contributor to policy and public debates." This kind of call for more socially relevant organization research has been a standing issue in the business school setting for a longer period of time (see, e.g., Pfeffer, 1993; Pfeffer and Sutton, 2001; Starbuck, 2003), a social institution with an idiosyncratic history and tradition, standing with one foot in the world of practice and the other in the world of science and desperately seeking to combine and mutually reinforce the two. Khurana's (2007) thoughtful account of the social role and position of the business school and competing institutional logics regulating the research and teaching underlines how business school faculty are struggling to reconcile various goals and objectives: "Anyone who spends time in an elite business school today knows that it is a place riddled with contradictions. Faculty are hired and promoted on the basis of discipline-oriented research that . . . often has little or no bearing on the practice of management," Khurana (2007: 369–370) argues. As a consequence, the MBA students and the faculty no longer identify with one another, having a sense of shared interests and obligations. For Khurana (2007), the scientific ideology privileges contributions to the formal theory of organizations, while the teaching is based on practically relevant and useful knowledge, not of necessity of scholarly interest (see also Bennis and O'Toole, 2005). For commentators like Pfeffer (1993), a key concern is that organization theory and management research are not capable of influencing policies and politics, and for Pfeffer the role models for organization researchers are the economists, increasingly broadening their domain of jurisdiction and successfully locating their discipline as some kind of master-discipline for all social sciences (Mackenzie, Muniesa, and Siu, 2007; Fourcade, 2006, 2009). Zald and Lounsbury (2010: 975) on their part put the issue of competing institutional logics aside, but rather "[e]ncourage scholars to become more ambitious with their research aims, and more aggressively pursue more integrative theoretical approaches that cross narrow sub-disciplinary specialization." Zald and Lounsbury (2010) thus call for research that is of political and practical relevance, which cuts through the narrow fields of specialisms in organization theory and the social sciences more broadly.

In an attempt at following Zald and Lounsbury's (2010) recommendations, this volume is presenting a thoroughly cross-disciplinary framework examining the intersection between the life sciences and their commercialization.[3] In this account, the very organizing of the activities in the life sciences is treated as a key aspect of the growth of the bioeconomy. It has been frequently pointed out that if there is a key to the success of the sciences, it lies in their organization (Fuchs, 1992: 18). The ability to enact standards, institute procedures, establish routines for peer review, and the formation of institutes and university departments––these are only a few examples of how the sciences have been gradually established (Latour, 1988; Shapin, 1994; Serres, 1995; Koyré, 1959). Many sciences were born as amateur activities or are indebted to pseudo-sciences such as alchemy (Bensaude-Vincent and Stengers, 1996), and only after decades and centuries of hard work and political campaigns have the sciences gained the position they hold today, as the providers of advanced technoscientific know-how, helping humans dominate nature. This volume addresses a relatively recent phenomenon, that of the commercialization of the life sciences, know-how produced on both the molecular and tissue levels (as in the case of organ donation), and this domain of research is a truly transdisciplinary field of research engaging anthropologists, sociologists, medical researchers, political scientists, etc. In contrast, this volume is embedded in an organization theory framework, in itself a multi or transdisciplinary domain of research, inasmuch as not only the very production of new life-science know-how is emphasized but also how such know-how is instituted and used through a variety of social practices such as patent laws (Carolan, 2010; McAfee, 2003), market-based activities (Åsberg and Johnson, 2009), juridical practice (Leslie, 2010; Dumit, 2004; Daemmrich, 1998), and in the day-to-day organization of scientific work (Owen-Smith, 2001; Barley and Bechky, 1994; Holmqvist, 2009). In other words, the technosciences may appear as if they are totally immutable and self-enclosed, but the authority of the sciences was accomplished through the organization of a multiplicity of activities.

Organization theory is a diverse field of research, including a variety of theoretical and methodological perspectives (for an overview, see, e.g., Perrow's [1986] classic and highly personal account). Organization theory does not provide a single integrated and unified view of organization but rather a series of theoretical frameworks, each having its own analytical strengths and weaknesses, which may be applied to cases. Some of the organization theory literature is highly normative (in many cases being labeled management), while many contributions avoid such standpoints. Whereas much writing about the bioeconomy—the field of the commercialization of the life sciences—is presented by scholars outside the field of organization theory, the organizational arrangements of the bioeconomy are relatively undertheorized. This volume seeks to make a contribution to the study of the bioeconomy by stressing the organization of the activities; the organization of the laboratory work, the organization of the intellectual property right arrangements, the organization of the marketing and promotion of, e.g., new therapies, and so forth. In this analysis, the life sciences will not be examined as if they were operating in their own self-enclosed sphere, detached from pubic interests and concerns, but rather as being fundamentally open to external influences and interests (see, e.g., Hilgartner, 2000; Jasanoff, 2004, 2005). As a consequence, concepts such as *managerialism*[4]—the belief in management practices as universally applicable routines for leading, controlling, and monitoring all sorts of organized work—will be used to understand the success of the life sciences and their recent more accelerated commercialization. Managerialism is in turn embedded, it is further argued, in the neoliberal economic and political doctrine where the state and its authorities should not restrain and delimit economic activities. In the neoliberal era, beginning at the end of the 1970s and stretching into the contemporary period, economic performance and economic growth are the principal drivers of the economy, and therefore various managerialist practices are widely enacted as universal procedures for organizing and leading a manifold of activities. Seen in this view, the technosciences and the life sciences more specifically are not in a privileged position vis-à-vis other domains of the economy; the life sciences too must prove their worth and their financial investment, and consequently they are increasingly exposed to managerialist forms of control. However, the technosciences are also strongly determined by professional norms and ideologies, locating them in a position where they have to constantly balance two institutional logics, those of professional and managerialist modes of control. Leslie (2010) provides a fine example of how "quality assurance" (QA), a managerialist practice to monitor the quality of the data and information provided, is used in a Canadian forensic biology laboratory. Leslie (2010) argues that the two principal categories of co-workers, the technicians and the scientists, operated under diverse conditions, leading to different uses of the QA: the technicians experience QA as "[a] precise, quantified, objective, thing-oriented QA process administered from above. On the other hand, scientists experience QA as the gaze of their peers. In contrast, there is an often vague, unquantifiable, intimate, person-oriented activity that is part of a collegial environment," Leslie (2010: 297) says. Leslie (2010: 299) suggests that the forensic biologists, both technicians and scientists, are engaging in a science that is "outward-looking," actively used in public settings such as in court, and therefore they can tolerate the use of QA as it is perceived as a "major source of credibility" inasmuch as "QA creates objectivity with its emphasis on audible processes." Still, as a "managerialist control structure," the QA is "both a technology of trust and mistrust." Since the work in court is fundamentally based on the juridical routines of systematic mistrust, the "institutionalization of mistrust" of the QA and managerial oversight are regarded as being "simply part of the work" (Leslie, 2010: 299). Leslie (2010) here points at the establishment of organizational routines, addressed in terms of "managerial oversight," as being an important element in the constitution of the forensic biologists' professional status as credible and disinterested experts in their domain of jurisdiction. While the technoscientific instruments, practices, and routines of the field of forensic biology may have given an adequate degree of authority, both in court and elsewhere, there is a perceived demand for accompanying these more intra-scientific procedures with managerial routines providing more opportunities for "credibility." Leslie's (2010) study is thus illustrative of how technoscience and the life sciences are bundling "intra-scientific resources" and organizational resources (managerial practices) into assemblages enabling actions to be taken. Under the auspices of "quality assurance," the forensic biologists were given the prerogative to present their scientific evidence. This case also suggests that managerial routines and forms of control are penetrating all domains of society, including the highly professionalized technosciences. As a consequence, an organization theory perspective on the life sciences further extends the understanding of how commercialization of advanced life-science know-how is enabled. Life-science expertise is by no means isolated from broader social interests, and consequently the capacity to bridge "the laboratory and the world" (Latour, 1988) is of key importance. This bridging is essentially a matter of the capacity of organizing the sciences and bringing them into society.

OUTLINE OF THE BOOK

The book is composed of five chapters: In Chapter 1, *The Concept of the Bioeconomy*, some of the key terms and issues in late modern society wherein the life sciences are demonstrating remarkable advancement and emerging opportunities for intervening in human bodies on a variety of levels, ranging from cosmetic surgery (on the surface) and organ transplantation (in the interior of the body) to the cellular level or in the genetic structure, are discussed. The chapter will provide an analytical framework for the understanding of the bioeconomy, the field where life-science know-how and economic interests are combined and where new organizations, professions, goods, and services are produced.

In Chapter 2, *Biopolitics, Neoliberalism, and the Calculative Worldview*, the broader social, cultural, and economic setting or field of emergence (Foucault, 1972) is sketched. With Foucault's work on governmentality and bio-politics as a major shift in political doctrines and practice at the end of the eighteenth century as a starting point, the gradual shift in perspective from the regulation of public health to the management of life is envisaged as an important reformulation of the political and economic objective to handle increasingly urbanized populations in the modern state. Pointing at the neoliberal economic and political doctrine, developed over the course of the twentieth century but taking off at the end of the 1970s as the regime of Keynesian economic policy increasingly failed to handle macroeconomic challenges, as an important framework enabling the economization of the life sciences, the chapter suggests that the emphasis on freedom of choice, enterprising ideologies, and a general skepticism regarding the legitimacy of state control and regulation has played a key role in paving the way for the bioeconomy.

In Chapter 3, *New Drug Development, Biotechnology and the Enactment of Life*, the pharmaceutical industry, with its roots in the pharmacies of the nineteenth century, and the biotechnology industry, a more recent spin-off from academic research work in the life sciences, are discussed as the principal agents serving to bridge life-sciences research and economic interests. The major multinational pharmaceutical industry is a finance-intense and highly sophisticated industry often criticized for failing to address a variety of illnesses and diseases or for overcharging the public sector health care organizations for their life-saving drugs. That is, "Big Pharma" often plays the role of being the faceless, capitalist corporation caring for little more than bottom line profit and shareholder value. This view may be appealing in many ways but unfortunately conceals the everyday work in major pharmaceutical companies where thousands of dedicated researchers work hard to advance therapies that would help patient groups. In comparison to the major pharmaceutical companies, the relatively small biotechnology companies are surrounded by a much more positive aura as being the hotbed for creative thinking and innovative applications of life-science know-how. Such affirmative images are not of necessity misnomers, but the biotechnology industry suffers from its constant needs for cash and its inability to deliver as much as promised, making the industry in general appear to be underperforming. The chapter is aiming at portraying both the pharmaceutical and the biotechnology industry in more tempered terms, as providers of advanced and highly specialized know-how, tools, and procedures for exploring the elementary components of life.

In Chapter 4, *The Tissue Economy*, a number of economic activities embedded in life-science know-how complementing the pharmaceutical and the biotechnology industries are accounted for. Addressing a variety of practices such as reproductive medicine and in vitro fertilization, organ donation, and cosmetic surgery, the chapter points at the remarkable breadth and scope of the bioeconomy. Not only are therapies and technologies developed to intervene into the human body and its biological pathways, but also the renewable (e.g., sperm or blood) and non-renewable (human eggs and organs) biological resources may be subject to various manipulations and circulation in the bioeconomy. The tissue economy is a phrase used to denote that in the bioeconomy, a variety of, and at times surprising, human tissues may acquire an economic value that may be further translated into economic value. The tissue economy is thus fueled by the combination of advanced life-science know-how and the access to biological materials., Such materials may be in short of supply (in, e.g., the case of human organs) or may be widely accessible (as in the case of sperm), ultimately regulating the economic activities of these fields.

In Chapter 5, *Living in and Managing the Bioeconomy*, the last chapter, a number of issues and concerns regarding the future bioeconomic society will be addressed. Since there are clear indications of the bioeconomy having gendered and racial and ethnic underpinnings, feminist and postcolonial theories will be discussed as important theoretical perspectives helping social theorists understand, e.g., reproductive medicine or the international trade of human organs. In addition, the bioeconomy has many implications for organization theory and management studies, including the emergence of new professional groups, the consumption and marketing of goods and services, the development and implementation of new technologies, and the collaboration between industry and universities. These issues and topics will be addressed in the final chapter. The chapter ends with a discussion about what the bioeconomic future may look like and how policies, regulations, consumer preferences and choices, and, most important, the advancement of the life sciences may affect everyday life in the future.

While the volume is clearly couched in an organization theory and management studies tradition, the literature referenced is by no means restricted to this corpus of texts. Instead, the bioeconomy is a field wherein contributions from a range of disciplines are helpful in creating a patchwork of images of how life-science expertise and enterprising activities may be brought together and may lead to new goods, services, and forms of know-how. Having said that, the volume includes references to works published in anthropology, sociology, science and technology studies, accounting, feminist theory, and so forth. At the same time as the variety and heterogeneity of texts are recognized, there is a clear focus on the bioeconomy as being the outcome of organized sociomaterial practices wherein both intangible and material resources are brought together.

1   The Concept of the Bioeconomy

INTRODUCTION

One of the key benefits of organization theory and management studies is that this discipline seeks to be opportunistic in the non-pejorative sense of the term, that is, that emerging events, new technologies, or new buzz-words used in industry may be subject to analysis and critical reflection. Rather than being enclosed within theoretical frameworks and relying on well-entrenched methodological traditions, organization researchers are entering the world to understand how new ideas and beliefs are enacted and serve to regulate actions and economies. This does not suggest that organization researchers are devoid of theoretical resources. Instead, they are equipped with a great number of analytical frameworks and theoretical models. The crux is that these frameworks and models do not of necessity translate into meaningful studies; there is always the need for aligning empirical observations and theoretical frameworks—empirics does not speak for itself, and nor is theoretical framework always capable of explaining what has been observed. A quote from the American anthropologist Paul Rabinow (Rabinow, et al., 2008) indicates this mismatch between empirics and theory:

> Today, the pedagogic challenge is to rethink the established combination of fast and slow operations that remains at the core of what inquiry should be. One may say, "Let's go to Chernobyl, but don't leave Weber behind." Of course, Weber is not going to tell you directly what's going on there—that would be ridiculous to expect. But surfing the internet is not going to tell you what is significant, either. (Paul Rabinow, cited in Rabinow et al., 2008: 56)

What Rabinow suggest is that particular events cannot be explained by the canonical work of an academic tradition, but nor can popular culture at the time. Instead, the researcher needs to carefully combine empirical observations, theoretical frameworks, and contemporary discussions into a coherent and credible narrative. In other words, the social world is never speaking on behalf of itself, but is always spoken for by the researcher. In addition, the language being establish to speak about matter never only draws on past accomplishments and contributions but is of necessity a form of theoretical Creole where both synchronic and diachronic resources are drawn on. The skilled organization researcher is thus working on an idiosyncratic body of literature, at best capable of making sense out of fluid and ambiguous empirical realities. A key skill in the researcher arsenal of resources at hand is then the capacity of interpreting events and occurrences and reflecting on the interpretations. Organization research is then always seeking to address contemporary issues but does so on the basis of theoretical frameworks that are composed of heterogeneous elements.

This volume aims to discuss what has been called the bioeconomy (Rose, 2007), a term denoting the intersection between the production of economic and financial value and biological know-how and opportunities. This definition is rather loose in its outline, and it is purposely presented in such terms because the connections between the advances in the life sciences (medicine, pharmaceutical production, biotechnology, and so forth) are still in an early stage of their development. In addition, the potentials for generating economic and financial value on the basis of biological know-how and the life sciences are far from realized. In late modern society, where material standards have risen enormously during the last hundred years, and where ageing populations have a large stock of capital to invest, there is a fertile soil for the introduction of goods and services derived from the life sciences. For instance, the democratization of higher education in combination with a widespread belief in meritocratic principles has pushed the age for couples to have their first child to the first half of the thirties or even later in some strata, giving quite a number of aspiring parents the unpleasant surprise of discovering that they suffer from infertility problems. It is today estimated that somewhere between 10 to 20 percent of all couples share this predicament. However, today there are opportunities for technoscientific interventions into conception, to "give life a little help on its way" as the slogans for infertility clinics suggest, helping couples in despair to have their much-awaited first child. This is a remarkable contribution from the life sciences, eliminating so much grief and sorrow among women and men not able to have a child of their own. At the same time, infertility clinics and reproductive medicine constitute a business in its own right. Deborah Spar (2006) actually uses the term "the baby business" to denote the totality of economic activities evolved around the social problem of childlessness.[1] The intersection of, and mutual dependence on, economic activities and the life sciences is the terrain where the bioeconomy develops and thrives. The role of the organization researchers is then to study the relationships between on the one hand the advancement of the technosciences and the life sciences, giving rise to new possibilities but also new trade-offs and ethical concerns, and, on the other hand, the processes of economization and financialization of this new form of knowing.

The technosciences and the life sciences are often portrayed as leading societal change, where new remarkable findings and contributions gradually trickle down to social practices and eventually new social beliefs and expectations. The sciences in this ideology are envisaged as the jewel in the crown of the human pursuit to master and control nature. Such a view is criticized by Franklin and Roberts (2006), suggesting that rather than being "'ahead of,' 'beyond,' or 'outside' society" the technosciences are instead part of the social fabric; there is in short no isolated or pristine extra-social position from which the sciences may be developed. "While it is not helpful to underestimate the radical novelty of many of the new techniques, choices, and dilemmas encountered in the context of new reproductive and genetic technologies, or the difficult issues they present, it is equally unhelpful to overprivilege technological innovation as if they were a force unto itself," Franklin and Robert (2006: 13) argue.

In this volume, this view of the life sciences will be maintained––the idea that the life sciences serving as the prime motor in the bioeconomy are not developed in isolation from wider social debates and interests. We may here also make reference to Jasanoff (2004), who suggests that science and society are "co-produced":

> Briefly stated, co-production is shorthand for the proposition that the ways in which we know and represent the world (both nature and society) are inseparable from the ways in which we choose to live in it. Knowledge and its material embodiments are at once products of social work and constitutive of forms of social life; society cannot function without knowledge any more than knowledge can exist without appropriate social support. Scientific knowledge, in particular, is not a transcendental mirror of reality. It both embeds and is embedded in social practices, identities, norms, conventions, discourses, instruments and institutions—in short, in all the building blocks of what we term the social. The same can be said even more forcefully of technology. (Jasanoff, 2004: 2–3)

Franklin and Roberts (2006) and Jasanoff (2004) suggest that rather than thinking of the sciences in exceptionalist terms (Figueroa and Harding, 2003), the sciences are always of necessity bound up with social relations and interests (Epstein, 1996). In other words, what here is referred to as the bioeconomy—the life sciences turned into economic activity—is by no means advanced by the life sciences alone. The bioeconomy is instead the co-production of socially legitimate and marketable goods and services that have their origin in the use of technoscientific know-how and expertise but that nevertheless fall short unless there is a market demand. This does not, however, mean that one can ignore the key role played by the life sciences. The remarkable, even unprecedented, advancement of the life sciences in the last fifteen years is today capable of offering new opportunities to intervene into the processes of life and biological systems in a manner that appeared as mere science fiction only a few decades earlier. The trick is to avoid being mesmerized by these impressive contributions and by the very products of the research in the life sciences as the outcome of social agreements on what kind of research to pursue in the interest of contemporary society and perhaps even humankind at large.

THE CONCEPT OF THE ORGANISM

One of the first modern definitions of the concept of organism was provided in Immanuel Kant's *Critique of Judgment,* wherein an organism is conceived of thus: *"an organized natural product is one in which every part is reciprocally both end and means.* In such a product nothing is in vain, without end, or to be ascribed to a blind mechanism of nature" (Kant, [1790]2005: 166. Emphasis in the original. See also Keller, 2000: 107). Kant here also speaks of what he, after J.F. Blumenbach's (1752–1840) term *nisus formativus,* referred to as *Bildungstrieb,* "the inscrutable self-organizational power present in organisms but not in mere aggregation of matter" (Bennett, 2010: 65).[2] In addition, Kant used the term *Anlagen,* "purposive dispositions" (Bennett, 2010: 71) to refer to the organism's innate structure regulating this "self-organizational power." For Bennett, Kant's talk about an organism as being "self-organizing being" and the *Bildungstrieb* suggest that Kant advocated what would a century later be referred to as *vitalism,* the belief in a life-force regulating organisms and any organic life (Lash, 2006; Fraser, Kember and Lury, 2005).

Prior to Kant, René Descartes advanced the idea of an organism as a form of "machine" in the fifth part of his *Discourse on Method* (Lewontin, 2000). The Kantian view of the organism, emphasizing the self-regulating and self-forming quality of the organism, and the Cartesian view, stressing the entitative view of the organism—its integrated but yet separated mechanisms and processes—have complemented one another through the history of biology. Keller (2000: 108) defines the organism as "[a] bounded, physiochemical body capable not only of self-regulation—self-steering—but also, and perhaps most important, of self-formation. An organism is a material entity that is transformed into an autonomous and self-generating 'self' by virtue of its peculiar and particular organization." In Lewontin's (2000: 100–101) understanding of the term, the organism is, similar to Kant's conceptualization, a dynamic concept formed by both its hereditary material and the environment: "Taken together, the relational of genes, organisms, and environments are reciprocal relations in which three elements are both causes and effects. Genes and environment are both causes of organisms, which are, in turn, causes of environments, so that genes becomes causes of environments as mediated by organisms." The organism is thus irreducible to neither the hereditary material, nor the environment, but is recursively produced by both.[3]

Anatomical treatises on the human body were developed in the medieval period. The works of the Florentine physiologist Andreas Vesalius were particularly important in breaking with ancient medicine in the tradition of, e.g., Galen and his influential theory of the fluids of the human body. Vesalius's *De Humani Corporis Fabrica* (1543) instituted the study of anatomy as a visual (or perceptual at large) practice; i.e., observation and empirical work displaced theoretical speculation based on the Greek canon (Thacker, 1999: 325). Despite the advancement of the field of anatomy as an empirical field of research in the medieval and early modern periods, medicine as a practice and scientific discipline were relatively blunt until the end of the eighteenth century, when the first vaccine against smallpox was developed by Edward Jenner (1749–1823) in 1798 (Bynum, 1994). At the turn of the nineteenth century, experimentalists like the French physiologist Xavier Bichat (1771–1802) engaged in developing methods for the study of the human organism. Bichat coined the term tissue (in opposition to organs), a central term in physiology. As Canguilhem (2008: 43) remarks, the term tissue derives from *tistre*, "an archaic form of the verb *tisser* ('to weave')." The tissue is thus what holds the organs together, locating them in the intricate weave of the biological organism. Bichat also advanced the view of the human body as a set of interrelated but largely independent systems. Bichat is perhaps most well-known for his systemic definition of life: "Life is an ensemble of functions deployed to resist death" (cited in Rabinow, 1996: 80). However, it was not until 1865 when Claude Bernard published *An Introduction to the Study of Experimental Medicine* that medicine and physiology acquired a full, consolidated argument in favor of experimental methods and observations, serving as a seminal text well into the twentieth century. Bernard advocated a scientific method that included both theorizing and experimental approaches:

> To be worthy of the name, an experimenter must be at once theorist and practitioner. While he must completely master the art of establishing experimental facts, which are the materials of science, he must also clearly understand the scientific principles which guide his reasoning through the varied experimental study of natural phenomena. We cannot separate these two things: head and hand. An able hand, without a head to direct it, is a blind tool; the head is powerless without its executive hand. (Bernard, [1865]1957: 3)

In the nineteenth century, the concept of the cell, etymologically derived from the Latin word *cella*, "room," was developed and widely recognized as the elementary building block in organisms, primarily in the German-speaking university system, including physicians working in German, Czech, and Polish universities (Harris, 1999). The advancement of new visual media such as the microscope, first developed in the seventeenth century—Robert Hooke's *Micrographia* of 1665 was one of the first monographs examining the uses of microscopes (Schickore, 2007)—further advanced the field as new visual scientific practices enabled new laboratory practices. Over the course of the nineteenth century, both biology and experimental medicine established themselves as autonomous, scientific fields.

In the nineteenth century, there was an ongoing discussion between proponents of a physiology embedded in mechanism or in vitalism. While the mechanist view of the organism emphasized discontinuity and the role of the elementary functions, the vitalist view underlined continuity and epigenesis, the self-reproducing capacities of the biological organism. That is, while mechanisms essentially adhered to a Cartesian view of the organism, a system composed of individual elements, vitalism operated in the Kantian tradition and held "[l]ife to be a principle transcendent to matter, an indivisible and ungraspable form" (Canguilhem, 2008: 44). Since modern technoscience is essentially reductionist, mechanist views predominate, and vitalism has been criticized, even ridiculed, for encouraging metaphysical speculation about a "life force" transcending the brute matter of the organism. On the other hand, the mechanist view is still unable to provide a credible explanation of how life emerges, and even in contemporary medicine and physiology, there is a slippery slope between life and non-life; an amino acid is not life, but the DNA constituted by such amino acids is capable of generating life. That is, life can never be fully understood by analytical methods, but a synthetic view is needed in this pursuit: "Life is the formation of forms, knowledge is the analysis of in-formed matter . . . because they are totalities whose sense resides in their tendency to realize themselves as such in the course of their confrontation with their milieus. Living forms can be grasped in a vision, never by a division" (Canguilhem, 2008: xix). Even though vitalist epistemologies may be outmoded and antiquated, the question of life, both its beginning and ending, still haunts the biological sciences (see, e.g., Lock [2002] on the definition of brain death and other forms of scientific definitions of "deaths"). If life is just chemistry under determinate conditions, then it would be possible to provide a full understanding of the biochemical processes constituting life. For the time being, life is yet to be explained, and consequently neo-vitalist theories may be advanced where mechanist and reductionist theoretical frameworks fail to explain the emergence of life.

If the nineteenth-century medicine and physiology enacted the human organism as a fleshy structure composed of tissues, organs, and more mysterious systems such as the central nervous system, the twentieth century shifted the perspective to the elementary levels of the organism. The very idea that there is a heredity material constituting the organism "from within" is generally credited to the Austrian physicist Erwin Schrödinger, in his book *What Is Life?* (1946) about a specific form of "code-script" underlying all forms of life (Kay, 2000: 59). With Schrödinger's view, modern biology was born, and he refused to recognize any purposeful (*zweckmässig*) adaptation in nature (Schrödinger, 1958: 67), contributing to the master narrative of the organism as being more determined by the hereditary material than by the organism's capacity to respond to external changes. For instance, for the French Nobel prize laureate Jacques Monod, an organism is nothing but "a cybernetic system governing and controlling the chemical activity at numerous points" (Jacques Monod, *Chance and Necessity*, 1970, cited in Kay, 2000: 17). The organism has thus during the most recent period of time been more Cartesian than Kantian, underlining the elementary components of the organism at the expense of a broader perspective.

The concept of the organism has also played a key role for the economic sciences inasmuch as the emerging science of political economy of the eighteenth century took not the existing social institutions—all-too-human, too idiosyncratic, and too imperfect to serve as fruitful model for a grand theoretical framework—but the "broader divine natural economy" as portrayed in Carl Linnaeus's biological framework. In the eighteenth century, "'oeconomy' was a word with wide circulation, commonly referring to matters of physiology," Gammon (2010: 223) stated. In addition, modern biology also uses the term organization as a somewhat equivocal term denoting "either state and process, or both" (Atlan, 1974: 296). For Atlan (1974), the crystal is an excellent example of how organization is both a state and a process:

> On the one hand, organization is meant as constraints between parts, or regulatory and order, where order is viewed essentially as repetitive order, i.e., redundancy. According to this view a model for the best organized system is a perfect crystal. On the other hand, under the influence of information theory, organization is means as non-repetitive order, which is measured by an information content in Shannon's (1949) sense, i.e., a degree of unexpectedness directly related to variety and unhomogeneity. Therefore, the ideas leading to a formal quantitative definition of organization should involve a kind of optimization process so that any optimum organization would correspond to a compromise between maximum information content (i.e., maximum variety) and maximum redundancy, and this is in fact the idea that I propose to use as a basis for the definition of organization. (Atlan, 1974: 296)

Classic and modern biology has thus advanced a vocabulary that has been imported to the economic sciences, and, over time, concepts such as organization further developed in organization theory have been reappropriated by the life sciences. In both biology and the life sciences and organization theory, the paradox of state and process, stability and change is mediated by the concept of organization and more specifically the concept of organism, a term that manages to de-paradoxify the opposition between fixity and fluidity. "The truth is that we change without ceasing, and that the state itself is nothing but change," Bergson (1998: 2) suggests, pointing to the need for developing vocabularies capable of apprehending life as a flow of ceaseless change that yet is temporarily stabilized into discrete organisms. In the modern bioeconomy, the concept of biological organism is conceived of both as an entity and a process depending on perspective, and the biological organism is thus a dynamic term capable of being connected to various technoscientific frameworks of analysis. The biological organism is similar to Michel Serres's concept of the quasi-object, moving back and forth, betwixt and between different positions.

THE LIFE SCIENCES AND TECHNOLOGY

Thinking of the bioeconomy as what is inextricably entangled with social interests and social concerns leads to an analytical position where students of bioeconomic practice have to untangle a rather complex texture of sociomaterial practices (Suchman, 2007; Orlikowski, 2010, 2007; Orlikowski and Scott, 2008). Such sociomaterial practices include, as indicated, the co-alignment of social and material resources. The social resources include everything from regimes of representations such as concepts, numerical inscriptions, and routines for making graphs and diagrams, to more abstract resources such as scientific ideologies and socially enacted routines for evaluating contributions to the life sciences. The material resources also include a heterogeneous blend of assets and resources that are integrated into ensembles of technoscientific apparatuses, often located in laboratories and research institutes, such as tools, machinery, computers, laboratory animals, human voluntary subjects, and so forth. It is, however, complicated to fully separate the social from the material as they are always present in all instances; social practices are maintained through the use of material resources, and materiality is itself examined and used on the basis of socially enacted frameworks of analysis. More specifically, the concept of technology plays a key role in the technosciences, and therefore an elaborated view of the concept of technology—indeed a *theory* of technology—is helpful. As the French archaeologist André Leroi-Gourhan (1989) has suggested, the development of the human into the *homo sapiens*, "the thinking man," is strongly co-evolutionary with the development of tools and technologies. Early humanoids were capable of developing a few tools helping them collect more food, leading to better nurturing and eventually to higher intelligence. Later on, the use of, for instance, pottery helped humans save food, thereby releasing time for intellectual pursuits leading to further innovations; humans were no longer strictly bound to an ongoing search for foodstuff. André Leroi-Gourhan is here talking about the co-evolutionary process of humanity as *orthogenesis*, the process wherein better living conditions helped increasing the intellectual capacities of humans, leading to better technologies and practices. In this virtuous circle of the mutual advancement of better technologies and more sophisticated modes of thinking, humankind developed from being an advanced primate to the species we are today.

Taking a somewhat less grand perspective, anthropologists such as Pfaffenberg (1992) have underlined the social embedding of all technology: "[T]hose who seek to develop new technologies must concern themselves not only with techniques and artifacts; they must also engineer the social, economic, legal, scientific and political context of the technology," Pfaffenberg (1992: 498) says. In this perspective, technologies are not invented by individuals and relatively isolated geniuses but are on the contrary always of necessity both derived from and influence social and economic conditions. "Every technology is a human world, a form of humanized nature, that unifies virtually every aspect of human endeavour," Pfaffenberg (1988: 249) argues. "To construct a technology is not merely to deploy materials and techniques; it is also to construct social and economic alliances, to invent new legal principles for social relations, and to provide powerful new vehicles for culturally-provided myths" (Pfaffenberg, 1988: 249). Studies of, for instance, electricity (Hughes, 1983), the telephone (Fischer, 1992), the phonograph (Gitelman, 1999), or music instruments (Pinch and Trocco, 2002; Beijsterveld and Schulp, 2004) show that rather than being immediately appropriated on a broad scale and being celebrated inventions, new technologies and media have been approached with skepticism, and it has even been pointed out that new technologies may have negative consequences for society. There is no deviation from this common pattern when it comes to the life sciences. Advances in transplant technologies, the uses of prostheses, and the possibilities for manipulating the reproductive processes have led to a general concern regarding the righteousness and possibilities of human interventions in "life per se." For instance, religious leaders (in, e.g., the Catholic Church) have criticized stem cell research, and abortion practices continue to be a source of great controversy in many parts of the world. The life sciences qua a set of sociomaterial practice are by no means protected from criticism based on ethics and religious beliefs. Therefore, as suggested by Pfaffenberg (1992, 1988), technology can never be examined isolated from broader social interests and discussions. In the bioeconomy, these kinds of debates are commonplace as the life sciences are translated into products and services. In some cases, for instance in the field of reproductive medicine, there is little debate regarding the run-of-the-mill routines, while in other areas, say organ transplantation (Lock, 2002; Sharp, 2003; Cherry, 2005; Sanal, 2011), there are many concerns regarding where the new possibilities derived from the new sociomaterial practices may take us.

DEVELOPING THE LIFE SCIENCES

The life sciences are, taken together, a rather recent domain in the totality of the sciences (today commonly referred to as the technosciences, emphasizing the technological constitution of any contemporary scientific practice). The life sciences are by and large conceived of as the outgrowth of speculative and theological reasoning and thinking in the medieval period and more systematized in the seventeenth century during the so-called scientific revolution propelled by the works of, for instance, the Florentine astronomer Galilei Galileo and the French mathematician and philosopher René Descartes (Koyré, 1992). Having their roots in the medieval cloisters, which led to the creation of universities where, e.g., theology and medicine were studied, the modern sciences were not originally conceived of as being of very significant practical value. During the early period of more systematic scientific research, the sciences were financed by royal courts and academic societies, by and large driven by individual curiosity and even the entertainment value of various scientific demonstrations. For instance, in the eighteenth century, demonstrations in the bourgeois salons played a key role in making the discipline of mathematics legitimate:

> The social acceptance of science in the eighteenth century depended on the cultivation of a larger, elite audience. Genteel audiences evinced enthusiasm even for mathematics—satirists made much of the early eighteenth-century mathematical rage among fashionable women—and most notably for experimental demonstrations of balls arcing through hoops, birds suffocating under air pumps, and electrically charged orphans discharged great sparks while suspended from silk strings. All this sound frivolous, and maybe it was, but serious careers, including the career of science itself, were sustained by such performances. By the end of the century, science was increasingly taking account of, and sometimes addressing, larger audiences. (Porter, 2009: 299)

In Porter's account, by the end of the eighteenth century, co-aligned with the growth of a more developed civil modern society, "sciences became of interest for the regulation of the state" (Porter, 2009: 300). In the nineteenth century, the social sciences were also born, serving to support the administration of an expanding state apparatus where larger and urbanized populations were increasingly subject to management and political objectives. In the nineteenth century, statistics and criminology were established as scholarly disciplines (Desrosière, 1998; Matthews, 1995; Hacking, 1990; Gunning, 1995). The modern sciences were thus brought into society not as what was immediately practical but rather interesting or capable of demonstrating many puzzling curiosities. Only after society was developed into a more differentiated structure in the nineteenth century did the sciences start to play a more practical role. Today, the sciences strongly influence social policy and practice.

The life sciences, as being a combination of medicine, biochemistry, and other specialized disciplines, demonstrate a rather crooked path toward contemporary accomplishments (Löwy, 2011; Pickstone, 2011). Medicine was established already in the antique period as a prestigious professional field, but the ancient ideas of medicine, for instance Galen's theory of the "four fluids" circulating in the body, were in many ways insufficient in explaining or curing illnesses. While medicine has always had some prestige in all societies regardless of its clinical value, there was an alarming lack of what today is called "evidence-based medicine." By and large, medical doctors were incapable of accomplishing very much until the first vaccines were developed in the last years of the eighteenth century. Since then, medicine has developed into being perhaps the most prestigious of the sciences, capable of demonstrating significant progress in terms of therapeutic effects and enhanced longevity. In the nineteenth century, medicine developed into being a highly empirical science, based on observations and descriptions of various biological processes and pathways. For instance, Xavier Bichat, the great French physician, whose classic work was *Recherches physiologiques sur la vie et la mort* (first published in May 1800), collected animals whereon he "provoked injuries in specific organs . . . to observe the consequences of such actions for the rest of the body" (Haigh, 1984: 88). Bichat was notorious for using animals in abundance. In addition—and quite disturbing for the contemporary reader—Bichat is reputed to have "frequently attended executions by guillotine so as to be able to make observations on the severed heads and trunks of the victims" (Haigh, 1984: 88). Besides being one of the great contributors to modern medicine, Bichat is famous for his definition of life as the "the totality of those functions which resists death" (Haigh, 1984: 10). Bichat took a systems view of the human body, conceiving of it as a bundle of interrelated but essentially separate systems capable of sustaining life. Death is therefore the event of all these interrelated systems collapsing, and death is then not a discrete event but the termination of a process where separate systems close down over time. With Bichat and his contemporaries, medicine was transformed from a relatively futile practice of curing illnesses to a modern application of scientific principles and routines to unravel the secrets of life (Foucault, 1973; Jordanova, 1989; Collins and Pinch, 2005). Always located in the clinic, the site where physicians were operating and encountering their patients, medicine has by tradition been a practical pursuit, only recently been accompanied by scientific ambitions (Dunn and Jones, 2010).

Chemistry, the discipline today widely addressed as biochemistry or microbiology in the life sciences, demonstrates a rather different trajectory. Just like medicine, chemistry has ancient roots. Etymologically, the term derives from the Egyptian word for "black" and from the Greek word *cheo*, meaning, "to pour a liquid or cast a metal" (Bensaude-Vincent and Stengers ([1993]1996: 13). However, the origin of the term has been disputed. In the period of AD 800–1000, Alexandria was a major intellectual center of the Arabic world, where the first formal descriptions of chemistry were developed under the name of the "Alexandrian corpus" (Bensaude-Vincent and Stengers ([1993]1996: 13ff.). In these texts, techniques and reagents were described with great care and precision. Arab scholars thus devoted themselves to the production and transmission of "reproducible, practical knowledge" (Bensaude-Vincent and Stengers ([1993]1996: 16). Among the pioneers of chemistry was Mary the Jewess, an Alexandrian scholar making many important contributions to the field. In the seventeenth century, Robert Boyle invented the concept of elements. In 1789, Lavoisier made a table that contained 33 simple substances. In 1834 Thénard "named 54 simple bodies in his textbook," and a few decades later, in 1869, Dmitri Mendeleev "counted 70" (Bensaude-Vincent and Stengers ([1993]1996: 111).

However, it was not until well into the eighteenth century that standard references and a unified operative vocabulary were established in the field of chemistry. Bensaude-Vincent and Stengers ([1993]1996) account for the confusion encountered by the modern reader in chemistry treatises from the period:

> One becomes lost, without landmarks, in a jungle of exotic and obscure terminology. Some products were named after their inventor (Glauber's salt, Libavius's liquor), others after their origin (Roman vitriol, Hungarian vitriol), others after their medicinal effects, and yet others after their method of preparation (flower of sulfur, obtained by condensing vapor, precipitate of sulfur, spirit or oil of vitriol, depending on whether the acid was more or less concentrated). On every page: what is he talking about? What substance is he describing? (Bensaude-Vincent and Stengers ([1993]1996: 46)

However, in the mid-nineteenth century, chemistry became, prior to physics, the leading science. Playing a decisive role in the mining industry in Germany and Sweden, chemistry became one of the first professional scientific university disciplines, organized into professional interest organizations and university departments and running its own conferences and congresses (one of the first conferences was organized in Karlsruhe in 1860).

What today is referred to as biochemistry (or biotechnology) has its own idiosyncratic history. In 1697, the great Prussian court physicist Georg Ernst Stahl (1659–1734), one of the "founding fathers" of modern chemistry besides Antoine Laurent de Lavoisier (1743–1794)—the French chemist who ended his days on the guillotine because the new regime famously declared it had "no need for his services"—published a work entitled *Zymotechnia Fundamentalis*. The Greek term *Zymo* means "leaven," and zymotechnology here denoted all forms of "industrial fermentation" (Bud, 1993). For Bud (1983), zymotechnology "constitutes a vital stage in bridging the gap between biotechnology's ancient heritage and its modernist associations." Stahl proposed a general theory and accompanying practice about how to use yeast and other biological species to produce certain substances. For instance, using yeast in brewing beer is an early and well-known example of how biological elements can be combined to produce new substances. In Budapest, a major agriculture center in the last third of the nineteenth century, the chemist Karl Ereky coined and popularized the concept of biotechnology (Bud, 1993: 32–37). In 1828, the German chemist Friedrich Wöhler managed to synthesize urea, thus helping to break down the barrier between natural and chemical, i.e., artificial products. From now on, chemistry was used to produce substances on a large scale, indeed on an industrial basis. Advances in the zymotechnology and chemistry more broadly eventually converged into what today is still being developed as biotechnology. In 1939, MIT started its first "biological engineering" and "biotechnology" unit, and in 1947 UCLA followed suit. However, not until the mid 1970s when the Stanford professor Stanley Cohen and the University of California professor Herbert Boyer managed to patent their discovery of a method to split and reproduce DNA strings, did biotechnology play a significant role economically (Smith Hughes, 2001). However, ever since the 1970s, biotechnology has been gradually established as a key industry in advancing new technologies and methods for the life sciences.

The life sciences are today a highly theoretically and methodologically diverse field where the classic disciplines of medicine and chemistry—relentlessly being further differentiated into new sub-disciplines and domains of expertise—have been accompanied by new scientific fields such as biocomputation, computer science, biophysics, and other highly sophisticated analytical frameworks. As will be discussed in this volume, the recent advancements in mathematics and computer science hold a promise in terms of handling large-scale data sets produced in clinical research work. Using what Thacker (2004) calls *biomedia*, translating data derived from biological systems into numerical representations without reducing them to the level of mere representations, biocomputation means that there are new opportunities emerging for seeing previously ignored connections between biological pathways. The most recent major shift in focus in the life sciences has been the interest in the human genome and genomics, and the accompanying so-called post-genomic methods and technologies developed in the wake of genomics technologies (Quéré, 2004). While the genomics research project was largely legitimized as being an atlas or "book of life" for the regulatory mechanisms of biological systems (Kay, 2000; Rabinow, 1999; Parry, 2004a), experienced actors in the life sciences have learned the hard way that knowledge of the human genome does not easily translate into adequate therapies. For instance, recent research has shown that rather than regulating the biological system more or less directly, sequences of genes (so-called SNPs, Single Nucleotide Polymorphisms, pronounced "snips," single base variations in the genetic code) are switched on and off in somewhat unexpected ways and that each sequence may produce different proteins. The new interest is thus in the field of proteomics where the proteins being encoded by the genes play a central role. Therefore, one may say that rather than ending up with a book of life where the inner workings of biological systems would "reveal themselves," life-science researchers found an entire library where the different books are not even sorted out and related to one another in a particularly intelligible manner. Still, even though the genomics program did not produce the immediate effects in terms of curing cancer and neurodegenerate diseases, the advancement of genomics has led to a massive growth in know-how regarding the elementary matter of biological systems. What is also intriguing from a social science perspective is the narrative and rhetorical function of concepts such as genome or gene. Being in themselves contested concepts in scholarly circles, they nevertheless denote an anchoring point for a joint understanding of how the human body functions. Thinking of the genome as some kind of script or framework from which a manifold of biological variation derives helps create a viable and (potentially) meaningful image of the biological system. This view also implies, as Hacking (2007: 78) points out, a return to a "mechanical view of the body": "[W]e are returning to an increasingly mechanical view of the body. Our organs—such as the brain or the kidneys—are big parts of our bodies. Our genes are often thought of as tiny parts, although the image of a gene as a physical entity is increasingly strained." Such a mechanical view of the biological system is not very compatible with empirical data, which underline the remarkable complexity of the biological organism, including many self-regulatory systems capable of accommodating both changes in the external system and in the biological system per se. However, one of the key benefits of the genome perspective is actually its bioeconomic value and functioning terms providing a shared ground for understanding concepts such as health and illness. Hacking (2006: 89) stresses this aspect of the term in his prediction: "The intersection of medical, social, personal, and profit-making interests ensure that the avalanche of genetic information available about individuals and populations has only begun."

In summary, the life sciences have an ancient origin but only recently, beginning in the 1970s and especially the early 1990s, have the life sciences been developed into coherent frameworks where they may accrue economic value for the various parts involved in executing life-science know-how in specific settings.

INTRODUCING THE BIOECONOMY

As we have seen, there are a series of historical conditions and occurrences that have led to the situation we have today, that is, a great number of resources at hand to intervene into biological systems and organisms to cure, correct, modify, and enhance their functioning. Infertility, high blood pressure, ulcers, and breast cancer tumors are some examples of biological concerns, illnesses, or health conditions, which may be treated or eased with the use of life-science know-how. What is new in the contemporary period is the ability to translate such life-science know-how into economic and financial terms, in what representatives of "new economic sociology" (see, e.g., MacKenzie, 2009; Zelizer, 2007; Fligstein and Dauter, 2007; Yakubovich, Granovetter, and McGuire, 2005; Zajac and Westphal, 2004) call *economization* or *financialization*. That is, rather than being a free resource for the benefit of humanity at large, life-science know-how is at the same time a communal resource *and* an economic asset in organizations or firms. When Stanley Cohen and Herbert Boyer tried to patent their ground-breaking discovery of recombinant DNA, many members of the scientific community were outraged because patenting scientific findings was at odds with the predominant scientific ideology (Smith Hughes, 2001: 542), but eventually the Bayh-Dole Act of 1980 gave universities the opportunity to patent their research findings even though the research was originally funded by public financiers (Mowery and Ziedonis, 2002). In many ways, the Cohen-Boyer affair seems in hindsight to be a key event in the emergence of the bioeconomy. Of course, such a major shift in focus is produced on the basis of a heterogeneous body of interacting events and changes, but this specific event in California once and for all undermined the century-long tradition of thinking of scientific work as a strictly public good. Instead, neoliberal political doctrines and economic regimes (discussed in greater detail in the next chapter) emphasized the need for property rights to fully enable an exploitation of research findings. In addition, the Cohen-Boyer case also underlined the economic value of scientific research, potentially derived from the capacity to package and market research findings into commodities such as therapies or analytical models.

The key term here is the bioeconomy. As a concept, the bioeconomy is yet another term using the prefix bio- (meaning "life," from Greek), with a great number of such neologisms—Oliver (2000) excels in creating such neologisms as "BioEntrepreneurs," "Bioterials," "BioBureaucrats," and "BioLuddits" (denoting individuals demonstrating their skepticism regarding genetically modified organisms, GMO)—that seeks to exploit the positive connotations of the prefix. The concept of bioeconomy was coined by Nikolas Rose (2007) to denote a wide-ranging series of changes in how human health, well-being, illness, and disease were received. Drawing on Michel Foucault and his writings on "the birth of biopolitics," the emergence of political, state-run programs to handle health and demographics in the nineteenth century, Rose (2007) sees a shift in focus from the governance of health to the "management of life":

> At the risk of simplification, one may say that the vital politics of the eighteenth and nineteenth centuries was a politics of health—of rates of birth and death, of diseases and epidemics, of the policing of water, sewage, foodstuffs, graveyards, and of the vitality of those agglomerated in towns and cities . . . [t]he vital politics of our own century looks quite different. It is neither delimited by the poles of illness and death, nor focused on eliminating pathology to protect the destiny of the nation. Rather, it is concerned with our growing capacities to control,

manage, engineer, reshape, and modulate the very vital capacities of human beings as living creatures. It is, I suggest, a politics of life itself. (Rose, 2007: 3)

In addition, such a change in focus is not, just like Foucault's biopolitics, a haphazard event emerging *ex nihilo* but is rather the outcome of a series of technological, political, economic, and cultural changes over a significant period of time. For Foucault, biopolitics represent a new form of governmentality wherein new technologies and analytical tools such as statistics and demographic classification models are used for governing and regulating larger, increasingly urbanized populations. Similarly, in Rose's (2007) case, there are "five tendencies" that precede the emergence of the bioeconomy. The first is named *molecularization,* meaning that the contemporary life sciences and biomedicine "envisage life" on the "molecular level" as "a set of intelligible vital mechanisms among molecular entities that can be identified, isolated, manipulated, mobilized, recombined, in new practices of intervention, which are no longer constrained by the apparent normativity of a natural vital order" (Rose, 2007: 5–6). That is, the sources of life and death, health and disease, are primarily to be sought on the molecular level; in DNA, in the proteins regulating the body, and so forth:"Molecularization strips tissues, proteins, molecules, and drugs of their specific affinities—to a disease, to an organ, to an individual, to a species—and enables them to be regarded, in many respects, as manipulable and transferable elements or units, which can be delocalized—moved from place to place, from organism to organism, from disease to disease, from person to person" (Rose, 2007: 15). Second, Rose speaks of *optimization* as the tendency for life and health to become an individual and social and demographic resource that should be managed wisely to achieve the highest degree of utility. Health care and medicine are then not only a matter of curing illnesses but take a wider and more ambitious perspective on the human body, which becomes a resource to manage. "Technologies of life not only seek to reveal these invisible pathologies, but intervene upon them in order to optimize the life chances of the individual," Rose (2007: 19) argues. Third, Rose names *subjectification,* i.e., the production of new subjects within the discourse of the bioeconomy. For instance, being concerned about and caring for one's health becomes a central component in the constitution of oneself as a moral and ethical subject. As new regimes of knowledge emerge, new subject positions are enacted. Fourth, Rose speaks of the emergence and growth of *somatic expertise,* that is, new groups of experts are born as the life sciences advance. These expert groups are in charge of either increasingly specialized domains of expertise or serve to integrate or mediate such specialized fields. For instance, the emergence of the so-called bio-ethicist (discussed by Sunder Rajan, 2006) is one such example of a new category of expert. Fifth and finally and perhaps most important, Rose (2007) speaks of a *new economies of vitality,* wherein a "new economic space has been delineated—the bioeconomy—and a new form of capital—biocapital" (Rose, 2007: 6). Rose (2007) here distinguishes between on the one hand the *bioeconomy*, the totality of economic action and markets produced, and, on the other hand, *biocapital*, a new form of symbolic capital comparative to Pierre Bourdieu's symbolic, cultural, and economic capital (see also Novas and Rose, 2000). Clarke, Shim, Shostak, and Nelson (2009: 22) define bio-capital (with a hyphen) rather loosely as "capital organized in and through bios—life in its many forms." They also introduce the term biolabour as being "the heterogeneous forms of labour that goes into the production of biocapital." The new economic regime also demonstrates how new alliances and joint ventures are made across boundaries. For instance, much of the biotechnology industry is producing new research methods and frameworks that are applied by pharmaceutical companies "downstream": "[B]iotech companies do not merely 'apply' or 'market' scientific discoveries: the laboratory and the factory are intrinsically interlinked—the pharmaceutical industry has been central to research in neurochemistry, the biotech industry to research on cloning, genetech firms to the sequencing of the human genome. Thus we need to adopt a 'path dependent' perspective on biomedical truths" (Rose, 2007: 31). The combination of what Rose (2007) calls bioeconomy and biocapital are generating what Waldby (2002: 310) refers to as *biovalue:*

"The term biovalue refers to the yield of both vitality and profitability produced by the biotechnical reformulation of living processes. In vitro tissues can be technically altered to make them productive in a variety of ways, for example, transformed into cell lines, genetic sequences, or genetically modified organisms that can be used in the generation of both health and commercial returns" (Mitchell and Waldby, 2001: 336).

In many cases, the concept of biovalue rests both on the access to biological tissues *and* the biography and "health story" of the donor. Biovalue thus derives from both from the *materiality* of the tissue and the *information* (see, e.g., Preda, 2009) associated with it:

In the context of a national biobank, the use of banked or registered tissues, fluids, or genetic information is dependent on the fact that these *remain* linked to the particular individuals from which they were derived. Moreover, the value of such tissues increases to the extent that further information about the individual, such as a new health problems and health-related behaviors, can be linked to these biospecimens. (Mitchell and Waldby, 2001: 346)

Ultimately, the production of biovalue and the circulation of biocapital are based on the ability to extend the domains of jurisdiction of the life sciences. "Biomedicine," Rose (2007: 25) writes, "throughout the twentieth century and into our own, has thus not simply changed our relations to health and illness but has modified the things we think we might hope for and the objectives we aspire to." For instance, one of the key and most hotly debated processes is what is called biomedicalization or medicalization (to be further discussed in Chapter 3, this volume), namely, the gradual reformulation of perceived physical or psychological deficiencies and limitations into actual medical conditions subject to available therapies (Beck, 2007; Blech, 2006). For instance, a lack of perceived interest in sexual activity among women, previously widely regarded as a part of the human condition and the outcome of the ebbs and flows of the biological life cycle, is today addressed as a medical condition—"female sexual dysfunction"—that may be treated with a range of so-called sexuo-pharmaceuticals (Fishman, 2004; Roberts, 2007; Marshall, 2009; Oudshoorn, 2003; Watkins, 2001). Biomedicalization is thus the gradual shift in focus from common concerns into medical conditions calling for therapeutic approaches. "Medical jurisdiction extended beyond accidents, illness, and disease, to the management of chronic illness and death, the administration of reproduction, the assessment and government of 'risk,' and the maintenance and optimization of the healthy body," Rose (2007: 10) writes. While a range of illnesses and medical conditions may benefit from being subject to biomedicalization, the common criticism is that the pharmaceutical companies are more interested in developing therapies for "lifestyle drugs," targeting markets characterized by affluent consumers rather than developing therapies for common and in many cases severe illnesses, such as tropical diseases like malaria, having less financially endowed end users. The statistics speak for themselves regarding the interest in common diseases for the developing world: "Of 1,393 new chemical entities brought to market between 1975 and 1999, only 16 were for tropical diseases and tuberculosis. There was a 13-fold greater chance of a drug being brought to market for central-nervous-system disorder or cancer than for a neglected disease" (Rose, 2007: 261, n. 1).

Rose (2007) outlines a general framework for the analysis of a new economic regime wherein the life sciences are capable of generating large economic value (for a critique of the Rose's work, see Raman and Tutton, 2010)—biovalue—on basis of the commodification of life-science know-how into products and services. Sunder Rajan (2006) is more concerned about the very term biocapital, the gold standard of the bioeconomy. Similar to Rose's (2007) view, Sunder Rajan (2006) emphasizes the shift in focus from health to life, from actual care of the sick to the management of life at large:

> Biocapital is creating a series of cultural transformations in the materiality and exchangeability of what we call 'life.' These transformations are created through shifting and variable use of market

commodification versus public commons or public good formation, both of which are disciplined by new forms of capitalist logic, conforming neither to those of industrial capitalism nor to those of so-called postmodern information capitalism. This is the rationale for the term 'biocapital,' which asks the question of how life gets redefined through the contradictory processes of commodification. (Sunder Rajan, 2006: 47)

For Sunder Rajan, biocapital is precisely the outcome of the wedding of the technosciences dealing with life and health and the neoliberal economic regime: "Biocapital is the articulation of a technoscientific regime, having to do with the life sciences and drug development, with an economic regime, overdetermined by the market" (Sunder Rajan, 2006: 111). There have always been substantial economic interests involved in maintaining health and longevity, but traditionally the life sciences have been restricted to the curing of diseases, and only recently has the shift in focus to life at large taken place. In Sunder Rajan's account, the bioeconomy (as an institutional field) and biocapital (as the main economic principle regulating the relationship between actors) are thus the outcome of the combination of advanced technoscience and a supporting economic and political regime. Given the emphasis on stable economic growth and financial performance, it is little wonder that the biopharmaceutical companies have by and large ignored human suffering in the developing parts of the world and aimed for exploiting the demand for, e.g., obesity drugs and type 2 diabetes therapies. If the pharmaceutical industry has traditionally been rather successful in taking on a heroic role as the provider of drugs that improve quality of human life, this image has been stained by recent critiques of the lack of interest in less lucrative markets and illnesses (Busfield, 2006; Angell, 2004).

Taken together, the bioeconomy is the economic regime wherein all sorts of know-how pertaining to the management of health and life per se are turned into marketable commodities and services. While the technosciences and the life sciences have traditionally been grounded in the scientific ideologies outlined by Robert Merton (1973), that is, being a communal resource for the betterment of humankind, from the mid 1970s, the focus shifted to discussions about intellectual property rights and the ability to reap the benefits from invested efforts, not only in terms of academic credibility but in terms of economic income: "Basic and applied biological research—whether conducted in biotech companies or in the universities—has become bound up with the generation of intellectual property; illness and health have become major fields of corporate activity and the generation of shareholder value," Rose (2007: 11) notes. The bioeconomy is undergoing a wide-ranging and comprehensive change in focus, producing many discourses and subject positions that open up new possibilities but also new concerns, debates, and ethical discussions.

TECHNOSCIENTIFIC ANXIETIES

At the same time as technoscience is remarkably complex in terms of its high degree of specialization and demand for developing idiosyncratic skills in just managing and monitoring an experimental system, it is, seemingly paradoxically, very transparent. Scientists produce data that are related to—some would say inextricably bound up with—a prescribed theoretical framework. What counts as legitimate knowledge claims (expressed in the form of a "fact") depends the ability to follow collectively enacted standards for how such theory-laden data should be produced, brought into this world. Therefore, Porter (2009: 296) says, "we trust scientists . . . for the same reasons we trust the mechanics who repair our cars; not on account of their superior rationality, but because they have the skills and expertise to do this work, while we do not." Still, one of the puzzling concerns for students of the life sciences is that trust in the sciences seem to be lower today than previously, and this despite the significant contributions made by the life sciences during the last decades."[I]t is clear," Franklin (2001: 342) says, "that both governments and industries increasingly fear the costs of miscalculating public distrust in science, and these fears are, if anything, especially predominantly in the fields of biomedicine and biotechnology." Marks (2006) identifies three forms of "biopolitical anxieties" in the contemporary debates: First is the fear of the "gradual reappearance of eugenic practices" to handle "social deviancy," that is, that we are witnessing a revival of "Nazi medicine" serving to eliminate social problems on the basis of scientific know-how. Second is the concern regarding the status of the human being "in the face of biotechnological advances," i.e., a sense of humanity being integrated into or even dominated by a technoscientific framework praising transhuman or posthuman possibilities and futures. Third, the fear that the "collective human genetic inheritance—the germ line—might be irreparably damaged by genetic modification or manipulation" (Marks, 2006: 334). In all three cases, the concept of the human and humanity is brought to the forefront, being implicitly staged as in opposition to technological and scientific advancement. Braidotti (2008: 10), for her part, speaks about outright "technophobic reactions" to the advancement of the life sciences: "Seldom has the future of human nature been the subject of such concerns and in-depth discussions by our wise public intellectuals as in our globalized age . . . This technophobic reaction to our bio-technological progress has led to a return to Kantian moral universalism." When Braidotti (2008) refers to "moral universalism" in the Kantian tradition, she points to the general statements derived from the religious credo that humans should not "play God" and intervene into the process of life. Habermas (2003) has expressed his concerns regarding the long-term consequences of the possibilities of the life sciences. Braidotti (2008) is not worried about the implications of some kind of essentialist humanist perspective, assuming that humans have an inner constitution that must not be manipulated, but is more concerned about the everyday practices that the contemporary "bio-political capitalism" may give rise to: "Contemporary capitalism is bio-political, in that it aims at controlling all that lives; it has already turned into a form of bio-piracy in that it aims at exploiting the generative powers of women animals, plants, genes and cells" (Braidotti, 2008: 10). The debate between humanists advocating a more restricted use of the new possibilities and proponents of the less restrained development of the life sciences may continue. However, no matter if one endorses progress or believes in a more regulated and controlled development, there are always of necessity trade-offs and negotiations between what may be done or not. The interesting thing to notice is, as Franklin (2001) suggests, that the general trust in the sciences has lowered despite its apparent possibilities for helping humans live healthier, happier, and longer lives. Apparently, there is a concern regarding the effects of a too far-driven and unrestrained technoscience that cannot be overcome only on the basis of sheer performativity.

SUMMARY AND CONCLUSION

The massive growth in the technosciences and the life sciences more specifically has opened up many new possibilities for humanity—at least in privileged classes in the affluent parts of the world—to improve the quality of life. The life sciences have traditionally been financed and organized into public sector organizations and universities adhering to principles of transparency and joint knowledge sharing, but since the mid 1970s, cohering with the growth in importance of neoliberal economic and political doctrines, know-how generated in the life sciences has been increasingly protected by patents and other intellectual property right legislation. During the growth of the biotechnology sector in the 1980s and 1990s, appearing at the same time as the large-scale human genome mapping projects (HUGO), the tendency to think of life-science know-how as intellectual capital subject to commodification continued and became widely institutionalized. Today, we can take advantage of a fully functioning bioeconomy wherein biocapital and biovalue are produced and circulate among a variety of actors. While the emergence of the bioeconomy has been, by and large, a positive thing for the individual, there are also concerns that the pharmaceutical and biotechnology industries are not only producing therapies for identified diseases or disorders but that they are also taking part in translating common conditions into legitimate and therefore "drugable" conditions. That is, rather than responding to existing conditions, the actors of the bioeconomy are actively imposing new beliefs and analytical frameworks helping to establish new diseases and illnesses.

2 Biopolitics, Neoliberalism, and the Calculative Worldview
The Economics of Life

INTRODUCTION

In this chapter the broader historical and politico-economical conditions for the emerging bioeconomy will be addressed. The growth and advancement of global technoscience are undoubtedly the *primus motor* for the bioeconomy, but to assume that the growth in know-how will eventually produce its own demand of market conditions is an undersocialized (in Granovetter's [1985] apt phrase) view of innovation and of market formation. Instead, consistent with studies of what Hughes (1999) calls "large technological systems" such as the electricity system (Hughes, 1983), the telephone system (Fisher, 1992), or the telegraph (Israel, 1992; Standage, 1998), the bioeconomy is examined in more sociological terms where practices, routines, rules, and standards are established over time and under the influence of social interests and political concerns (Yakubovich, Granovetter, and McGuire, 2005). Expressed differently, the new economic sociology (see, e.g., Fligstein, 2001; MacKenzie and Millo, 2003; MacKenzie, 2006; Zelizer, 2007) suggests that there is no such thing as an "invisible hand" regulating markets, but instead that the great variety of actors and interests in place needs to be coordinated to create a market or a large technological system. While the totality of the life sciences by no means is one single unified technological system in analogy with the electricity system, there are still similar trajectories in terms of the enactment of standards and routines for how to proceed in the work.

The principal economic and political regime serving to advance the bioeconomy is the neoliberal doctrine that emphasizes the de-regulation of markets and the central importance of individual property rights. As have been pointed out by many commentators, without the very idea that life-science know-how can be legitimately protected by intellectual property rights, it is complicated to advance interesting research findings to integrated, registered, and marketable commodities. This chapter thus addresses the neoliberal doctrine as one of the key political and economic changes in the last century, having direct influence over the emergence of the bioeconomy. However, the roots of the bioeconomy stretch back to the late eighteenth century and especially the nineteenth century—the century of swift urbanization in parts of Europe (Gay, 1984; Bynum, 1994: 63)—and the growth in political initiatives to regulate and monitor growing populations. Michel Foucault speaks of this change as a new forms of biopolitics, a new regime of governmentality, emphasizing demographics and specific tools such as descriptive statistics being developed during the course of the nineteenth century (Hacking, 1990). In the latter half of the chapter, it is demonstrated how numerical representations (figures, mathematical algorithms, and formulae) have increasingly served a key role in both neoliberal governance centered on finance theory but also in the life sciences, in the use of what Thacker (2004) calls *biomedia*. Biomedia thus exploits recent changes in both media and in computation (mathematization of underlying materials and modes of calculation) to render biological systems open for inspection and analysis through the use of numerical representations. That is, the biological body is examined no differently than a stock broker examines the changes in financial markets. The two activities, life sciences and financial trading, are thus operating on the basis of the same epistemology, emphasizing the possibility of using numerical presentations to capture an underlying material substratum (e.g., biological organism) or the circulation of capital (in financial markets). Seen in this way, the insistence on transparency, calculability, and computation is part of the master narratives (Star, 1999) of the neoliberal doctrine, where what can be measured and rendered visible to inspection and therefore open to public evaluation is capable of being economized. In short, the neoliberal gaze is operating on the basis of numerical inscriptions and representations and their computation.

GOVERNMENTALITY AND BIOPOLITICS

The works of Michel Foucault have generally been praised as being a major contribution to the social sciences, and his *oeuvre* contains a large number of concepts and analytical models and metaphors that have informed social science research over the last forty years (Hindess, 1996). In addition to his highly sophisticated theoretical framework, Foucault also presented important historical studies of, for instance, penal practice, psychological illness ("madness"), sexuality, and medicine as professional disciplines. One of the key terms in his vocabulary is *governmentality*, a term used to denote, in McNay's (2009: 57) view, a "peculiar modern form of political rule, the legitimacy of which is derived not from the wisdom, might or religious sanction of the sovereign but from the 'rational' ordering of men and social affairs." In Foucault's discourse theory framework (Foucault, 1972), a new regime of governmentality emerges on basis of a new formation of knowledge (referred to as *savoir* in French), producing many different practices and forms of specialized knowledge (*connaissance*).[1] These forms of discursive formations, playing a key role in the regulation and governance of modern society, started to be consolidated in the eighteenth century:

> The eighteenth century was the century when knowledges were disciplined, or when, in other words, the internal organization of every knowledge becomes a discipline which had, in its own field, criteria for selection that allowed it to eradicate false knowledge or nonknowledge. We also have the forms of normalization and homogenization of knowledge-contents, forms of hierarchicalization, and an internal organization that could centralize knowledges around a sort of de facto axiomatization. So every knowledge was organized into a discipline . . . Science in the singular did not exist before the eighteenth century. Science existed, knowledges existed, and philosophy, if you like, existed. (Foucault, 2003: 181)

The amateur scholars that dominated in the eighteenth and nineteenth centuries were replaced by a new academic class, located at the universities and organized in the disciplines and domains of expertise (like the schools for engineering, mining, politics and administration, and commerce in the French *Grandes Écoles*). This growth of civil society, based on institutions rather than the presence of a king, led to a shift in focus from techniques of power "centered on the body" (see Foucault, 1977) to the organization of larger populations:

> [W]e see something new emerging in the second half of the eighteenth century: a new technology of power, but this time it is not disciplinary. This technique of power does not exclude the former, does not exclude disciplinary technology, but it does dovetail into it, integrating it, modify it to some extent, and above all, using it by sort of infiltrating it, embedding itself in existing disciplinary techniques. The new technique does not simply do away with the disciplinary techniques, because it exists on a different scale, on a different scale, and because it has a different bearing area, and makes use of very different instruments. (Foucault, 2003: 242)

Foucault names this new form of governmentality *biopolitics*, a totality of techniques of power that controlled and organized populations rather than punishing individual deviant cases through bodily violence (Lemke, 2001, 2011). However, Esposito (2008: 16) points out that the Swede Rudoph Kjellén, a relatively obscure thinker not playing a central role in Foucault's work, was the first to use the term "biopolitics" as an extension of "geopolitics" in 1905. McNay (2009: 57) suggests that there are two key elements in the new biopolitical regime: (1) "regulatory and massification techniques" (e.g., statistics and demographics) aimed at controlling the increasingly urbanized population, and (2) "individualizing, and disciplinary mechanisms" that "shape the behaviours and identity of the individual through the imposition of certain normalizing technologies and practices of the self." In the new regime of governmentality, populations are not only controlled and monitored "from above" but also "from within" through the imposing of individualizing and disciplining mechanisms. For instance, in Sweden the eighteenth century was a period during which large scale social movements aimed at reducing the consumption of alcohol. Alcoholism was widespread in all social strata, and in many cases the abuse of alcohol caused much social suffering. For instance, in the case of Sweden, the non-drinking associations condemning alcohol, and helping people getting over their alcohol consumptions played a key role in forming the social organization that eventually would lead to the formation of a labour movement and trade unions at the end of the century. This kind of engagement to deal with social problems on the basis of individualizing and disciplinary practices is highly representative of the new regime of governmentality. Helmreich (2008) sees a direct connection between Foucault's concept of biopolitics and the more recent term biocapital:

> Biocapital . . . extends Foucault's concept of biopolitics, that practice of governance that brought 'life and mechanisms into the realm of explicit circulation' (Foucault, 1978, p. 143). Theorists of biocapital posit that such calculation no longer organizes only state, national, and colonial governance, but also increasingly formats economic enterprises that take as their object the creation, from biotic material and information, of value, markets, wealth, and profit. The biological entities that inhabit this landscape are no longer individuals and populations—the twin poles of Foucault's biopower—but also cells, molecules, genomes, and genes. (Helmreich, 2008: 461)

While biopolitics was the main regime of governmentality during the eighteenth and the first half of the nineteenth centuries, granting the state apparatus and its institutions a key role to play, the neoliberal change in focus downgraded or even condemned state-interventions as a means of pushing individual economic enterprises to the periphery. If biopolitics is the governmentality of the state-regulated monitoring of health and life, the bioeconomy is the comparative regime of governmentality in the neoliberal regime. Rather than representing a radical shift in focus, it is important to recognize the continuity over time while recognizing the small shifts in emphasis and nuances.

I. NEOLIBERALISM, FINANCE THEORY, AND THE BIOECONOMY

Neoliberalism

Harvey (2005) locates the breaking point for neoliberalism to the end of the 1970s. During this decade, there had been two major oil crises, and the mass production regime that worked smoothly during the decades after World War II apparently had come to an end. Stagflation (inflation in combination with rising unemployment) was a confusing phenomena not being fully explained by the predominant Keynesian economic theory. Harvey (2005) points at three (seemingly) interrelated political processes. In China, in 1978, Communist Party chairman Deng Xiaoping declared that he intended to start to deregulate the Chinese economy and transfer it from a planned economy to a more market-based form, using "capitalist slogans" such as "to get rich is glorious" to signal a break with the former Maoist doctrine (Fang, 2010: 162). In the U.K., Margret Thatcher was elected prime minister in 1979 and started to deregulate the financial markets and fight the trade unions. The year after, in 1980, Ronald Reagan took office in the U.S., more or less continuing the deregulation of the markets and implementing other neoliberal reforms that had been initiated during the Carter administration. These three events were not very spectacular at first sight and were not treated as major historical events from the outset, but Harvey (2005) suggests that historians may conceive of this period as being revolutionary in terms of breaking with the state-governed economy and opening up more market-based economic activities. Several authors point out that the term neoliberalism is a complex term with an interesting and diverse history. "It is impossible to define neoliberalism purely theoretically . . . neoliberalism straddles a wide range of social, political and economic phenomenon at different levels of complexity," Saad-Filho and Johnston (2005: 1) claim. Similarly, Plehwe and Walpen (2006: 2) argue that "neoliberalism cannot be understood as a *singular* set of ideas and policy prescriptions, emanating from one source." Adam Smith, neoclassical economics, the Austrian School of economics and its critique of Keynesianism and Soviet-style socialism, the University of Chicago monetarism, libertarianism, and "supply-side economics" are some of the elements in the neoliberal doctrine. Wacquant (2009: 306) emphasizes the distinction between the "lay idiom" of neoliberalism and its meaning in social science discourses: "Neoliberalism is an elusive and contested notion, a hybrid term awkwardly suspended between the lay idiom of political debates and the technical terminology of social science, which moreover is invoked without clear referent." He continues: "Whether singular or polymorphous, evolutionary or revolutionary the prevalent conception of neoliberalism is essentially economic: it stresses an array of market-friendly policies such as labor deregulation, capital mobility, privatization, a monetarist agenda of deflation and financial economy, trade liberalization, interplay competition, and the reduction of taxation and public expenditures." Pulley (2005) names the specific form of neoliberalism that was developed in the U.K. and U.S. in the 1980s and 1990s the "The U.S. model," a model characterized by "[d]eregulation of financial markets, privatisation, weakening of institutions of social protection, weakening of labour unions and labour market protections, shrinking of government, cutting of top tax rates, opening up of international goods and capital markets, and abandonment of full employment under the guise of the natural rate" (Pulley, 2005: 25). In Wacquant's view (2009: 306. Emphasis in the original), neoliberalism is to be understood as a "[a] *transnational policies project* aiming to remake the nexus of market, state, and citizenship from above." This "project" engages a great many actors and institutions and is "[c]arried by a new global ruling class in the making, composed of the heads and seniors executives of transnational firms, high-ranking politicians, state managers and top officials of multinational organizations (the OECD, WTO, IMF, World Bank, and the European Union), and cultural-technical experts in their employ (chief among them, economists, lawyers, and communication professionals with germane training and mental categories in their different countries)" (Wacquant, 2009: 306–307).

Griffin (2009), examining the spread of neoliberal practices as a process of interested and situated gendered politics, lists four basic principles in the neoliberal tradition of thinking:

1. A confidence in the market (*marketization*) as the mechanism by which societies should be made to distribute their resources (although market imperfections may hamper distributive patterns; should we remove these the 'allocative efficiency' of the market is restored);
2. A commitment to the use of private finance (in place of public spending) in public projects (*privatization*);
3. *Deregulations*, with the removal of tariff barriers and subsidies ensuring that the market is freed from the potential tyranny of nation-state interventions, thereby granting capital optimal mobility;
4. A commitment to *flexibilization*, which refers to the ways in which production is organized in mass consumption society (i.e., dynamically, and flexibly) (Griffin, 2009: 9).

Wacquant (2009: 307) suggests that while neoliberalism is essentially "economic" in nature, it establishes a "new institutional logic" having four elementary components: (1) "Economic deregulation," (2) "Welfare state devolution," (3) "The cultural trope of individual responsibility," and (4) "an expensive, intrusive, and proactive penal apparatus" (Wacquant, 2009: 307). In general, Wacquant speaks of the "masculinization" of the state apparatus as penal practices are expanding at the expense of the public welfare. In Griffin's (2009) account, studying the work in the World Bank, an international regulatory financial institution set up to govern and monitor the global economy, in many cases in the economies of so-called developing countries, the four principles of *marketization, privatization, deregulations,* and *flexibilization* are not axiomatic principles in a politically value-neutral scientific framework but rather constitute a highly politicized and gendered set of economic governance principles (i.e., that of neoliberal economic theory). Griffin (2009) says that many commentators on her work have claimed that the term gender is of minor importance in her research project, and in order to understand the role of the World Bank there are other, more relevant issues to address. Griffin (2009: 9) responds to such claims as "trivializing" the role of gender into a matter of populating key positions in organizations such as the World Bank with a least a minimum number of female experts and directors, and points at gender as a more deep-seated issue in economic governance: "Gender is not, as many would have it, marginal to relations of economic governance, but the belief that it is remains persistent, not least among those who believe economics, even politics, to be neutral sciences peopled by functionally similar, rational actors." For Griffin (2009), the neoliberal doctrines put into work by institutions such as the World Bank need to be understood on the basis of gendered ideologies and beliefs. Whether or not Griffin's approach to the study of economic institutions is fruitful, neoliberal doctrines have been articulated by primarily male social theorists and economists, with a few central female actors such as Margret Thatcher and the Russian-American writer Ayn Rand—"the closest one can get to an ideologist of the 'greed is good' form of radical capitalism," in Žižek's (2009: 21) view—as notable exceptions.

Notwithstanding Griffin's (2009) emphasis on gender, neoliberal thinking is perhaps best known for its emphasis on the market as a principal *topos* for the rational regulating of economic activities. "For neoliberalism, the market symbolizes rationality in terms of an efficient distribution of resources. Government intervention, on the other hand, is deemed undesirable because it transgresses that rationality and conspires against both efficiency and liberty," Munck (2005: 61) states. However, critics contend that an idealized image of the market might work fine in conceptual models and theoretical elaborations, but in real life settings, markets are not of necessity inherently rational (see, e.g., Willse, 2010; Ericson, Barry, and Doyle, 2000):[2] "Markets never operate freely. The assertion they do so is part of neoliberal ideology. Both markets themselves and the environments they operate in are always created by government regulations, and cannot exist without them," Campbell (2005: 189) argues. Even in cases where markets apparently fail (either in terms of not being able to uphold I their key functions such as in the 2008 financial meltdown, or fail to value and appraise assets correctly), proponents of neoliberalism tend to blame the actors rather than the capitalist system per se. For Clarke (2005: 31), neoliberalism is not so much a "scientific theory of capitalism" as it is its "theology," a set of religious beliefs that cannot be abandoned in the face of unpredicted or unexpected events.[3] Economic breakdown in what is supposed to operate as a well-functioning capitalist system—Latin America has for instance been the scene for numerous failed neoliberal experiments managed by the IMF and the World Bank, including the Argentine recession in 2002 (Chorev and Babb, 2009)—thus constitutes a form of secular theodicy problem for neoliberals; how can there be economic glitches in an economic system that works perfectly well in theory?

The neoliberal tradition stretches back to the at least the 1920s and 1930s. In his history of neoliberalism, Michel Foucault examines a group of German economists located in Freiburg, publishing the Journal *Ordo* and favoring limited state intervention in the economy. These so-called ordoliberals expressed their concern for a common and recurrent theme in neoliberal thinking, namely, "excessive state intervention." This anxiety was based on the idea that "if one governs too much one does not govern at all" (McNay, 2009: 58) and postulated that state intervention should be regarded as exceptional. The ordoliberals favored individual action, governed by economical principles and preferences, rather than political forms of control. For the ordoliberals, McNay (2008: 56) claims, political control may lead to social conformity while individual difference is allowed in an economic matrix of regulation.

A few decades after the ordoliberals, leading American and European proponents of neoliberalism such as the Austrian School economists Friedrich von Hayek, Ludwig von Mises, and Milton Friedman and the renowned philosopher Karl Popper met in the Swiss resort of Mont Pèlerin in 1947 to discuss how to promote neoliberal thinking and politics. Hayek and Mises were prominent representatives of the Austrian School of Economics, advocating limited state interventions in the economy and liberal policies, and eventually Milton Friedman became a leading economist in the so-called monetarist school emphasizing low inflation policies and commonly associated with the economics department of University of Chicago where Friedman spent most of his career. Mises, the oldest of this core group, was a life-long enemy of state-controlled economy, bordering fanaticism in his beliefs. For instance, in his rant about bureaucracy (1944), Mises claims that this very organization form is "[i]mbued with an implacable hatred of private business and free enterprise" (von Mises, 1944: 9). For Mises, bureaucracy is a "disease" and an "outcome of government meddling with business" (Mises, 1944: 12). Mises here speaks—anticipating the work of, e.g., Crozier (1964) a few decades later—of a "bureaucratization of the mind," a decline of initiative and entrepreneurial capacities: "It [bureaucracy] kills ambition, destroys initiative and the incentive to do more than the minimum required. It makes the bureaucrat look at instructions, not at material and real success" (Mises, 1944: 56). In a society thoroughly based on bureaucratic organization, such portrayal of bureaucracy appears somewhat curious and not very tempered. Hayek proposed a theory of a self-organizing economy in his *The Road to Serfdom* (1944) and in his *Constitution of Liberty* (1960)—a key reference for the Thatcherist policies in the U.K.—wherein economic conditions and policies were giving privilege over political rights; for the first time in liberal thinking, economic doctrines are given more weight than that of human rights and liberties. This neoliberal cutting of the Gordian knot of politics and economics opened for the way for neoliberal economic policies. In Milton Friedman's *Capitalism and Freedom* (first published in 1962), this characteristic neoliberal separation of "political" and "economic" power is underlined: "Economic arrangements play a dual role in the promotion of a free society. On the one hand, freedom in economic arrangements is itself a component of freedom broadly understood, so economic freedom is an end in itself. In the second place, economic freedom is also an indispensable means towards the achievement of political goals" (Friedman, [1962]2002: 8). In this view, the distribution of resources and wealth is not a political objective but should be regulated by a "market organization of economic activity" (Friedman ([1962]2002: 14–15) wherein there is no "coercion." This assumption about the lack of coercion may be disputed.[4] This relatively simplistic assumption that there may be an economy devoid of politics in the conventional sense of the term is commonly associated with the rational choice theory of the Chicago School of Economics. More specifically, the Chicago doctrine rearticulated the entire political agenda in such terms:

> Notoriously, it was the Chicago School that innovated the idea that much of politics could be understood as if it were a market process, and therefore amenable to formalization through neoclassical theory. Politicians, it was claimed, were just trying to maximize their own utility, as were voters. Unfortunately, this doctrine implied that the state was merely an inferior means of attaining outcomes that the market could provide better and more efficiently; and that in turn led to another jaundiced assessment of the virtues and benefits of democracy. (Mirowski and van Horn, 2009: 162)

In this view, the economy can operate effectively outside a well-functioning democratic society. Politics and all the groundwork demanded to uphold a political system are here treated, at best, as a mere complement, a "support function," to economic action. Therefore, just as Hayek claimed, Friedman ([1962]2002) stresses that economic freedom is more important than political freedom precisely because the former will lead to the latter: "Viewed as a means to the end of political freedom, economic arrangements are important because of their effect on the concentration or dispersion of power. The kind of economic organization that provides economic freedom directly, namely competitive capitalism, also promotes political freedom because it separates economic power from political power and in this way enables the one to offset the other" (Friedman, [1962]2002: 8).

In the neoliberal doctrine of thinking, it would be to put the cart before the horse to assume that politics can regulate economic action. Instead, a deregulation of the economy to pave the way for "competitive capitalism" will lead to the "constitution of liberty." Friedman is not a political theorist or social thinker of the highest rank but a practicing economist, and his defense of economic liberty is in many ways confusing in terms of offering no substantial vision of society beyond the presence of competitive capitalism. As Mirowski and van Horn (2009: 167) notice, Friedman does now even bother to define freedom, the central concept in his treatise, justifying all kinds of political and economic action. Besides the separation between politics and economy being highly problematic, the entire philosophy pursued by Friedman ([1962]2002) is circular in argumentation, as freedom is not carefully defined, but is exactly the very absence of political control in the economic sphere. Therefore, "political freedom" is to be accomplished on the basis of "economic freedom." "In a further imitation of natural science, freedom was redefined as a purely mechanical 'choice' that could be exercised in each and every sphere of public life," Mirowski and van Horn (2009: 163) say a propos the Chicago School of neoliberal economic theory. "Chicago [economists] *saw* (sees) the world in a very distinctive manner: natural economic reality *is* the world of perfect competition," Fourcade (2009: 96) adds. Still, Friedman's arguments in combination with explicit instructions for economic policy have been remarkably influential, and *Capitalism and Freedom* has never gone out of print despite its "crude arguments" in Mirowski and van Horn's (2009: 167) view. Friedman was awarded one of the first Nobel Prizes in economic sciences in 1973—a year before his great master Friedrich von Hayek won the same prize—and has been a lifelong defender of neoliberal economic doctrines and a symbol for neoliberal economic policy and neoconservative political doctrines. Friedman's contributions to economic theory and political policy remain disputed; for some, he is a heroic figure while for others he merely served to justify the greed and inequality of an uncontrolled "competitive capitalism" and for deconstructing the legitimacy of the welfare state.

FINANCE THEORY

In addition to these political alliances leading up to the event of 1970, there were a number of changes in the underlying economic doctrines. While Hayek, Mises, and Friedman based their political convictions on macroeconomic theory, the growth of finance theory provided the tool for the financial markets that were developed in the 1980s. Path-breaking work done by a number of economists in the U.S. including Merton Miller and Franco Modigliani created a shared framework for the option-pricing model developed by Fischer Black and Myron Scholes, a contribution that eventually won them the Nobel prize in Economics. In MacKenzie's (2006) seminal work, the new finance theory developed in economics is not envisaged as cameras, capable of capturing the movements and patterns of the market, but rather as engines, having the capacity of producing large values through aligning a number of actors and imposing shared standards for how to trade risks across large number of actors. Finance theory may seem largely separated from the neoliberal political doctrines, but the advancement of new mathematical models and algorithms enabled an unprecedented growth in a calculative mode of thinking favoring numerical representations and other forms of mathematization of underlying assets and resources (Miller, 2001). Even though the relationships and connections between neoliberal doctrines and finance theory have been only marginally subject to systematic scholarly reflection, recent managerialist practices such as auditing are strongly related to a neoliberal tradition of thinking and a preference for calculation derived from finance theory. In MacKenzie's (2006) account, finance theory is the intermediary theory between abstract political systems and actual practices. If nothing else, the thriving finance sector in cities like London, New York, and Chicago (the latter the center for American derivative instrument trading) produced immense economic values benefiting at least some groups in society. Given the importance of the finance sector in late-modern contemporary society, it is little wonder Harvey (2005) reserves the term "neoliberal state" for the state primarily serving to ensure the free circulation of capital.

Peet (2007) grants much of the impetus of these neoliberal advancements to the field of economics. Just as suggested by MacKenzie (2006) and McCloskey (1986), Peet (2007) claims that economics is performative in terms of creating the behavior the discipline sets out to predict, and is by no means, as instituted by scientific ideologies, value-neutral or disinterested: "My claim is that economic theory is ideological in the sensed of being committed to class and national interest. Economic ideas follow logics that are constructed rather than discovered—that is, made up with interest in mind, rather than discovered innocently, latent in reality. This social construction includes the economic ideas and terminologies employed in policy-making power" (Peet, 2007: 53). A handful of economics departments at elite universities in the U.S. and in the U.K. supply neoliberal *bien pensant* economists serving to advise neoliberal governments on how to cut down public spending and otherwise pave the way for corporations in the neoliberal state. In this small but enormously influential group, 88 of the world's leading economists are working in America and 10 in the U.K. (Peet, 2007: 63).[5] The Anglo-American dominance of the economic doctrines is thus massive. Peet (2007: 82) portrays economics as being hegemonic, operating on the basis of knowledge that cannot be legitimately criticized from the outside (see Lyotard [1988] for an illustration) and concealing its own interests: "Economics is not an interest-neutral science of society. Economics is a liberal ideology devoted to the bourgeoisie. Modern economic theory, the pride of social science, rests on an empirical based (i.e., a set of generalized facts about the world) that is precarious to the extreme." Like perhaps no other science, economics remains highly contested in terms of making claims of being objective while critics suggest that is not the case.

CONSEQUENCES OF NEOLIBERALISM

At the same time as neoliberalism has produced massive amounts of wealth in some strata, for instance, in the emerging community of finance trading professionals (once referred to with the acronym *yuppies*—young professional people), neoliberal doctrine has served to widen the gap between the richest (few) and the poorer (multitude) at an alarming rate. Leslie Sklair (2002: 21) uses the term "the transnational capitalist class" to denote a small but very influential economic and political elite, and maintains that "despite real geographical and sectoral conflicts, the whole of the transnational capitalist class share a fundamental interest in the continued accumulation of private profit" (see also Hull, 2006; Carroll and Carson, 2006). This transnational economic class is the powerful elites of the globalized and international late-modern capitalism populating transnational corporations and resting on the "culture-ideology of consumerism."[6] There has been a significant redistribution of wealth from traditional sectors such as manufacturing to, for instance, the finance sector and the so-called professional service sector. Ericson, Barry, and Doyle (2000: 554) stress that economic inequality is one of the pillars of neoliberal economic doctrine, not as an inevitable consequence of economic policy but as a driver for economic growth: "Neoliberalism chooses inequality. Within a neoliberal regime of responsible risk taking all difference, and the inequalities that result from it, is seen as a matter of choice. If one ends up poor, unemployed, and unfulfilled, it is because of poorly thought-out risk decisions." Since neoliberalism "fosters the ethics of being responsible" (Ericson, Barry, and Doyle, 2000: 554), much agency is granted to individual subjects, and consequently a series of social problems is enacted as being a matter of free choice and agency in the neoliberal doctrine. Davis (2009a) points at the consequences of neoliberal doctrines for the economy and stresses the relative downgraded role of manufacturing in for instance the U.S. . By March 2009, more Americans were unemployed than were employed in manufacturing, and "all signs pointed to further displacement in the goods-producing sector" (Davis, 2009a: 27). By 2009, Walmart, the largest American company in terms of numbers of employees, "employed about as many Americans (1.4 million) as the 20 largest U.S. manufacturers *combined*." In addition, nine of the twelve largest employers were retail chains (Davis, 2009a: 30). The future of the labor markets lies in retailing, not in manufacturing. However, the principal reason for manufacturing being offshored to economies with lower costs is, Kollmeyer (2009) argues, that the general growth in the economy in the Western world has produced a demand for services that have been able to attract parts of the workforce. That is, the main reason for companies moving abroad is not the higher productivity accomplished elsewhere but because there is less competition over labor in less-developed countries than in the West. One of the consequences of the shift in focus from large manufacturing companies to smaller service-producing companies is the decline of what Davis (2009a) calls, after Peter

Drucker, the "society of organizations." Rather than being characterized by large-scale organizations, the Western economies are increasingly based on smaller firms collaborating over organizational boundaries (Owen-Smith and Powell, 2004; Powell and Grodal, 2005; Raab and Kenis, 2009). "Large corporations have lost their place as the central pillars of American social structure," Davis (2009a: 27) says. Even seemingly large corporations like Nike or Coca-Cola Company, are primarily engaged in managing their intellectual properties—brands, patents, advertising copy, distribution, knowhow—while most production activities are outsourced. These companies are, Davis (2009a) says, just like universities and pharmaceutical companies, in the "idea business." As opposed to the "society of organizations," the present economic regime can be characterized as a "portfolio society," a society where smaller firms are collaborating and where all sorts of economic assets become subject to what Dore calls (2008: 1097–1098) "financialization," "[t]he increasing role of financial motives, financial markets, financial actors and financial institutions in the operation of domestic and operational economies." Davis continues:

> In a portfolio society, the organization man has become replaced by the daytrader, buying and selling various species of capital, from homes reconceived as options on future price increases, to college education whose estimated net present value informs the choice of school and course of study, to children whose Little League games might be an apt context to cultivate potential clients. (Davis, 2009a: 39)

In the portfolio society the corporate governance structure of the corporation is changing since the ownership move from individual owners to institutional ownership: "Nearly three-quarters of the average Fortune 1000 corporations' shares were owned by institutional investors in 2005, with mutual funds making up the most concentrated block" (Davis, 2009a: 33). These institutional investors increasingly set the pace for global capitalism inasmuch as they increasingly regard firms analytically as bundles of financial resources, not as organizations populated by human beings, machines, material resources, and intangible assets (brands, patents, etc.). Instead, these firms are treated as financial assets whose investment needs to pay off in a relatively short time perspective. The dominant economic doctrine regulating this portfolio management is the idea of shareholder value, a term that we will address in some detail.

SHAREHOLDER VALUE IDEOLOGIES AND THE REDISTRIBUTION OF ECONOMIC WEALTH

The capacity of producing shareholder value is today the single most important performance indicators in listed companies (Engelen, 2002;

Cooper and Robson, 2006; Ezzamel, Willmott, and Worthington, 2008). Ho's (2009) ethnography of Wall Street provides insights into how the ideology of shareholder value structures the economy. According to Ho, an anthropologist and Princeton graduate with experience working on "the street," Wall Street is a community of about between 600,000–700,000 workers (depending on the economic cycle), recruited from elite institutions such as Princeton (the recruitment base *par préférence*) and Harvard, fueled by an interest for making quick and substantial amounts of money (bonuses range from between U.S. 300,000–500,000 per annum), and characterized by razor-sharp competition, excessive overwork (around 100 hours per week seems to be fairly standard, and one interviewee claimed he worked about 90 percent of the weekends during his first two years on Wall Street), endemic sexism and racism, and virtually no job security. This combination of blatant elitism—virtually all of Ho's interviewees claimed they were "working with the smartest people on earth," a central belief in sustaining the industry—massive amounts of pay, and hard work produce, Ho suggests, a lack of empathy with people working in other sectors. For instance, Wall Street investment bankers tend to see themselves as upholders of socio-economic Darwinist principles where only the strongest survive and where performance is singlehandedly evaluated in terms of shareholder value. Says Ho:

> My informants conflated the characteristics of brightness and motivation with work ethic to frame their own industry as the cutting edge of efficiency, radically transforming the mediocrity of regular corporations. Wall Street beliefs about 'complacent' workplaces in the 'outside world' certainly help to justify programs of downsizing and narratives of doing more work with less people and suggest how corporate America should reframe its very approach to work and employment. (Ho, 2009: 104)

The sense of superiority, derived from the perceived and affirmed extraordinary talent and intelligence of the elite-university graduates, and a self-declared mission to put capital into more effective circulation, lead to a disregard for "the real economy": "Most corporate work, from Wall Street's perspective, is neither change oriented, financially innovative, nor directed towards spiking stock prices; it is not forward-thinking nor in lockstep with the market, and as such is inherently *unproductive*. It does not 'add value' according to the financial parameters by which investment bankers measure success" (Ho, 2009: 105–106):

> [One informant talked] about the struggle between the owners of capital versus managers, where managers had squandered the fruits of capital by sharing them with other constituents. He spoke passionately about the poor stewardship and excess of managers and how it was

Wall Street investment bankers who realigned managers to their true purpose of increasing shareholder value . . . Wall Street's shareholder value perspective is that employment is thought to be outside the concern of public corporations. Job loss was certainly a sad event, but beyond the responsibility of corporate America. (Ho, 2009: 128)

The concept of shareholder value is the central theoretical construct legitimizing Wall Street's authority to take control over various corporations not effectively enough handling the interests of the owners. One of Ho's interviewees,' a certain Stan Clark, was explicit about the role of investment bankers in governing capital in the interest not of society more broadly but only in the shareholders' interest:

'If you look at the old days,' Stan Clark told me, 'all the companies were basically fat, dumb, and stupid. [T]hey did not change. They were not making [enough] money. The [managers] didn't care. Now, you have Wall Street with all their shareholders . . . You can't just be dumb, fat, and happy . . . You have to change. Shareholders are looking at. . . . your excess expenses . . . Back in the old days, wide town employment was big a thing. They didn't even hardly lay off. Nowadays, they have to lay off because shareholders say, "Look, you have all this excess overhead . . . You have to cut out the fat. We want a lean, mean operation." So . . . Wall Street is definitely making a much more efficient corporate America.' (Ho, 2009: 130–131)

Stan Clark's opinion and stern belief in the righteousness of the shareholder value doctrine were representative of Ho's sample of interviewees. Wall Street is guarding capital against lazy bureaucracies and managers having little interests in changing or performing better. The cure for "big, fat, and lazy" bureaucracies is "corporate restructuring" and downsizing, commonly under the more positive-sounding banner of becoming "lean," a term brought into the management vocabulary from the Toyota manufacturing system (e.g., Liker, 2004). Such restructuring and downsizing naturally produce "surplus labor" whose future after Wall Street is only vaguely fathomed by Ho's interviewees. Says a Wall Street investment banker apropos the emphasis on shareholder value ideology: "Well. That's just a matter of making the economy efficient. In the end that is good because you take people out of dead-end jobs anyway and sort of force them to find something in an industry that is growing. But I am sure, if you are on the other side of that equation, it is a lot harder" (Ho, 2009: 158). Even though Wall Street investment bankers are thinking of shareholder value as "a natural way" to manage and govern organizations, Ho traces the idea of shareholder value to a complex history of ideas derived from neoclassical economic theory and the long-standing debate over the role between professional managers and owners (see, e.g., Berle and Means, 1971; Chandler, 1977). The idea that shareholders are the only group to be concerned about is in this perspective representative of an analytical framework and model where the complex and manifold social relations of the firm are reduced to a univariate calculus anchored in the neoliberal doctrine that it is capital per se that is the prime motor of the economy and that the circulation of capital is the only valid measure for economic efficiency: "The neoclassical critique of managerialism turns on a compelling narrative of the abused shareholder, rendered powerless by the dispersal of concentrated shareholding and the rise of self-serving managers running companies in their own interests. In this drama, the owner is positioned as the victim, denied his rightful role in the modern corporation by managers-usurpers" (Ho, 2009: 190). Rather than enacting a more integrated model of the corporation wherein many stakeholders and interests are considered, the shareholder value ideology put to use on Wall Street is overly neoliberal in terms of both its disregard of the social accomplishments of bureaucracy and management and its one-dimensional emphasis on unrestrained capital: "The precarious balance that corporate America had wrought between catering to stock prices and administering to the multiple and conflicting participants of the corporations has been tipped decisively in favor of financial values and interests," Ho (2009: 158) concludes. She continues: "To hear Wall Street tell the narrative of stock markets and shareholder ascendancy in the late twentieth century is to hear a narrative of justice prevailing after prolonged hijacking of the modern corporation by a 'fat, dumb, happy' bureaucracy." It is against this historical background that Stan Clark's indignant exclamation that "they didn't even hardly lay off" needs to be understood. Wall Street may have helped making American and overseas business more competitive by reducing "excessive overhead," but it has also—which may be the principal aim, not a by-product, some would argue—transferred wealth from the multiple corporate stakeholders to a smaller number of shareholders, including some Wall Street investment banks. In addition, Wall Street professionals were used to getting fired occasionally and arguably did not see the laying off of employees as a major issue. The difference is that these downsized corporations did not pay their former employees annual bonuses in the range of USD 300,000–500,000. Seen in this perspective, shareholder value ideology theoretically, politically, and, perhaps more important, ethically legitimizes cutting pay for employees and downsizing corporations to transfer a larger share of the wealth produced by corporations to the owners of the capital at work. Mirrored against the recent debates about corporate social responsibility (CSR), shareholder ideology may be disputed on the basis of the governance of corporations in late modernity. Is the performance of corporations solely evaluated on the basis of the value produced for the owners of capital, or are there other parameters that need to be taken into account to ensure sustainable long-term performance? If you safeguard the interests of the owners of capital, you get adequate performance and healthy corporations for free, neoliberal economists and financial analyst claim. Other commentators are less certain of the validity of such a doctrine. Above all, as Milton Friedman declared, economic freedom has a value in its own right, and shareholder value is such a doctrine operationalized into actual practices.

In summary, the neoliberal economic and political doctrine has gradually been established in the Western world as a predominant, close to hegemonic, idea. While the neoliberal economy has brought new industries and made a number of industries more effective (e.g., health care and public transportation), there is also a lingering concern regarding the long-term viability of a world economy governed by financial markets, financial analysts, and what may be called "shareholder gaze"—the insistence on seeing heterogeneous underlying assets in numerical and financial terms exclusively. In industries like the pharmaceutical industry, demanding long-term investment in R&D, shareholder gaze may easily underrate the value of investment in know-how paying off in the future (Ramirez and Tylecore, 2004). There is, in short, a risk of market failure in valuing certain economic activities properly and correctly, thereby undermining long-term investment. Investments that will yield income many years in the future are often less valued than relatively safe investment in a shorter time perspective. Especially after the 2008 economic downturn, starting as a financial crisis and leading to a worldwide economic recession throwing states like Greece, Latvia, Dubai, and Iceland into major budget deficits and sharply growing debts, there is widespread skepticism regarding an unregulated or poorly regulated financial market (see Stiglitz, 2010). The case of Iceland is informative in this respect. Being a small Nordic country (approximately 250,000 inhabitants), primarily engaged in fishing and tourism, Icelanders developed a large international banking sector that collapsed during the financial crisis. Many Icelanders had taken large loans in foreign currencies and found themselves on the brink of bankruptcy as the Icelandic *krona* sank like a stone on the international capital markets. The macroeconomic situation became so severe that McDonald's decided to close down its Iceland branch because it was too expensive to import meat and other ingredients, a seemingly peripheral event that nevertheless played a key symbolic role. Also major economies like the U.S. had to take massive loans to stabilize the economy and boost demand in the home market. The consequences of the 2008 finance crisis and the accompanying economic recession are still today complicated. One thing is however clear and that is that the credibility of neoliberal economic doctrines and especially the idea of self-regulating markets, so dear to the first generation of American neoliberal economists such as Friedrich von Hayek and Milton Friedman, has been lowered. How this will affect the long-term economic policy remains to be determined.

NEOLIBERAL THINKING IN THE BIOECONOMY

The neoliberal economic and political doctrines have influenced the study of the many branches of the life sciences in, e.g., health care and new drug development (Pitts-Taylor, 2010; Fischer, 2009; Prasad, 2009; Cooper,

2008; McAfee; 2003). In this literature, neoliberalism is not only tangential to the advancement of the life sciences but is constitutive of such accomplishment, and therefore there are strong and complex relations and causalities between economic and political ideologies and actual research work. The perhaps most salient effect of neoliberal doctrine is the emphasis on intellectual property rights (IPR) in late modern capitalism, defending one of the pillars of liberal and neoliberal thinking. McAfee (2003) talks about "neoliberalism on the molecular scale" in her study of the use of patenting of biotechnological species and processes. McAfee (2003) speaks of a "double reductionism," the "molecular-genetic reductionism" assuming that epistemic objects (Rheinberger, 1997) such as genes or gene sequences may be patented and that they serve as enclosed and stable entities, and the "economic reductionism," the emphasis on "private ownership and market-based management of biotechnology." The discourse on molecular-genetic reductionism "[c]onceptualizes genes as discrete entities: functional units of information which can be characterized precisely, counted, added or subtracted, altered, switched on and off, moved from one organism or one species to another by means of genetic engineering," McAfee (2003: 204) suggests.[7] This perspective is highly debated and increasingly outmoded in biomolecular sciences, but since it is strongly supported by economic reductionist doctrines it still play a key role when thinking about biotechnology notwithstanding its limited accuracy: "[F]rom an economic-reductionist perspective, genes and genetically modified organisms can be priced and traded, so long as clear rights of ownership to genetic information and its products are established and enforced" (McAfee, 2003: 209). In other words, economic interests overrule technoscientific models under the auspices of private property rights. Carolan (2010: 111) addresses the same topic, claiming that the biotechnology industry poses a real challenge to American patenting law in terms of not seeking to patent stable and self-enclosed entities:

> [B]iotechnology patents require a degree of flexibility in the thing they are said to protect because biotechnologies are by their very nature ontologically mutable. Not unlike earlier patented forms . . . the stability of biotech patents is produced. Yet, unlike conventional patented forms, the thing produced with regard to biotech patents retains a significant degree of flexibility to it, which is to say, at least in part, there has been so much activity in the courts in recent years over just what constitutes patents infringement. (Carolan, 2010: 111)

While McAfee (2003) emphasizes private property rights as the prime motor in the reductionist doctrine of molecular-genetic research, Carolan (2010) points at the ontological and epistemological challenges for juridical bodies granting the patents. "[Patents] create," Carolan (2010: 111) writes, the "illusion of an immutable, ontologically independent object. This socio-legal maneuver is necessary if these objects are to be distinguished from the unwieldy (and thus unpatentable) realm of the natural world." The unruly world of nature, being too fluid, changeable and fluxing to be tamed by any juridical system based on clearly distinguishable and compartmentalized entities and processes, still needs to be packed and distributed as neat parcels. Just as McAfee (2003) suggests, science loses against the institution of private property rights and the juridical system instituting such rights by law: "While no molecular biologist actually believes biology is just chemistry . . . it is this very view of reality that underlies biotechnology patents. In patent law, the fundamental unwieldiness of these artifacts is denied, leaving only discrete, isolated bits of reality to claim ownership over (e.g., chemicals, DNA, etc.)," Carolan (2010: 117) argues. While concepts such as genes and gene sequences (e.g., SNPs) came in handy for the juridical systems, the recent change in perspective to bioinformatics, conceiving of the biological system as essentially informational, poses a new challenge for patent law inasmuch as now-familiar terms such as genes and gene sequences are displaced by other technoscientific frameworks and epistemic objects, not anchored in the doctrine that "DNA-based technology is chemistry by another means" (Carolan, 2010: 119). In the wake of such changes, Carolan (2010) encourages us to think of patented technoscientific objects as being "fluid objects," more changeable and inherently unstable and distributed than the traditional patent law prescribes: "It might . . . be useful to think of biological patents as fluid objects. . . . self-replicating intellectual property, at least under the current patent regime, which demand a degree of interpretative flexibility. Without this mutability, biotechnology patents would likely not continue to exist. Yet conversely, too much flexibility would also threaten the patent regime" (Carolan, 2010: 122). Carolan (2010) and McAfee (2003) suggest that the neoliberal doctrine of intellectual property rights have helped protecting private interests in the work to develop new techoscientific know-how but that the price paid is the reduction of complex and distributed biological processes to stable, immutable entities, examined as being freestanding entities. That is, even the authority of the technosciences has not been able to resist what McAfee calls the "double reductionism" of neoliberal doctrines.

Besides IPR issues, neoliberal doctrines influence other domains of the bioeconomy. Needless to say, health care has always been heavily surrounded by norms and regulation.[8] In many countries in Europe (Sweden and the U.K., for instance), the health care sector has been located in the public, non-profit sector, to prevent a situation where individual economic interest should not interfere with issues of health, illness, and death. Over time, in the 1980s and subsequently, the public sector monopoly over health care has been weakened, and private interests have been allowed in the health care sector. Still, there is some concern in, e.g., Sweden, whether health care organizations should have the right to make money on the basis of health care operations, and there is a great anxiety surrounding the health-profit nexus in many quarters. A company producing furniture or gasoline, goods individual consumers may refuse to buy at will, may make a profit, but when it comes to health and illness, individuals may not have any choice but to seek medical expertise. Such anxieties have been mediated by public control organizations and the regulation of how much profits are made in health care organizations. When it comes to the broader bioeconomy, outside immediate patient care, there have been relatively few restrictions regarding privatized initiatives. Most of the biotechnology, pharmaceutical, and medical technology companies are private companies operating on the basis of sound economic principles shared with any other industry or business. Cooper (2008) suggests that the neoliberal economic regime serves as the bedrock for the emerging bioeconomy and strongly underlines the economic interest, i.e., *financiation*:

> What neoliberalism seeks to impose is not as much the generalized commodification of daily life—the reduction of the extraeconomic to the demands of exchange value—as its financiation. Its imperative is not so much the measurement of biological time as its incorporation into the nonmeasurable, achronological temporality of financial capital accumulation. (Cooper, 2008: 10)

Based on finance theory, neoliberal economic ideas are translated into practices of calculation where all kinds of biological assets are transformed into numerical (i.e., financial) representations. Fischer (2009: 15), studying the outsourcing of clinical trials, uses the term to "medical neoliberalism" to denote a variety of procedures and beliefs that "commodifies the body itself" through fragmenting the body into "specific problem areas" and thereby transforming the patient into a "consumer." For Pitts-Taylor (2010), "neoliberalism replaces an ethic of state care with an emphasis on individual responsibility and market fundamentalism." She continues:

> Market-based health care policies construct populations of individuals who are encouraged to ensure their own health and promote their personal wellness and success in the face of economic insecurity and globalization; they simultaneously render patient population consumers. Health maintenance becomes a responsibility or a duty rather than a right, and bodies and selves are targeted for intense personal care and enhancement. (Pitts-Taylor, 2010: 639–670)

Using the specific case of what is called *brain plasticity* or *neuroplasticity* the capacity of the brain to "[m]odify itself in response to changes in its functioning or environment" (Pitts-Taylor, 2010: 636). Pitts-Taylor (2010) suggests that neurology research is brought into a neoliberal discourse wherein individuals are expected to conceive of themselves as what Pitts-Taylor (2010: 639) names "neuronal subjects." In this view, it is the individual that is held responsible for a continued enhancement of "learning, intelligence, and mental performance, and to the avoidance of various risks associated with the brain, including mental underperformance, memory loss, and aging" (Pitts-Taylor, 2010: 639). In the regime of medical neoliberalism (Fischer (2009) or what Pitts-Taylor calls "biomediated capitalism," individuals are expected to care for the self even on the molecular scale through engaging in a variety of prescribed activities helping to maintain a healthy and vigorous brain. That is, the popular brain plasticity literature suggests, neurodegenerate disorders such as Parkinson's and Alzheimer's could be kept at a distance through thoughtful and regular mental exercises. Pitts-Taylor summarizes:

> The ideal subjects constructed here [in popular brain plasticity literature] should see herself in biomedical terms and should relate to her body at the molecular level, taking on a regimen of practices to ensure her neuronal fitness . . . Overall, brain potentiality represents a competitive field in which one's willingness to let go of sameness, to constantly adapt, and to embrace a lifelong regimen of work on the self (and one's children) are the keys to individual success. (Pitts-Taylor, 2010: 644)

In Pitts-Taylor's account, the literature on brain plasticity and neuroplasticity is translated and enacted within a neoliberal political framework, a particular regime of power, advancing the neuronal subject as an active and enterprising self in the position to determine one's "neurological fitness." This wedding of neoliberal ideology and life-science know-how is representative of biomediated capitalism wherein "biology derives production and it is the resource mined, excavated, and produced" (Pitts-Taylor, 2010: 642). One example of how the biological image of the self is produced is the research on the relationship between "pathological gambling" and neurology (Vrecko, 2008). The American gambling industry, holding substantial financial capital, has funded neurology research identifying certain neurotransmitters such as dopamine in the human brain's so-called reward system, which, arguably, determines compulsory gambling. Financial capital is then translated into "facts" about the human biology and the human brain:

> The capital ventures into biology that have occurred as the gambling industry has engaged in remaking neurobiological nature suggests as much, demonstrating how social actors and organizations are able to translate their economic resources into new forms of capital, via investment that reorganize institutions (e.g., academic and funding structures), scientific priorities and the directions of research and, ultimately, the standards for knowing (and contents of) biological nature. (Vrecko, 2008: 64)

For the gambling industry, such a scientific theory of pathological gambling is useful because it effectively separates social problems and biological constitution into two separate domains, nature and society: "Biological facts are powerful precisely by virtue of their distinction from the social: pathological gambling as a factual matter of neurobiology can be mobilized by the gambling industry precisely because those facts are understood to be a world apart from the social" (Vrecko, 2008: 63–64). The neurology sciences help establishing new, fact-based ways of thinking of gambling, pushing responsibilities toward the neurological self in need of monitoring and controlling her own cravings for gambling.

In terms of excavating biological resources, Prasad (2009) emphasizes neoliberal ideology as a principal driver in the contemporary bioeconomy: "[T]he market within neoliberal governmentality is 'naturalized' in terms of formal rules of economic order and subsumes within itself the other anchorage of liberal governmentality—utility . . . Utility is defined though exchange and that too in relation to the market" (Prasad, 2009: 2). Expressed in less abstract terms, the neoliberal doctrine has helped both to justify the treatment of biological assets in economic terms and provide the tools and theories for translating these assets into financial terms. The neoliberal doctrine is thus both the ideological framework wherein the bioeconomy is thriving and a box of tools for calculating the value of certain biological assets. To exemplify this thesis, the relentless transformation of "biology" into economic value, Prasad (2009) points to the growth of so-called Clinical (or Contracting) Research Organizations (CROs) in India. CROs are small, specialized companies helping major multinational pharmaceutical companies develop various parts of the drug trial process, for instance, to manage large-scale clinical trials during the development phase of new drug development (Petryna, 2009; Fischer, 2009). Prasad (2009) here makes reference to the home page advertisement of the CRO iGate Clinical Research, pointing out that there are "10 reasons" for coming to India to conduct clinical trial studies, namely:

40 million asthmatic patients
34 million diabetic patients
8–10 million people HIV positive
8 million epileptic patients
3 million cancer patients
>2 million cardiac-related deaths
1.5 million patients with Alzheimer's disease. (Prasad, 2009: 5)

This list of sick people, traditionally regarded as being indicative of the relative lack of progress of Indian society, is here overtly displayed as economic assets of the nation, a spreadsheet displaying the human suffering ready to be studied on the basis of commercial interests. "These characteristics of the Indian population," Prasad (2009: 6) writes, "which were for long considered a hindrance to India's development and, not to forget, a blot in the healthcare of citizens, have become 'assets.' They have come to constitute a human capital with starkly different characteristics from, say, the software engineer who has become the iconic Indian human resource." In a neoliberal economic doctrine, commodification is the prime motor of economic activity and economic development. If there is a lack of research subjects (i.e., patients) in the Western world (Drennan, 2002) because patients here are consuming too much medicine and thereby may jeopardize the clinical trial results, or may simply not want to participate in clinical trials (Petryna, 2006), there are ample opportunities for going to India to find a stock of patients to safeguard the trial. Prasad (2009) conceives of this kind of commercial as a form of neocolonialist practice: "Drug testing in India seems to be an ideal-typical case of continued capitalist exploitation of people of poorer countries by multinational companies based in the U.S. or some European nations" (Prasad, 2009: 6). However, even though Prasad (2009) makes a distinct point about the blatant display of human suffering in the form of a menu to choose from, the connections between the multinational pharmaceutical companies and the new drug development practices are not simply reduced to a matter of universal narrative of neocolonial exploitation, but the outcome has a rather complex historical trajectory. While it is true that pharmaceutical companies have been only modestly concerned about tropical diseases and other therapies where there is little economic potential, their activities are governed by political and scientific regulations and economic prospects. Major multinational companies are, like any other business, based on the concern for the bottom line result, and it would be unfair to expect them to act more "ethically correct" than any other industry. When pharmaceutical companies move their clinical trials to new parts of the world, they develop new drugs that both create employment in that part of the world and develop drugs that are (at times) of relevance for all of humankind. For instance, so-called lifestyle diseases like obesity, potentially treated by obesity drugs in the future, are by no means a health concern in the richer parts of the world. For instance, the working class in the U.S. is obese to a higher degree than the middle class in the U.S., and in relatively poor pars of the world such as in Pacific islands like Samoa, the degree of obesity is among the highest in the world.

The lack of research subjects willing and capable of participating in clinical trials has forced the multinational pharmaceutical companies to new parts of the world to conduct studies. In 1980, a new law limited the access of prisoners in the U.S. for clinical trials, and more or less overnight, a stock of volunteers was lost (Prasad, 2009: 12). In addition, the drug consumption has skyrocketed in the U.S. during the last three decades and today, Shah (2006) claims, a patient is more likely to die from eating too many drugs rather than eating too few. These drugs, interacting with the biological system in their own idiosyncratic ways, may interfere with the targeted drugs being tried out and therefore the research results may be blurred. To escape this problem, clinical trials are set in parts of the world were people consume less drugs, in most cases because they are poorer. In South America and in Eastern Europe (Ukraine, Russia, the Baltic states), regions where the phenotype is shared with the targeted American and European consumers, clinical trials may be organized and managed at a relatively low cost. This new migration of the clinical trials to regions characterized by what is called "drug naivité" is indicative of what Cooper (2008) and Prasad (2009) speak of as the neoliberal underpinning of the bioeconomy. In the bioeconomy, operating on the basis of biocapital and biovalue, access to, say 34 million diabetic patients may have a direct, calculable economic value—a biovalue. That is, the neoliberal practice of calculating on basis of biological assets represents an evident example of what McNay (2009: 59) speaks of as "the economization of social relations." Neoliberal doctrines are in other words providing an ideological framework and a set of practices helping translate previously neglected resources (e.g., the multitude of the sick in India) into economic value. Drawing on Pierre Duhem's (1996: 25) phrase *mise-en-équation*, one may say that the neoliberal analytical framework is capable of locating illness in calculation and ending up with a positive net present value. How this mathematization and representation of biological systems and organisms take place in practice will be discussed in the next section as the use of biomedia, media for translating biological systems into representations without reducing the material substratum to a mere regime of representation.

II. INSTITUTING CALCULATIVE AND COMPUTATIONAL WORLDVIEWS

Managing by Numbers

The neoliberal economic and political regime is characterized by its reliance on finance theory when economizing and financializing of virtually all kinds of commodities (Dore, 2008). Underlying the circulation of both capital and the more specific case of biocapital is then a series of transformational and computational practices, enabling a translation of material substrata into numerical representations and computations. What has been called the "new economic sociology" has been concerned about how this regime of economic and financial thinking, manifested in models and calculus (Miller [2001] uses the term *calculative practice*), has penetrated a variety of spheres of contemporary life. This represents a shift in focus from seeing the economy as a texture of relations and exchanges to a more detailed interest of the various procedures and technologies used in the very process of economization. Beunza and Stark (2004), studying financial trading, refer to this shift in focus as a "post-Parsonian economic sociology": "Just as post-Mertonian studies of science moved from studying the institutions in which scientists were embedded to analysing the actual practices of scientists in the laboratory, so a post-Parsonian economic sociology must move from studying the institutions in which economic activity is embedded to analysing the actual calculative practices of actors at work" (Beunza and Stark, 2004: 369–370). Institutions are needed for a market to function properly, but in order to understand the reproduction of institutions, "the calculative practices" need to be examined. The new economic sociology also emphasizes that such calculative practices are far from being objective and disinterested practices but are instead an embodiment of underlying ideologies and assumptions. In addition, calculative practices are not representing some extra-social domain of pure mathematics but are instead grounded in social relations and enacted assumptions. Expressed differently, new economic sociology does not postulate a pure economic domain devoid of social interests but conceives of markets and other economic arenas as being supported by and maintained by social relations. In the words of Neil Fligstein (2001: 4): "[T]he dynamism of market society is made possible by the extensive social organization. Competition and technological change are themselves defined by market actors and governments over time. These forces are not exogenous to market society, but endogenous to these social relations." Freese (2009) continues:

> Simple, uniform actors have had their greatest run anyway in orthodox economics, with its assumptions of uniform, unchanging preferences and actions as optimal given preferences . . . Sociologists traditionally look at the world and see actors who have biases, are swayed by emotions, respond to how information is framed, are influenced by affiliations and identity, internalize rules, and so on. (Freese, 2009: S21)

The difference between the economists' view of the market and the sociologists view is a matter of the belief in efficiency (see, e.g., Fama [1970] for an argument regarding market efficiency).[9] Says Fligstein (2001):

> Economic theories start with the premise that social institutions would not persist if they were not efficient. In the new institutional economics this assumptions is not meant to be tested. Instead, the general research tactic is to examine situations where different amounts of sources of uncertainty exist and then predict whether or not one will observe a certain social relation . . . Sociological theories are more descriptive and usually agnostic or skeptical as to the ultimate effect of social structures on efficiency. I, too, doubt that all social structures are efficient. (Fligstein, 2001: 9)

Economic theory and more specifically finance theory do not just assume that markets are effective (i.e., that all available information is accessible for all actors instantly) but actually enact that assumption as one of the axioms in the finance theories used in financial trading. What for the new economic sociologist would be a remarkable accomplishment, observable at best only at a few occasions, "effective markets," are for the economist an elementary theorem upon which a variety of theoretical elaborations is derived. However, as have been shown by MacKenzie and Millo (2003), economic theories do not have to be accurate as long as social practices converge toward their use and there is a wide agreement that the theories in use are, under determined conditions, the most useful models for guiding economic action.

In terms of actual practices, new economic sociology conceives of economic action taking place in markets as including both "cognitive understandings" and "concrete social relations" (Fligstein, 2001: 32). In practical terms, this means that agency is dependent on both tools and resources for serving in economic activities and that these tools and resources are always of necessity located in a social and cultural domain wherein they acquire their meaning. For instance, in financial trading, tools and resources include the various calculative practices enabling a mathematization of individual assets and some kind of socially sanctioned functions for these activities, for instance, trading risks, creating wealth, or even making money for oneself. The concrete social relations also include how different actors interact in their work. In the field of organization theory, there have been a variety of studies of how underlying social practices or resources become subject to calculative practices and how such new practices are related to a wider framework of managerialism and auditing, in short a new regime of managerial control through instituted calculative practices (Frandsen, 2009; Hummel, 2006). Zaloom's (2006) study of financial market trading in Chicago and London provides some interesting insights into the calculative practices of the traders. Zaloom (2006) suggests that traders have been trained in finance theory wherein the capacity to translate marketable assets is a "cornerstone" for the entire theory and its accompanying practice:

> Traders base their interpretations of financial conditions on the numbers that represent the market. Numbers are a cornerstone of economic calculation, the essential tool for rationalized action. Yet the practice of economic judgment in futures markets challenges this representation of economic action and requires a shift in the way we think about numbers. Numbers have often been considered elements of knowledge production that increase objectivity and certainty . . . The provisional nature of market numbers and the approximate character of traders' conclusions suggest that their practices are best characterized as interpretation rather than calculation. But scholarly theories of numbers and quantitative representations are insufficient to provide a full reading of the power of numbers in financial future markets. (Zaloom, 2006: 142)

Zaloom thus says that rather than being capable of containing all the relevant information, the financial figures are used in a broader social setting wherein they acquire their meaning, which in turn leads to certain decisions and actions. Financial traders have recently moved from an open trading floor—widely referred to as "the pit"—to a digital interface where fellow traders' body language and behavior cannot be observed and interpreted. Arnoldi (2006: 387) emphasizes the role and function of bodily communication in the previous practice of floor trading: "[T]he body language and look of a given trader make it possible to know which state of mind the trader is in, information which the counterpart will seek to exploit." Such body language provided the trader with a "feel for the market" (Arnoldi, 2006: 389). When floor trading was succeeded by "electronic trading" on the computer screen, old "practices of looking became obsolete. One of the traders complained about the new situation: 'It is like suddenly being blind and deaf. It is a complete cut-off from the information flow. Being a focal point, centre of all market activity, is suddenly gone. Instead of being in the centre, I suddenly found myself outside'" (Market trader, cited in Arnoldi, 2006: 388). As a consequence, financial trading is not strictly a matter of evaluating large sets of strings of numerical representations, but is also a matter of understanding this information in a wider socio-economic setting:

> The presentation of the market as a set of numbers is critical to the production of informational transparency. But the visual and auditory contexts of open outcry pits create opportunities and ambiguities that are not present in the graphic user interface of a digital exchange offer. In the transition from the pit to the screen, the contrasting representations of 'the market' demand that traders develop new strategies for using numbers to understand it. (Zaloom, 2006: 144)

At the same time, it is important to portray financial trading as a scientific, objective practice anchored in mathematical analysis to provide financial trading with the necessary image of being a socially legitimate and beneficial activity, a familiar narrative of "progressive rationalization." Says Zaloom (2006: 153): "This spare visual depiction embodies a commitment to reducing the intermediation between trader and market and to providing a simple and unadorned numerical representation of the market. The use of numbers as a means of transparency draws the trader toward a distilled idea of the market where disembodied action displays supply and demand for futures contracts." Zaloom (2006) suggests that numbers have a "synecdochal" relationship to markets; the individual figures are "parts" representing the "whole." In fact, however, market traders need additional competencies to excel in their profession. Zaloom (2006) is thus suggesting that even in the most mathematized forms of economic activity, operating primarily on the basis of financial information that may be examined through the use of various "inscription devices" (Beunza and Stark, 2004: 390) that help detect changes and movements in the market, there is still room for social elements guiding the work. The strong emphasis on the mathematical constitution of financial markets and financial trading is an ideological framework portraying the trade as being objective, fair, and socially legitimate. The ability to push subjective beliefs and preferences to the side for the benefit of effective market activities is one of the key benefits of financial trading, this ideology proposes. From the perspective of (new) economic sociology, the strong reliance and emphasis on calculative practices are indicative of the precarious role of financial trading. Century-long religious doctrines and common-sense thinking, denouncing money-making on the basis not of hard work and the transformation of nature into commodities and services but on the basis of usury and money-lending, will not vanish because influential doctrines such as the Black-Scholes option pricing model is rewarded the Nobel Prize. In the financial crisis of 2008, there were many alarmed voices being raised against the allegedly harmful effects of a free-wheeling and unregulated financial market populated by greedy financial traders having little interest besides making money for themselves. Such critique tends to surface in periods of turmoil while during the regular run-of-the-mill trading work there is relatively little concern. During economic recessions, financial traders serve the role of scapegoats since they are still today widely regarded as being complementary to regular so-called real economy. Perhaps in the future, there may be a wider acceptance for the financial markets.

However, the major facts in this setting are that numerical representations play a key role in enabling and structuring calculative practices in financial markets, that financial traders are not only, as proposed by the accompanying ideologies, strictly looking at the numbers when making their decisions, and that the financial markets have served as the archetypical domain where a calculative and mathematizing mindset has been successfully established. As Zaloom (2006) points out, the well-known narrative of "progressive rationalization" associated with mathematization and calculative practice is perfectly connected to the neoliberal worldview where transparency and effectiveness are highly valued and praised. Therefore, it is little wonder that the calculative practices of financial markets have served as a general role model for other managerial practices in other domains of the economy.

THE HUMAN BODY AS NUMERICAL REPRESENTATION

The human body is increasingly examined as a material substratum that can be translated into numerical representations, which in turn can be used in calculations and computation. At the end of the eighteenth century, leading medical authorities in France started to develop methods for using statistical analyses in their practice (Matthews, 1995). Over the course of the next century, more elaborated statistical methods were developed to produce what today is called "evidence-based medicine."

Today, medical practice is widely based on the idea that observations on human bodies and biological systems may be translated into numerical data. For instance, Frandsen's (2009) study of psoriasis patients in Sweden shows the complex translations of diagnostic data into figures and their continued circulation in the health care sector. In some domains, the increased reliance on numericals, calculation, and computation has improved practices and enhanced the overview and control of the operations, but there are also, critics like Hummel (2006) contend, cases where the mathematization of activities has led to a reification of underlying resources. Samuel, Dirsmith, and McElroy (2005) argue that "cost management" and accounting procedures widely used in health care organizations have produced a new image of the patient and of health care work. Prior to the development of health care accounting procedures, work done by engineers and economists paved the way for the new cost management procedures: "On a parallel path with the engineers, economists elaborated concepts of health economics that changed the perception of the doctor-patient relationship into one between self-interested producers and consumers who trade in a commodity called 'care'" (Samuel, Dirsmith, and McElroy, 2005: 251). The engineers modeled health care processes as a form of industrial system where logistics and throughput of patients were key parameters for efficient care:

> According to the precepts of industrial engineering, the difficulty in defining a product for the hospital lay in constructing one that would subject medical judgment and practice to cost and production management. Therefore, engineers explicitly redefined medical care as an industrial process by asserting that costs were practically triggered by medical judgments and theoretically incurred for a product. (Samuel, Dirsmith, and McElroy, 2005: 258)

In this "restructuring" or "re-engineering" of health care processes and organizations, the human body has been functionally examined and reduced to 23 "major diagnostic categories," e.g., the nervous system, the respiratory system, and the hepatobiliary system. (Samuel, Dirsmith, and McElroy, 2005: 272). This body subject to health care treatment is, indeed, as suggested by Mol (2002), "multiple" as it is distributed across a number of therapeutic areas and domains of professional expertise. The next generation of work contributing to the change in perspective was made by economists who instituted what is called "health care economics." The gradual formulation and implementation of such a framework has led to a new view of health care, where the key actors including doctors, nurses, and technical staff behave in accordance with economic theory, thinking of their work in terms of "incentives, choices, and risks" (Samuel, Dirsmith, and McElroy, 2005: 270). The work of engineers and economists thus reshaped the very idea of health care: "By statistically reducing the professional practice of medicine to a factory product, the engineers gave the accountants a new object for which to calculate the costs of production. Similarly, by theoretically reducing the professional service of medical care to a commodity, the economists provided accountants with new arenas for financial management" (Samuel, Dirsmith, and McElroy, 2005: 270). In the present economic regime, doctors and patients are referred to as "providers" and "consumers," and "care" is rephrased as the delivering of enhanced "health status." In addition, and perhaps more alarming, "ill-health people are no longer viewed as a social problem but increasingly as a 'budget-deficit problem,'" Samuel, Dirsmith, and McElroy, (2005: 270) argue. They continue: "Doctors, nurses and clinicians are increasingly seduced by the language of efficiency, costs, and management in speaking about what they do." Samuel, Dirsmith, and McElroy (2005: 274) here announce the emergence of what they refer to as a "physico-fiscal body," a human body that is both examined in medical terms and regarded as a potential source of income or (in the worst case) uncovered costs. The gaze of the medical doctor is no longer strictly concerned with medical issues but is simultaneously interpenetrated by the accountant's gaze, specifying therapies in monetary terms. Say Samuel, Dirsmith, and McElroy (2005: 274):

> We suggest that since the DRGs [Diagnostic Related Groups] statistically tie organ-systems to fiscal categories they constitute the components of a 'physico-fiscal body.' As DRGs circulate throughout the healthcare industry, knotting together patients, doctors, insurers, and state agencies among others, they spread the illusion that the body is an artifact fabricated by engineers, economists, doctors, and accountants. People are being seduced to understand themselves through the physic-fiscal categories which professionals, jostling the jurisdiction, have imputed to them. (Samuel, Dirsmith, and McElroy, 2005: 274)

For the cynic, this "physico-fiscal body" is indicative of a far-driven reification of the human body, being no more no less than a source of good or bad economic performance. For the proponents of such a construct, it would be overtly naïve and irresponsible to believe that health care could be sheltered from the same demands for economic transparency and sound householding of resources that any other industry needs to pay attention to. In a society where economic resources are scarce and where the use of resources is governed by neoliberal beliefs, the presence of physico-fiscal bodies is indicative of a well-functioning control system that clearly demonstrates the costs and the trade-offs involved in all health care activities. As we will discuss in the next section, the uses of biomedia is another example of numerical representations and computation to produce a transparent and non-situated, mediatized view of the body.

THE MANAGEMENT OF BIOLOGICAL SYSTEMS: BIOMEDIA AND THE INFORMATIZATION OF MATTER

Agential Realism

The single most important social practice derived from neoliberal doctrine, more explicitly finance theory, pertaining to the bioeconomy is the practice of mathematizing (Lynch, 1988) underlying resources, that is, capturing underlying resources in numerical representations allowing mathematical analysis. In the following, the concept of biomedia will be examined in details as the key technoscientific framework for circulating bioinformation in the wider economic setting of the bioeconomic regime. However, prior to the examination of specific biomedia, some ontological and epistemological issues will be addressed in more detail. Rather than thinking of biomedia as disinterested and devoid of broader technoscientific assumptions, the biomedia strongly influence how specific research problems are conceived of and articulated. Understanding biomedia is thus to pay attention to the apparatus and instruments that produce the data and the information that are widely regarded as valid and unproblematic instants of an underlying biological substratum. In the discussion of the role and function of biomedia, we are here drawing on the writings of Karen Barad (2003, 2007), American physicist and social theorists at the University of California, Santa Cruz, advocating a specific form of realism that she calls "agential realism." Barad's (2003, 2007) work is of great help when theorizing how biological systems are turned into numerical representations and further into a circuit of data and information enabling various forms of calculation.

The main influence for Barad's ontological and epistemological writing is Niels Bohr, the Danish physicist and one important contributor besides for instance Erwin Schrödinger and Werner von Heisenberg to the quantum theory in physics. The well-known "Copenhagen interpretation" of quantum physics, one version of quantum theory, was based on Bohr's philosophical thinking about the connection between reality and representation. For Bohr, language is not merely representative; it fails to autonomously account for what is in fact being observed. That is, language is not *outside* the research work but is instead an integral component of the very research setup. As a consequence, a detailed description of the experimental apparatus must accompany the data produced therein. Says Bohr:

> While the scope in classical physics, the interaction between objects and apparatus can be neglected or, if necessary, compensated for, in quantum physics this interaction thus forms an inseparable part of the phenomenon. Accordingly, the unambiguous account of proper quantum phenomena must, in principle, include a description of all relevant features of the experimental arrangement. (Bohr, 1963: 4, cited in Barad, 2007)

This is a central idea in Barad's agential realism, the idea that language cannot properly represent what is being produced through scientific practice and apparatuses. Instead, similar to Bohr, there are intimate connections between the apparatus and the entities or events produced, and they are always of necessity entangled and cannot be fully separated. Barad is here critical of what she calls "representationalism," the epistemological position that matter can be properly represented:

> The agential realism . . . is a non-representationalist form of realism that is based on an ontology that does not take for granted the existence of 'words' and 'things' and an epistemology that does not subscribe to a notion of truth based on their correct correspondence . . . *experimenting and theorizing are dynamic practices that play a constitutive role in the production of objects and subjects and matter and meaning.* As I will explain, theorizing and experimenting are not about intervening (from the outside) but inter-acting from within, and as part of, the phenomena produced. (Barad, 2007:56. Emphasis in the original)

In Barad's (2004) view, the experimental system, the totality of techno-scientific tools and technologies, produces both reality and also forms of agency and subject positions; "reality is not composed of things-in-themselves or things-behind-phenomena but 'things'-in-phenomena," (Barad, 2003: 817) claims. This is a radical point of view, insisting that matter (i.e., reality), which Barad calls "inter-active becomings," is not "a thing" but a "doing": "*matter refers to the materiality/materialization of phenomena,* not to an inherent fixed property of abstract independently existing objects of Newtonian physics" (Barad, 2003: 822. Emphasis in the original). In the experimental apparatus, both matter and agency are produced. Matter becomes visible or otherwise open to scientific inspection (in graphs, diagrams, photographic plates, etc.), and agency is the outcome of a form of activity that is grounded in the "intra-activity" where the subject interacts with the apparatus: "Agency is a matter of intra-acting; it is an enactment, not someone or something. Agency cannot be designated as an attribute of 'subjects' or 'objects' . . . Agency is not an attribute whatsoever—[it] is a 'doing'/'being' in its intra-activity" (Barad, 2003: 827–828). In Barad's view, matter/reality cannot be examined in isolation from the experimental system. Instead, matter is produced by the experimental system but is also what cannot be discussed or examined in such terms outside the experimental system. The agential realism lies precisely in this association between matter, apparatus, and agency in one single unified process of "mattering." Just as Bohr thought of the quantum theory as being "objectively true" because it accounted for the experimental apparatus generating the data as an integral element of the experiment, so too does Barad claim that her agential realism is objective. "[A] condition for objective knowledge is that the referent is a phenomenon (and not an observation-independent object)," Barad (2007: 120) says. In a passage worth citing at length, Barad writes:

> The point is not merely that knowledge practices have material consequences but that *practices of knowing are specific material engagements that participate in (re)configuring the world.* With practices we enact matters—in both senses of the word. Making knowledge is not simply about making factors but about making worlds, or rather, it is about making specific worldly configurations—not in the sense of making them up ex nihilo, or out of language, beliefs, or ideas, but in the sense of materially engaging as part of the world in giving it specific material form. And yet the fact that we make knowledge not from outside but as part of the world does not mean that knowledge is necessarily subjective (a notion that already presumes the pre-existing distinction between object and subject that feeds representationalist thinking). At the same time, objectivity cannot be about producing undistorted representations from afar; rather, objectivity is about being accountable to the specific materializations of which we are part. (Barad, 2007:91. Emphasis in the original)

Based on the writings of Niels Bohr, Karen Barad proposes the theory of agential realism as an ontology and epistemology that seeks to escape representationalism on the one hand (inscriptions, representations, and theories represent underlying matter) and essentialist theories (e.g., matter does exist as brute fact, and there are clearly separated human subjects that can engage in revealing such matter) by thinking of matter and representation as being what is simultaneously produced as phenomena through the very use of the experimental system. Matter does not "reveal itself" through technoscientific practice but is instead what is inextricably bound up and co-produced with the experimental apparatus, presenting itself as phenomena. Barad's (2003, 2007) position is thus interesting as it points at the central role of the media used in the work. There is no position for matter outside media, but the media enable us to operate. This does not mean that Barad rejects any common sense claims that "there is in fact a reality whether we seek to know it or not," but she says that in order to make matter known to us, to gain legitimacy and credibility in technoscientific circles, there must be a technoscientific experimental apparatus to produce phenomena. That is, Barad's (2003, 2007) position emphasizes primarily the epistemological issue of knowing. To know, one must also produce matter, and such a production is mediated, co-produced by the technoscientific apparatus.

Uses of Biomedia

Pharmaceutical companies produce what Barry (2005) calls "informed matter," information regarding the interaction between a chemical entity, e.g., a molecule or an antibody and the biological system wherein the chemical entity is located (for a more practical description of the new drug development procedures, see Hara [2003]). In Thacker's (2004) seminal work, biomedia are portrayed as technoscientific tools and technologies that are capable of rendering biological systems and biological organisms subject to transformation into numerical or graphical representations, thereby enabling further calculative operations and mathematical analyses (Squire). In the recent contributions to the life sciences in what is called bioinformatics and biocomputation, numerical representations and mathematical algorithms are the principal resources for an extended analysis of biological systems. However, the trick here, Thacker (2004) says, is not to fully translate the biological system into a mere regime of inscriptions but to maintain the "biological" nature of the material substratum. That is, biomedia do not conceive of the biological system in analogy to mechanisms composed of linear relationships but recognize the emergent and highly adaptable nature of biological systems. Thacker (2004) explicates this position:

> Put briefly, biomedia is an instance in which biological components and processes are technically recontextualized in ways that may be biological or non-biological. Biomedia are novel configurations of biologies and technologies that take us beyond the familiar tropes of technology-as-tool or the human-machine interface. Likewise, biomedia describes an ambivalence that is not reducible to either technophilia (the rhetoric of enabling technology) technophobia (the ideologies of the technological determinism). Biomedia are particular mediations of the body, optimisations of the biological in which 'technology' appears to disappear altogether. With biomedia, the biological body is not hybridised with the machine, as in the use of mechanical prosthetics or artificial organs. Nor is it supplanted by the machine, as in the many science fictional fantasies of 'uploading' the mind into the disembodied space of the computer. In fact, we can say that biomedia had no body anxiety, if by this we mean the will to transcend the base contingencies of 'the meat' in favor of virtual spaces. (Thacker, 2004: 5–6)

Thacker (2004) is persistent in making this point: the body (or any other biological system or organism) is not simply subject to the "computerization" of biology or to the "digitalization" of materiality, and despite the integration of computer technology with bio-technology, "biomedia establish more complex, more ambivalent relations than those enframed by technological-determinist views," Thacker (2004: 7) asserts. "The 'goal' of biomedia is not simply the use of computer technology in the service of biology, but rather an emphasis on the ways in which an intersection between genetic and computer 'codes' can facilitate a qualitatively different notion of the biological body—one that is technically enhanced, and yet still fully 'biological,' Thacker (2004: 6) argues. Biomedia are a variety of integrated technologies that help examine the biological system in the form of numerical and mathematical representations enabling biocomputation and other forms of mathematical analysis. The term biomedia is consequently defined by Thacker (2004: 10) as "the technical recontextualization of biological components and processes." This is, to say the least, a rather loose definition, opening up many local and contingent interpretations. Thacker (2004: 16) speaks of biomedia in analogy to visual media wherein one material substratum is encoded into a digital, binary form. The same image appears in both forms (e.g., an actual oil painting being encoded into the digital photo accessed through a stream of binary digits), but the two media have translated the original image into a new medium that enables almost endless possibilities for manipulation (see Manovich, 2001). The biological system is still in place after being encoded by the media, but the new digital code enables many forms of computation that may provide new insights into the functioning of the biological system. Biomedia are thus only forms of encoding the biological system, but there is relatively little that is "speaking for itself" in the form. Instead, biomedia are still expected to formulate and test hypotheses and theories about the functioning of the biological system. The large-scale production of data on the basis of new technoscientific apparatuses, e.g., genomics, proteomics, and transcriptomics, has led to a situation where life scientists are up to their neck in data that they do not fully understand or can make sense of. Says one of the scientists interviewed by Shostak (2009):

> What does the data mean? That's the big question. There is so much data. It's like being given the Encyclopedia Britannica and ten seconds to find an answer . . . You know the answer is out there somewhere, but you have to learn the rules or what volume to go to, and you have to learn the rule within that volume. Where do you look it up? And you have to learn the rules for not only reading what's there, but understanding and interpreting. (Toxiocogenomics researcher, cited in Shostak, 2009: 384)

Advanced biomedia have enabled an ever-increasing speed of data production, but making sense of the data and structuring it into testable hypothesis are quite other matters. Calvert (2007) here makes the important distinction between information *about* biological systems (e.g., genes) and information *encoded in* biological systems, that is, how genes translate into different biological functions and mechanisms; the former is "[i]nformation in the very simple sense of a particular strand of DNA having a particular sequence (ATTTG, for example)," while the latter is "[t]he information possessed by the genetic material, which will tell us something significant, for example, about the phenotype of the organism." It is the second form of information that is used "[w]hen we hear talk of the gene sequence providing 'the blueprint' for the organisms" (Calvert, 2007: 217–218). Just because life scientists (like the toxiocogenomics researcher cited above) have information about the biological system does not mean that they are capable of predicting how the biological system will respond to various changes within or external to the system. This is one of the common critiques of the human genome mapping projects: the confusion of information *about* genes and *encoded* in genes would match perfectly. In the field of proteomics it has been found that a specific sequence of genes may or may not switch on in a manner that is not fully understood, and individual sequences of genes may encode different proteins. In other words, there is by no means a straight connection between gene and biological process. Instead, there is a variety of possibilities derived from single sequences of genes. Apparently, the biological system is more flexible, emergent, and malleable that previously thought.

Visual Biomedia

The concept of biomedia is relatively abstract in terms of being technologies for creating biological events and entities (in Karen Barad's view). In the digital media regime of the present period (see e.g., Waldby, 2000; Oudshoorn and Somers, 2007), biomedia are advanced technological systems, but the original biomedia were—from today's perspective—relatively elementary. Still, "old" biomedia helped reconfigure the social relationships between various social actors and instituted biomedia per se as credible tools for "revealing nature" (Kevles, 1997). Just as suggested by Barad (2003, 2007), there is close proximity between agency, phenomena produced, and technoscientific apparatus (biomedia) even in the earliest phases of biomedia. In Golan's (2004) study of the use of x-ray technology, the new professional groups of radiologists and orthopedics managed to establish domains of jurisdiction (Warwick, 2005). The ability to see inner injuries such as broken bones, blind to the unmediated human gaze, was also recognized among lawyers as excellent evidence in juridical practice. In fact, lawyers were more eager to use x-ray than many general practitioners because the x-ray was suspected of revealing cases of malpractice that would potentially threaten the reputation of the doctor. Golan (2004) explains how the new visual biomedia were embraced in some quarters:

> Regular and X-ray photography were part of a new class of machine-made testimonies that rose to dominance during the second half of the 19th century. Ever alert and never involved, machines such as microscopes, telescopes, high-speed cameras, and X-ray tubes threatened to turn human testimony into an inferior mode of communicating facts as they purported to communicate richer, better, and truer evidence, which often was inaccessible by other means to human beings. The emblem for this type of mechanical objectivity was visual evidence. 'Let nature speak for itself' became a watchword, and nature's language

seemed to be that of photographs and mechanically generated curves. (Golan, 2004: 474)

In addition to orthopedics, radiologists were the single group benefitting from the establishment of the new technology. They were however cautious to defend their entrenched positions vis-à-vis other groups:

> Mastering the technology, the radiologists emphasized time and again, was not enough. To read the images with any reasonable degree of accuracy—to be distinguished between normal and pathological appearances and between essential and accidental details—one needs to know autonomy, histology, and pathology in detail, and to be familiar with the various ways both normal and abnormal conditions appear on the X-ray plate, Without such knowledge, no meaningful reading of the images was possible. (Golan, 2004: 485)

Here, there is a noteworthy difference between on the one hand representatives of the juridical system, endorsing the use of x-ray photos (produced by an apparatus referred to as a *skiagraph*) as excellent evidence, and the radiologists, who were more concerned about the expertise involved in interpreting and examining the photos: "'The skiagraph is never wrong', the slogan ran, '[w]hen error exists it lies in its interpretations'" (Golan, 2004: 485). This debate thus existed between professional groups who regard biomedia as being overt representations of the human body, open for immediate inspection for each and everyone, and professional groups, who, as Karen Barad would do, claimed that visual representations cannot be fully separated from the biomedia producing them. In this latter view, only after substantial training and experience can the individual articulate some useful and credible information on basis of the data. In Dumit's (2004) study of the use of Positron Emission Tomography (PET) scanning of the human brain, there is a representative case of this clash of perspectives of biomedia. In the trial of John Hinckley, the man who shot President Ronald Reagan in 1981 to impress the actress Jodie Foster, the defense referred to PET images to claim evidence that Hinckley suffered from a medical condition which should be taken into account in the final sentencing. However, such images are by no means self-explanatory but demand a full explanation by a skilled PET expert. This makes the very use of PET a complicated juridical practice in Dumit's (2004: 112) view: "Expert images are objects produced with mechanical assistance that require help in interpreting even though they may appear to be legible to laypersons. The paradox of expert images in a trial is that if they are legible, then they should not need interpretation, but if they need interpretation, then they probably should not be shown to juries." Laypersons may see the images but they cannot understand what kind of information is encoded in the plates; when being accounted for, the plates are no longer "evidence" but are merely information provided to support some kind of case, loosely structured around the line of reasoning "abnormal brain = mentally ill = not responsible" (Dumit, 2004: 119, 125). Dumit summarizes his argument:

> [E]ven though the brain images are produced by people, they are coproduced by scientific machines, and it is the machines, especially computers, that leave their mark. Scientists . . . increasingly attempt to remove their marks from the image, even though they must still provide the text . . . At the crux of this relationship between the image that (objectively) speaks for itself and the expert who (subjectively) speaks is a desire by the court and by everyone else to reduce ambiguity, to make things clear, and clearly acceptable. (Dumit, 2004: 119)

Echoing Barad's (2003, 2007) argument, Dumit (2004: 159) here suggests that there are no "facts" per se, but facts are always of necessity part of a broader professional framework and cannot be properly understood outside such associations and joint frameworks. "Facts are bits of mastery in an expert culture. Expert culture is about being extremely knowledgeable about a very few things. We are all people who know a little about a lot of things, but, in their entirety, the facts are beyond reach. The very category of the person has become, in part, parceled out among expert discourses."

In summary then, neither the x-ray plate nor the PET image are "evidence" on their own but may become part of a wider juridical narrative of actions and responsibilities when being accompanied by the professional accounts of what the images say (Daemmrich, 1998). Similar to Calvert's (2007) distinction between information *about* genes and information *encoded* in genes, the x-ray plates and the PET images may provide some information to lay audiences about the skeleton or brain but not the information *encoded* in the images. That is, by the end of the day, matter *qua* instances of reality (the brain of a human being or the bone of a child) is co-produced with the expertise needed to encode the information and the technological apparatus employed in this work. A final example of this co-construction of agency, matter, and apparatus with little reference to juridical practice is Myers's (2008) study of protein crystallographers, a relatively new professional field of expertise wherein proteins are crystallized and visually represented as part of a general proteomics research program. Myers (2008) suggests that what she calls "matters of substance," not only sequences of data but also in the actual three-dimensional materiality and structure and function of elementary matter on the molecular level, are of interest (Myers, 2008: 163). However, Myers (2008) suggests that creating this three-dimensional image demands a relatively detailed understanding of the protein because protein crystallographers are always operating on the basis of inadequate or incomplete information. The role of protein crystallographers is thus to interpret the data provided into models that are likely, given the data, to represent actual molecules. Myers (2008) is here talking about the need for developing a "feeling for the molecule," a feeling that was only acquired over time and through experience from working with creating the images:

> The common lore in the lab is that even if well versed in crystallographic theory, a crystallographer remains a novice until they have fully built their own structure. Working in the tangible medium of interactive computer graphics, modelers-in-training learn how to see, feel, and build protein structures through their embodied interaction with the data. Model-building is thus a kind of training ground for crystallographers to acquire their 'feeling for the molecule,' to develop the tacit skills and craft knowledge required to visualize proteins and 'think intelligently about structure.' (Myers, 2008: 181)

During a trial-and-error procedure, the protein gradually emerges in its final form. The "feeling for the molecule" is also accompanied by what could be referred to as "molecular vision," the ability to think visually about how the three-dimensional object enfolds in space. Myers (2008: 169) explains: "More than visual traces, marks or inscriptions, three-dimensional physical models explicitly blur the boundaries between automated machinic productions and the skilled work of scientists, and between the intellectual and physical labor of research." The molecular vision is thus a form of embodied yet cognitive understanding of the protein and the capacity to illustrate this operative model in the computer-program used: "Keen molecular vision is, for her [Diane, an experienced crystallographer], an embodied practice of observation and manipulation, where seeing is also a way of feeling what the structure is expressing in its form" (Myers, 2008: 189). Myers thus says that protein crystallographers mobilize a variety of skills and forms of know-how in order to construct the three-dimensional structure of the protein. Again, there is a fundamental co-alignment of agency, technology, and forms of knowing when representing matter. The proteins are not captured by a camera but are instead constructed as three-dimensional instances of matter on basis of a variety of resources. As a form of biomedia use, protein crystallography is thus, like uses of other biomedia, a highly distributed practice that cannot be strictly located in linear practices of inscription and translation.

SUMMARY AND CONCLUSION

The period from the late 1970s on has been described as a period characterized by neoliberal politics. Neoliberalism and its emphasis on the free circulation of capital and on entrepreneurial and venturing activities as the prime motor of the capitalist economy have arguably served as a key factor in establishing the life sciences as a source of economic interest. Historically, scientific research has been either organized in academic institutions or in R&D departments in larger corporations. From the end of the 1970s, university researchers were given more opportunities for patenting publically funded research, and the increase of patent rights has been a warrant for a return on investment in the life sciences. In the present regime of the economy, the life sciences are treated no differently than other parts of the economy. On the contrary, both biotechnology and the major pharmaceutical companies are intimately bound up with the financial markets and regularly drop drugs from the R&D portfolios on the basis of market prospects. The neoliberal deregulation of the financial markets and the inflow of financial resources in, e.g., state-owned or state-governed pension funds have also increased the access to capital in the life sciences, benefitting an industry with long-term product development time horizons and substantial above-average return on investment (see next chapter in this volume). Although the connections between the neoliberal shift in economic policy may appear of only marginal importance, the life sciences' transformation into the backbone of the bioeconomy is arguably closely bound up with the general political ambition to deregulate market control and enhance the possibilities for venturing. In addition, the tendency to conceive of biological systems in informational terms—an epistemological position shared with, e.g., finance theory—has produced a wide variety of tools, techniques, and methods that have advanced the life sciences enormously. Life, like the economy, is a matter of flows and circuits of information.

3 New Drug Development, Biotechnology, and the Enactment of Life

INTRODUCTION

The multinational pharmaceutical industry naturally plays a key role in the bioeconomy as being the major instituted industry serving as the nexus between the life sciences and the market (Abraham, 1995). In this role, the pharmaceutical industry controls advanced research competence, juridical know-how, marketing capacities, and, perhaps most important, the financial resources needed to bring interesting but unrefined research work to the market in the form of new registered drugs. However, while the post–World War II period until the mid 1990s has been described as the "golden age" of "Big Pharma," the recent fifteen-year period has been characterized by a slowdown in output of new and innovative drugs. At the same time, the pharmaceutical industry continues to report significant return on investment, in many cases justified on the basis of the need for large investments in the future (Brody, 2007). Lexchin (2006: 11) reports that the profit margin in the industry has in fact grown rather than fallen during the last three decades of the twentieth century: During the 1970s, drug companies "averaged 8,9 per cent profit as a percentage of revenue" in comparison to 4.4 percent for all Fortune 500 industries in the 1970s. In the 1980s, the same figures were 11.1 percent compared to 4.4 percent, and in the 1990s, 15.1 percent compared to 4.1 percent. Brody (2007: 57) shows that in 2002, "the pharmaceutical industry accounted for 2 percent of the Fortune 500 companies, but 57 percent of these companies' total profit." The pharmaceutical industry is notwithstanding its large investments in R&D a reliable source of sustainable profits. Lexchin (2006: 11) emphasizes that one of the reasons for the industry's performance is its emphasis on developing drugs targeting profitable customer segments. At the end of the 1980s, 43 percent of drugs were terminated based on limited profitability prospects in comparison to 31 percent based on unsatisfying efficacy and 21 percent based on safety issues.

While new drug development has been traditionally organized into small units where a combination of pharmacology and synthesis chemistry has dominated, today there is a rich inflow of new scientific principles and approaches that have made some of the major companies open the door for new methods to develop new drugs. These new approaches include the use of various genomics approaches, high through-put screening molecule detection methods, and more recently more biocomputational and bioinformatics approaches (Hedgecoe, 2006; Hedgecoe and Martin, 2003; Drews, 2000). The adoption of these new analytical procedures has enabled a more detailed understanding of the elementary matter of the biological organism, but it has also been more complicated to transform this new know-how into new drugs and therapies:

> The advent of genomic sciences, rapid DNA sequencing, combinatorial chemistry, cell-based assays, and automated high-throughput screening (HTS) had led to a new concept of drug discovery. In this new concept, the critical discourse between chemists and biologists and the quality of scientific reasoning are sometimes replaced by the magic of large numbers . . . So far, this several hundredfold increase in the number of raw data has not yet resulted in a commensurate increase in research productivity, As measured by the number of new compounds entering the market place, the top 50 companies in the pharmaceutical industry collectively have not improved their productivity during the 1990s. (Drews, 2000: 1962)

What is especially puzzling about this tendency is that the slowdown in drug output happened during a period where the life sciences were advancing quickly. In Munos's (2009) account:

> The innovation crisis of the pharmaceutical industry is occurring in the midst of a new golden age of scientific discovery. If large companies could organize innovation networks to harness scientific discovery of biotechnology companies and academic institutions, and combine it with their own development expertise, they might be able to reverse the forces that are undermining their research model; that is, they might be able to lower their costs and increase their outputs. (Munos, 2009: 865)

Today, pharmaceutical companies are widely criticized for investing more money than ever in new drug development while still producing relatively few new innovative drugs. The literature, both academic and popular, is filled with worried accounts of the relative decline of output in the industry. For instance, in a *Harvard Business Review* article, Jean-Pierre Garnier (2008), the former CEO of GlaxoSmithKline, noted some of the challenges for the pharmaceutical industry for the future, for instance, the ability to overcome the far-driven standardization of work routines and standard operation procedures in new drug development:"[T]he leaders of major corporations in some industries, including pharmaceuticals and electronics, have incorrectly assumed that R&D was scalable, could be industrialized, and could be driven by detailed metrics (scorecards) and automation. The grand result: a loss of personal accountability, transparency, and the passion of scientists in discovery and development" (Garnier, 2008: 72). This view of the over-emphasis on "industrialization of R&D" in the industry has been widely shared among a number of critics (e.g., Dougherty, 2007). Munos (2009: 867) also emphasizes this belief in firmly established procedures: "During the past couple of decades, there has been a methodological attempt to codify every facet of the drug business into sophisticated processes, in an effort to reduce the variances and increase the predictability. This has produced a false sense of control over all aspects of the pharmaceutical enterprise, including innovation."

Also in the scholarly literature, there is a concern regarding the effectiveness of the pharmaceutical industry (Angell, 2004; Brody, 2007). "[A]lthough in the period of 1993–2004 expenditure on R&D increased by 147%, the number of drastic innovations, denoted as 'priority new molecular entities' (NMEs), has remained stable," Ganuza, Llobet, and Domínguez (2009: 539) report. While the pharmaceutical industry is happy to take on the role of a provider of advanced therapies helping humans live better and happier lives, there are some concerns regarding how the money is invested. Angell (2004) emphasizes that the pharmaceutical industry is investing more money in marketing and administration than in R&D and that the industry hires the highest number of lobbyists in Brussels and Washington of all industries. In addition, just like any other industry, there are concerns regarding corporate crimes such as bribery, unsafe R&D practice and manufacturing practices, and so forth (Braithwaite, 1984). Taken together, even though the industry is performing well in terms of cash flow and bottom line results, there is a concern in the industry that large-scale pharmaceutical companies may have lost their creative edge. The slowdown in new drug development output is significant but is partially explained by the increased investment in new costly technologies and in training to use the technologies. In this chapter, the new drug development activities in the pharmaceutical industry will be examined. The discussion includes a review of the history of the industry and the shift in focus from traditional pharmacology based on in vivo trials to more recent changes to biocomputational approaches.

The chapter is structured accordingly: First, some historical conditions regarding the emergence of a biopharmaceutical industry will be addressed. Second, the concept of biomedicalization and its importance for promoting new therapies is addressed. Third, the growth of new genomics and post-genomics technologies are discussed.

DEVELOPING THE PHARMACEUTICAL INDUSTRY

The pharmaceutical industry has its roots in the pharmacies that existed throughout Europe in the late eighteenth and early nineteenth centuries

(Swann, 1988; Gottinger and Umali, 2008) and, to some extent, in the chemical industry developed in Germany, Switzerland, and the U.S. in the period of what has been called the "second industrial revolution" starting around 1880 (Chandler, 2005). In the eighteenth century, prior to the development of scientific, experimental, and clinical medicine, a wide variety of actors such as "wise women, herbalists, good samaritans, midwives, itinerant drug peddlers, ladies of the manor, mountebanks, and quacks" (Bynum, 1994: 2) competed with physicians to offer health care services. The most difficult competitor was however the apothecaries in the pharmacies, who were more specialized in botany and chemistry than in physiology (Bynum, 1994). In the pharmacies, apothecaries used their pharmacological expertise to produce drugs prescribed by local doctors. The most advanced of these pharmacies were "small but well-outfitted laboratories" (Swann, 1988: 19). However, the leap from these small and relatively isolated pharmacies to today's large-scale businesses was not insignificant. The growth of large pharmaceutical companies began in the second half of the nineteenth century, especially in Germany, as the outgrowth or spin-off from the coal-tar dye industry (Swann, 1988: 20). That is, the chemical industry in Germany served as the starting point for the production of pharmaceuticals. Not until after World War II was there any significant collaborative research between the universities and the pharmaceutical industry (Swann, 1988: 6). Initially, the strong belief in the universities' role in conducting "fundamental research" (i.e., basic research in today's vocabulary) inhibited the full collaboration between industry and university. However, in the interwar period, there was a significant growth in the number of laboratories and research staff in the industry, from approximately 1,000 laboratories and 19,000 researchers in 1927 to 2,262 laboratories and 58,000 researchers in 1940 (Swann, 1988: 15). In the first decades of the twentieth century and especially after World War II, the pharmaceutical industry took advantage of a series of advancements in the life sciences. At the turn of the century, the germ theory of disease was established and led to much research effort and in the 1930s and 1940s, what Galambos and Sturchio (1998: 251) call the "chemo-therapeutic revolution," which instituted a variety of new research practices. The next important step came in the 1940s and 1950s when advances in virology provided new opportunities. Shortly thereafter, a new wave of breakthroughs in microbial biochemistry and enzymology "provided the basis of a new style of targeted pharmaceutical research and development" (Galambos and Sturchio, 1998: 252). More recently, the inception of a biotechnology industry developing new research tools and technologies has made valuable contributions to the new drug development research process. Another important step occurred when the human genome mapping project outlined the entire human genome. As an effect of this large-scale program, new perspectives on the role of the human genome emerged, suggesting that rather than being the underlying script determining the biological organism, the genome is encoded into proteins in various unpredictable ways. The massive amount of data provided by genomics research, often tens of thousands of data points, has led to analytical procedures that examine the biological system on what is at times called a "global scale," including all sorts of modeling and computation on the basis of the large data sets. Such biocomputation and bioinformatics practices have been advanced as a complement to the traditional "wet lab biology" centered on small-scale molecules, biological targets, and in vivo studies. Nightingale and Mahdi (2006) note the new importance granted to the *in silico* methods:

> While biologists in the late 1980s may have focused primarily on empirical 'wet' biology, today they may spend much of their time in front of computers engaging in more theoretical *in silico* science, experimental design, quality control, or trawling through large data sets. The process has made pharmaceutical R&D more theoretical, more interdisciplinary, and has meant that medicinal biologists may now find themselves working with clinicians in hospitals. (Nightingale and Mahdi, 2006: 74)

In this biocomputational approach, the cell is treated as "complex biochemical machinery" (Nightingale and Mahdi, 2006: 75) and must consequently be examined in accordance with the global scale analysis wherein the healthy, well-functioning cell is capable of self-regulating its functions. The biocomputation approach is then an attempt at constructing a model of the cell's pathways "from the bottom up," beginning with available data and constructing a coherent and unified framework. Proponents of biocomputation approaches tend to regard the "wet lab biology" approach as being anecdotal in terms of studying one-to-one relations (e.g., a molecule interacting with a protein serving as the target for a specific biological pathway. See e.g., Torgersen, 2009). In fact, biological systems tend to have emergent properties; that is, they are constantly responding and adapting to conditions in the environment of the biological system or in changes within the system. The biocomputation approach is therefore better suited for unraveling the complex pathways and relationships on the molecular level in, e.g., a cell. On the contrary, proponents of wet lab biology approaches believe it is impossible to predict the outcomes from interventions into biological systems on the basis of simulation models created with clinical data without having a proper model or theory of what kind of biological pathways and processes are involved.

REGULATION AND CONTROL OF THE PHARMACEUTICAL INDUSTRY

In addition to the growth in know-how in life sciences there has been an increased institutionalization of regulatory control of the industry. When interviewing researchers in pharmaceutical companies there is a recurrent theme that today's best selling household drugs such as aspirin probably would not be able to pass the evaluation in the contemporary regime of control. In 1938, one of the first decisions was made in the U.S. to control the industry via the Federal Food, Drug and Cosmetics Act. In 1962, the Kefauver-Harris Amendments of the 1938 act followed after the Thalidomide controversy (Mirowski and van Horn, 2005: 508), a common sedative medication producing severe birth defects. While the role of the FDA, the Federal Food and Drug Administration, in making decisions about what drugs will be approved and what criteria to use is constantly criticized for being too slow and non-transparent, the approval rate within six months after the submission of a new drug application has actually increased from 4 percent in 1992 to 28 percent in 1999 (Mirowski and van Horn, 2005: 510). Mirowski and van Horn (2005: 510) also point out that the increased effectiveness of the discovery phase in new drug development has led to "a tidal wave" of new clinical trials in Phase 1, from "386 in 1990 to 1512 in 2000"—representing a growth of 392 percent. Today, there is an abundance of new candidate drugs in new drug development work, and clinical trials, the costly and time-consuming development phase of new drug development, are the principal bottleneck in the research work.

Traditionally, the pharmaceutical industry has been heavily controlled by external organizations and has created alliances and joint ventures with other pharmaceutical companies or research universities and medical schools. New drug development work is thus heavily distributed across domains and institutions, making it a relatively complex matter, not only in terms of the life-science know-how and expertise involved, but also in terms of managerial and organizational capacities. Since the 19070s, the organization field has grown more complex as new biotechnology companies have been established as important players in the field, developing and providing important tools and technologies for the new drug development work.

THE GROWTH OF THE BIOTECHOLOGY INDUSTRY

The concept of biotechnology is, as suggested in the first chapter of this volume, not as new as one may think but has its roots in the food-processing industry. Today, the term has taken on a somewhat wider meaning as a general capacity to apply technoscientific know-how in industrial processes: "[b]iotechnology is defined as the application of knowledge of living organisms and their components, to industrial products and processes" (Brink, McKelvey and Smith, 2004: 21). The OECD offers a somewhat more specific definition: "The application of S&T to living organisms as well as parts, products, and models thereof, to alter living or non-living materials for the production of knowledge, goods, and services" (cited in Dahlander and McKelvey, 2005: 410). Brink, McKelvey, and Smith (2004: 21–22) point to the relatively diverse set of activities under the biotechnology label: "Examples of areas affected include human health care, drug development and pharmaceuticals, food production and processing, new materials and fine chemicals, energy, sensors and such environmental applications as bioremediation." Biotechnology has acquired a substantial interest in scholarly circles, and there is also a significant growth in patenting in the industry, indicating the activities of the field: "Between 1980 and 2003, the 80 incumbent pharmaceutical firms were granted a total of 15,607 biotechnology patents; and the 249 firms patenting in nanotechnology were granted a total of 3236 nanotechnology patents," Rothaermel and Thursby (2007: 835) report: "During the 1980–1990 decade, the average number of biotech patents generated per year was 3.97, while the average number of biotech patents generated per year in the second decade (1990–1999) was 10.97, a statistically significant increase of about 275% ($p<0.001$)" (Rothaermel and Thursby, 2007: 842). This growth is impressive in terms of sheer patent-counting, but some commentators note the relatively limited consequences of biotechnology in the development of therapies and the modest economic performance of the biotechnology sector. Pisano (2006: xii) defines the biotechnology industry as a "science-based business," an industry "that is not just a passive user of science, but also an active participant in the process of advancing science either directly (through in-house research) or indirectly (through sponsored research)." Biotechnology companies are thus both translating life-science know-how into products and services and also making contributions to the life sciences per se. While Pisano (2006) recognizes the contributions of the biotechnology sector, he is still rather explicit regarding the poor financial performance (see also Durand, Bruyaka, and Mangematin, 2008). Besides a few well-known flagship companies such as Amgen and Genetech, accounting for the majority of the profits generated in the industry, the overall economic performance "has been disappointing by any objective standard" (Pisano, 2006: 5). One of the main reasons for the relative lack of financial performance, Pisano says, is the absence of possibilities for organization learning, to accumulate know-how over time:

> [T]he conditions that allow it to work well in those sectors [other high-tech sectors]—codified technology, modular designs and standard platforms, and well-delineated intellectual properties—are often lacking in biotechnology. As a result of the system of innovation, the biotechnology sector has evolved an anatomy—small, specialized firms, integrated by means of alliances, etc.—that, while doing certain things well (e.g., generating many experiments, encouraging risk-taking, learning through imitation), falls short in other areas (integration, learning from experience). (Pisano, 2006: 156)

Among the most important contributions of the biotechnology industry is the development of recombinant DNA, Stanley Cohen and Herbert Boyer's groundbreaking discovery in the 1970s, leading to a number of therapies such as insulin and human growth hormone Factor VIII (isolated from human blood) (Pisano, 2006: 8–9). In general, the main contributions of the biotechnology sector lie not in the output of therapies but in various methodological developments. The traditional domain for therapies developed by the major pharmaceutical companies is small molecules (below the weight of 150 Daltons) aimed at one target, which in turn plays a key role in a disease or medical condition—a linear sequence wherein the biological system is affected at one single point. The concern is that the number of such so-called "drugable targets" has been estimated to be quite modest, around 600–1,500 (Hopkins et al., 2007: 572). This suggests that there are a limited number of small molecules that are useful from a therapeutic point of view, and consequently there may be a need to think about new strategies for discovering new therapies.

Biotechnology has to date had limited "impact on primary care medicine." Hopkins et al. (2007: 578) suggest. Instead, the biotechnology industry has developed a number of "upstream" tools and approaches for studying biological systems: "Biotechnology is being used within established heuristics and has broadened the scope of the technological options available to drug developers at a time when the industry is addressing quantitatively more complex medical problems" (Hopkins et al., 2007: 584). Mirowski and van Horn (2005) list a few contributions from the biotechnology sector:

> What is beyond dispute is that some of the earliest breakthroughs in genetic research were processes or entities that enabled genetic manipulation: The Cohen-Boyer recombinant DNA technologies of Genentech; the polymerase chain reaction (PCR) controlled by Hoffman-La Roche; and the Harvard Oncomouse—none of which were downstream products aimed at a consumer market. Therefore, some of the earliest money made from biotechnology was in the area of 'research tools,' rather than fully-fledged therapies. (Mirowski and van Horn, 2005: 524)

Unfortunately, as Nightingale and Mahdi (2006: 75) point out, "it does not follow that radical improvements in scientific research will lead to revolutionary improvements in productivity, because bottlenecks remain within the drug discovery process, particularly at the target validation stage. As a result, qualitative improvements in research capability do not necessarily translate into quantitative improvements in output." Growth in scientific know-how does not of necessity translate into increased output. Therefore, notwithstanding the contributions from biotechnology listed by Mirowski and van Horn (2005), Hopkins et al. (2007: 580) downgrade the influence of the biotechnology industry on health care: "[I]t has not yet boosted productivity" and has failed in "generating new types of drugs" that have "achieved significant impact on healthcare." Despite these contributions to both practical research methods and an extension of the knowledge base in the life sciences, Hopkins et al. (2007: 584) claim "[i]t is hard not to conclude that many of the widely held expectations about the impact of biotechnology are over-optimistic." At the same time as they recognize that there is a relatively limited influence over the output of therapies, Hopkins et al. (2007) are aware that the relative decline in the output of new innovative therapies may in fact hide qualitative improvements, i.e., an increased understanding of biological systems, that may lead to more significant breakthroughs in the future:

> *Quantitative declines in productivity may hide very real qualitative improvements*, as the pharmaceutical industry tackles increasingly difficult diseases . . . This is intuitive when we consider the nature of the industry's shift from infectious to chronic diseases. Many of the successes of the golden age (such as the sulphonamides, penicillin, and other antibiotics) were drugs that targeted invading (exogenous) organisms. The restoration of balance to a biological system composed of endogenous components or subsystems is an entirely different operational principle. (Hopkins et al., 2007: 584. Emphasis in the original)

For instance, the human genome mapping program demonstrated that the number of genes in the human is in the range of 25,000–35,000, relatively few more in humans than in what are regarded as less differentiated organisms. This insight was a disappointment for those who believed that the human genome was the "book of life" or a key to the inner workings of biological systems (Griffith, 2001). Since the pharmaceutical industry had a firm belief in the genomics approach and the genomics framework of new drug development, the industry's significant investments have led to relatively little impact on the development of new therapies. Against this background, it is tempting to say, like Higgs (2004. cited in Hopkins et al., 2007: 583), that "the genome sequence has a far greater capacity to mislead than it has to illuminate." However, the number of proteins produced in the human body may be around 29 million (Pisano, 2006: 34), and a key interest is then how different sequences of genes encode different proteins. The proteomics research program is thus one of the most promising approaches for developing new therapies.

In summary, the biotechnology sector has been one of the most recent innovations in the life sciences. Despite limited immediate effects on new drug development and overall a disappointing economic performance, there is still a significant growth in know-how in the biotechnology sector, which sooner or later may prove itself valuable when developing drugs. In terms of growth of patents, the biotechnology industry has performed very well.

(BIO)MEDICALIZATION AND THE
DEMAND FOR PHARMACEUTICALS

The pharmaceutical industry has its roots in the nineteenth century, whereas biotechnology is by and large an outcome of the 1970s liberalization of patenting laws, opening up new opportunities for transforming know-how in the life sciences into companies, patents, therapies, and—ultimately—money (Coriat, Orsi, and Weinstein, 2003; Casper, 2000). These two industries—at times merged into one biopharmaceutical industry—both draw on and make important contributions to the life sciences. The field of new drug development is thus an eminent example of a field where university and industry collaborations are widespread and can demonstrate a fine track record. The university-industry collaborations are however still located in a social setting that influence how the activities are structured and what drugs that are legitimate to develop (Shostak and Conrad, 2008). In this section, some of the recent debates and discussions regarding the role of the life sciences and the conditions for new drug development will be examined. We therefore shift the focus from the actors of the market to the researchers and commentators passing judgment on how the life sciences are organized, managed, and regulated. As will be shown, the life sciences are accompanied by strong norms and ethics regarding how the life sciences play an increasingly significant role in contemporary society.

One of the key concerns in the literature regarding the influence and role of the biopharmaceutical industry is whether the pharmaceutical industry is responding to actual medical needs and demands, or if it is in the position to either create a demand through marketing or, in more sophisticated cases, to turn social and personal worries and concerns into medical issues and problems to be treated medically (Rosenberg and Golden, 1997). In the first case, that of marketing, the pharmaceutical industry has been widely criticized for sponsoring of medical conferences and similar activities that, critics claim, seek to influence physicians and other relevant categories of decision-makers to choose specific therapies, namely, the ones provided by the sponsoring companies (Brody, 2007). The more complicated case, that of medicalization, includes a series of transformations of social individual concerns into legitimate medical conditions (Beck, 2007). This shifting of focus from the curing of actual illnesses to the active enactment of new standards turning specific social conditions into illnesses has been heavily discussed in the literature. DeGrandpre (2006), speaking about the U.S. as a market being fully penetrated by the pharmaceutical companies to the degree that there is little opportunity for further raising drug consumption in certain strata, introduces the term *pharmacologicalism,* to denote the ideology of prescribing pharmaceutical therapies whenever there is an opportunity for it. This ideology presupposes that it is the drug consumed that makes the difference in terms of therapeutic outcomes—not the social and cultural setting of the actual patient:

A key supposition of pharmacologicalism is that pharmacological potentialities contained within the drug's chemical structure determine drug outcomes in the body, the brain, and behavior. Accordingly, non-pharmacological factors play little role, whether the realm of the mind of the world of society and culture . . . As a result, pharmacological-ism dictates that the moral status of a drug exists as a purely scientific question that can be documented and classified once and for all, not as a social one that must be considered and unconsidered across time and places. Society, culture and history can be ignored. (DeGrandpre, 2006: 27)

Pharmacologicalism is thus a far-driven scientism, assuming that the human body is strictly regulated by the fluids and components that con-stitute it; medicine is then the science of affecting the biological system through pharmaceutical means and nothing else. The term biomedicaliza-tion or medicalization is therefore a key element in pharmacologicalism as being the translation of social and individual concerns into diseases that are amenable for therapies. Conrad (2007: 4) defines medicalization accord-ingly: "'Medicalization' described a process by which nonmedical problems become defined and treated as medical problems, usually in terms of illness and disorders . . . While some have simply examined the development of medicalization, the most have taken a somewhat critical or skeptical view of this social transformation." In the same vein, Clarke et al. (2003: 162) speak of biomedicalization as "the increasingly complex, multisite, multi-directional processes of medicalization that today are being both extended and reconstituted through the emergent social forms and practices of a highly and increasingly technoscientific biomedicine." The term medical-ization was first used by Irving K. Zola in 1972 to theorize the "theorize the extension of medical jurisdiction, authority, and practices into increas-ingly broader areas of people's lives" (Clarke et al., 2003: 164). Initially, the term medicalization was used to address particular social problems that were "morally problematic" (e.g., alcoholism, homosexuality, abortion, and drug abuse) that were moved "from the professional jurisdiction of the law to that of medicine" (Clarke et al., 2003: 164). For instance, rather than seeing alcoholism as a form of social deviancy that needs to be handled by juridical and penal practice, it became increasingly medicalized during the last decades of the twentieth century. The term biomedicalization denotes, Clarke et al. (2003: 165) suggest (similar to Rose, 2007), a shift in focus from the management and control of health to an enhanced control of life at large, that is, an extension of the medical jurisdiction into a wider set of concerns not of necessity being "morally problematic":

Biomedicalization is characterized by its greater organizational and institutional reach through the meso-level innovations made possible by computer and information sciences in clinical and scientific settings, including computer-based research and record-keeping. The scope of biomedicalization processes is thus much broader, and includes conceptual and clinical expansions through the commodification of health, the elaborations of risk and surveillance, and innovative clinical applications of drugs, diagnostic tests, and treatment procedures. (Clarke et al., 2003: 165)

Abraham (2010) argues that medicalization is not caused by the advancement of new and innovative drugs—a French review of 3,100 new drugs registered in the period 1981–2004 suggested that only 10 percent had "moderate to significant therapeutic advance" (Abraham, 2010: 615)—but that the prime motor behind medicalization is a consumerist ethos giving the patients a new role as clients in a position to negotiate with their doctors, thus partly by-passing the doctors as "gate-keepers" prescribing therapies (Abraham, 2010: 616). Therefore, medicalization and what Abraham (2010) calls pharmaceuticalization are propelled by consumerist ideologies rather than technoscientific advancement. Still, the process of biomedicalization is a complex social accomplishment, including a series of acts and decisions leading to a fully legitimate and treatable disease. "The key to medicalization," Conrad (2007: 5) continues, "is definition. That is, a problem is defined in medical terms, described using medical language, understood through the adoption of a medical framework, or 'treated' with a medical intervention." In order to serve as a legitimate disease, it is important that the disease acquire what Lackoff (2006) speaks of as "disease specificity":

> To circulate in the regulated system of biomedicine, a drug is supposed to operate according to its model of the relation between illness and intervention. According to this model—'disease specificity'—illnesses are stable entities that exists outside of their embodiment in particular individuals and that can be explained in terms of specific causal mechanisms that are located within the sufferer's body. Disease specificity is a tool of administrative management. It makes it possible to gather populations for large-scale research, and more generally, to rationalize health practice. (Lakoff, 2008: 744)

In order to be subject to effective therapies and biomedicalization, disease, illness, or medical condition must be relatively confined, have a stable and predictable etiology, and be connected to present regimes of knowledge (Collins and Pinch, 2005). In some cases, there are difficulties in accomplishing disease specificity because the life sciences have not yet enacted a widely shared theory or model of a particular medical conditions, as in the case of many central nervous systems disorders such as schizophrenia or Huntington's disease, where the biological pathways and biomarkers are not yet fully understood, or, as in the case of obesity, where there are controversies about whether obesity is a disease per se or is closely correlated with other metabolic disorders; i.e., it is not widely agreed upon whether obesity is a disease or not in the first place. If there is no specific and discrete disease specificity, there are significant problems in acquiring funding for research and approval from regulating bodies to conduct research and new drug development activities that would lead to a new therapy.

An alternative approach is that pharmaceutical companies turn the question upside down and start with the available drugs and "see where they work"—Brody (2007) refers to this as the "first shoot the arrow, then draw the target" research strategy. This may sound like an unexpected approach given the aura of scientific rigor surrounding the pharmaceutical industry, but is in fact quite common, the literature suggests. For instance, Pfizer's drug Viagra was widely regarded as a serendipitous discovery in terms of demonstrating an unexpected side-effect, in a new substance being clinically tested for a completely different therapy. Having the capacity to ease erectile dysfunction, Viagra became one of the blockbuster drugs of Pfizer, generating massive incomes on annual basis. Lackoff (2006) emphasizes that it is drugs that increasingly define diseases rather than the other way around:

> Illness comes gradually to be defined in terms of to what it 'responds.' The goal of linking drug directly to diagnosis draws together a variety of projects among professionals, researchers and administrators to craft new techniques of representation and intervention. These projects range from diagnostic standardization and the generalization of clinical protocols to drug development and molecular genetics. This constellation of heterogeneous elements is joined together by a strategic logic I call 'pharmaceutical reason.' The term 'pharmaceutical reason' refers to the underlying rationale of drug intervention in the new biomedical psychiatry: that targeted drug treatment will restore the subject to a normal condition of cognition, affect, or volition. (Lakoff, 2006: 7)

Rather than operating on the causal sequence disease therapy, a therapy may prove to have good results on additional diseases. Lackoff (2006) says that in the case of psychopharmacological drugs, there is a most troubling relationship between disease and available and applicable therapies. In addition, "fashionable" concepts in psychiatry strongly determine what diagnoses are actually made in patient groups. Lackoff (2006) provides an illustration when comparing the incidence of specific mental disorders in the U.S. and the U.K.: In a study, "one third" of American psychiatrists diagnosed schizophrenia, but none of the British did. It "turned out," Lakoff (2006: 29) writes, "that many American psychiatrists regarded 'schizophrenia' the general term for serious mental illness." At the same time, "the diagnostic rate of manic depression was as much as twenty times higher in British hospitals than in American hospitals." "In United States, clinicians simply did not 'see' manic depression," Lakoff (2006:

29) contends. In the U.S., schizophrenia was apparently a legitimate diagnosis to articulate, while in the U.K., manic depression was a term more widely used. This case is illustrative of the relatively low disease specificity of mental disorders during the period of the study. The professional community of psychiatrists did not share a unified and coherent model for the analysis of these disorders. "In conclusion," Lakoff (2006: 35) writes, "the study called for a standardization of disease definition in order to make disciplinary communication possible. Psychiatry desperately needed a common language, the authors argued." Micale (1993) argues that the entire history of psychiatry, more than other branches of medicine, is characterized by new phenomena and diagnoses fashionable during periods of time, including melancholia in seventeenth-century England, "vapors" in eighteenth-century Paris, neurasthenia in late nineteenth-century America, and psychogenic eating disorder in our own times. Micale (1993) examines how the perhaps most prominent psychological disorder of "hysteria"—a term closely bound up with, e.g., Freudian psychoanalysis—disappeared from the field of psychiatry in the first decades of the twentieth century. In the last few decades of the nineteenth century, hysteria reached its zenith in attention. In the early 1950s, the French historian Jacques Chastenet argued that hysteria was one of the primary *"névroses fin de siècle."* The term and diagnosis of hysteria gradually lost its prominence in psychiatric discourses as psychiatrists in Europe and North America adopted a "different set of diagnostic terms, ideas and practices, which they deemed to be more in accord with the medical science of a new generation" (Micale, 1993: 523). Lakoff (2006) and Micale (1993) demonstrate that rather than being stable and unified conditions, many psychiatric diagnoses are co-produced with wider social changes and beliefs; the line of demarcation between the domain of psychiatry and the surrounding society is always porous and permeable.

Greene (2007) examines three different drugs and points out that both therapies and underlying medical disorders are mutually constitutive, i.e., are co-evolutionarily developed: "Our contemporary understanding of chronic disease is the product of epidemiological practices and marketing practice that have come to configure their common subject in increasingly similar terms," Greene (2007: 4) suggests. For instance, Greene (2007) examines the case of Diuril, the world's first hypertension therapy developed by Merck Sharp & Dohme and marketed in 1958. Greene suggests that the underlying medical condition, hypertension, perhaps more commonly addressed as "high blood pressure," was gradually redefined and standardized after Diuril was promoted and brought into medical practice:

> Hypertension became a different drug after Diuril. It is equally true, however, that Diuril became a different drug after it encountered hypertension. If we look at a pharmaceutical as both a clinical entity and a branded consumer product, the relationship between drug and disease

emerges not as a story of design or serendipity, control or production, but rather as a narrative of cumulative negotiation and reciprocal definition. The history of Diuril and hypertension . . . illustrates the mutually constitutive processes of clinical research, clinical practice, and medical marketing in the postwar American pharmaceutical industry and traces the evolution of a set of hybrid structures that became central institutions of pharmaceutical promotion in the second half of the twentieth century. (Greene, 2007: 22)

For instance, after the registration of Diuril, new technologies and methods to measure hypertension were invented and brought into clinical work. In addition, the medical research community managed to establish widely shared norms for blood pressure; i.e., standards (see, e.g., Lampland and Star, 2009) for "normal blood-pressure" were enacted—a proper "disease definition" in Lackoff's (2006) vocabulary. These different resources—available therapies, diagnostic methods, and clinical standards—lowered the threshold for patients needing therapies for their hypertension:

> Diuril not only altered the options available for the treatment of hypertension but also changed irreversibly the tools available to 'think hypertension' with. By making antihypertensive therapy a sweeter pill to swallow, Diuril lowered the threshold for the prescription and consumption of antihypertensive medication, enlarged the population of potential hypertensive patients in both clinical trials and clinical practice, and contributed to the consolidation of a single threshold of hypertension. (Greene, 2007: 53–54)

Hypertension was thus established as a medical condition that larger strata of the population suffered from, thereby broadening the market for the drug. Greene's (2007) analysis thus shows that there are intricate relationships between medical conditions, available therapies, and enacted disease definitions, and that rather than appearing in a linear and sequential manner, they are co-produced and jointly further developed as new clinical data are produced. Greene (2007) thus demonstrates that medicalization is by no means instant and conclusive but rather emerges through the collaborative efforts of a variety of actors, including the joint establishment for procedures for collecting and evaluating clinical data and setting ethical and medical standards (Abraham and Davis, 2009; Abraham and Reed, 2002; Timmermans and Berg, 1997). In summary, then, therapies are not only developed by pharmaceutical companies to deal with clearly targeted and defined medical conditions but may equally help to identify patients or even to set the standards for what counts as "normal health." While this may be a common theme in the scholarly literature, this procedure is to some extent at odds with the public view of drugs as being developed to target specific medical conditions.

CRITICISM OF (BIO)MEDICALIZATION

In order to understand biomedicalization, there is both a supply side and a demand side. While much of the literature addresses the supply side, i.e., the activities of the actors in the field to establish possibilities for new therapies to be successfully launched in the market, there is also a demand side that plays a role. Conrad and Potter (2000: 560) underline, similar to DeGrand-pere (2006), that there is in fact an increased demand for drugs that can handle even what have traditionally been regarded as relatively "mild symptoms": "The American public's tolerance for mild symptoms and benign problems has decreased, which may be leading to a further medicalization of ills." Likewise, the role of marketing plays a role in strengthening the demand side of the equation. One may deplore the lack of tolerance for the natural swings in mood and health in contemporary society, but the supply side provides even more grist for the mill for students of consumption of drugs. Marshall (2009), studying the development of so-called sexuo-pharmaceuticals, therapies for perceived loss of sexual interests or performance, suggests that pharmaceutical companies have long-term strategies when it comes to medicalization, serving to provide tools and arenas for an increased demand: "Pharmaceutical companies have invested heavily in the development of diagnostic instruments and symptoms inventories, often well in advance of an approved treatment for the disorders they purport to identify" (Marshall, 2009: 144). Prior to any development work, there are activities aimed at rendering certain individual concerns subject to potential therapies. In the domain of psychopharmacological drugs, Healy (2004, 2006) has been explicit in his critique of the poor regulation and control of new drug development activities. Especially the relatively weak control of the field is problematic in his mind:

> Regulatory bodies. . . . essentially have only minimal audit functions. It is pharmaceutical companies that decide which trials should be conducted. And trials are conducted to fit the marketing requirements of the company, rather than being dictated by the effects of the drug. For example, SSRIs have greater effect on premature ejaculation than on depression, the decision to market these drugs as antidepressants is a business rather than a scientific decision. (Healy, 2004: 238)

It is market demands rather than the efficacy of the drug that determines the portfolio of new drug development trials in the industry. In addition, Healy (2006) is highly critical of the compromising of scientific standards when it comes to the publication of research results: for instance, the use of ghostwriting practices, where major multinational pharmaceutical companies hire skilled academic writers to produce journal papers that are submitted, signed by leading researchers in the field (Brody, 2007). Healy (2006) says that this practice of producing non-original texts is widespread and occurs in even the most prestigious journals: "[G]host-writing is no longer occurring only in peripheral journals and affecting only review articles. It happens in the most prestigious journals in therapeutics, and it probably happens preferentially for papers reporting randomized trials and other data-driven papers" (Healy, 2006: 72). The ghostwriting work is thus highly problematic in terms of short-circuiting the "economy of credibility" in scientific fields, where leading scholars and scientists are given much credit for their work. Exploiting this symbolic capital and translating it to economic capital are at odds with the academic liberties and tradition of transparency in which authorship is assumed to rest on some authentic or first-hand relationship to the published text. In Healy's view, the ghostwriting practice thus overturns the instituted symbolic and cultural order of the traditional university. Also Fishman (2004) expressed skepticism regarding the autonomy of the university vis-à-vis industry. She points to the obvious economic effects derived from collaborative efforts between individual researcher and research groups and the major companies in the industry:

> Pharmaceutical companies are not alone in standing to gain from such arrangements and performances [collaboration with academic researchers]. The researchers themselves, in addition to receiving financial rewards as consultants for pharmaceutical companies, also gain professional recognition, funds for their research departments and laboratories, publications and, often, media attention through related public and professional activities. (Fishman, 2004: 188)

Since the pharmaceutical companies, unlike many other industries, are dependent upon the legitimacy of the life sciences to get full approval for their products, there is a fertile soil for collaborative efforts. The concern is, however, that studies being conducted show that research sponsored by companies is more likely (3.6 times, to be specific) to present results favorable to the sponsoring company than studies not financed by an external part (Clarke et al., 2003: 169). Studying the highly controversial case of sexuo-pharmaceuticals and the specific case of so-called female sexual dysfunction, Fishman (2004) addresses the disease specificity for this condition:

> So-called lifestyle drugs such as sexuo-pharmaceuticals, have raised questions about how pharmaceutical companies can meet the approval guidelines for new drugs given their questionable status for treating 'diseases.' Such drugs will only be approved if they treat an established 'disease,' and lifestyle issues or even 'quality of life' issues have not traditionally fallen into this category. Hence, the biomedicalization of a condition . . . is in fact necessary for a lifestyle drug to gain approval. (Fishman, 2004: 188: 191)

In Fishman's (2004) view, there is a thin line between a medical condition and a general condition of human life (e.g., a reduced sexual interest during periods of life), and the tendency to medicalize, for instance, the relative lack of sexual interest among certain groups of women may have more to do with market potentials than with actual perceived human needs. There are thus highly performative consequences from defining the loss of sexual interest as a form of "dysfunction" or "disorder" in terms establishing ideas about normality and abnormality or pathology, where "standard" behaviors or preferences are established and where the outliers are given specific attention in terms of demonstrating behavior that is amenable for medicalization. Rather than being some kind of unproblematic external condition, existing as a *factum brutum*, female dysfunction syndrome and other similar "disorders" are fabrications produced on the basis of interests and situated knowledge. Using Canguilhem's (1991) important distinction between the "normal" and the "pathological," first used by the German neurologist Kurt Goldstein ([1934] 1995), pharmaceutical companies inscribe standards for evaluating or even measuring normality: "The relationship established between the FDA guidelines, clinical trials researchers, and the pharmaceutical companies helps to create a consumer market for a pharmaceutical product while also shaping ideas about normality, in this case, normal sexuality," Fishman (2004: 188: 194) writes (see also Abraham and Sheppard, 1999). The very idea of producing sexuo-pharmaceuticals is thus based on what are regarded as "normal" sexual interests and deviations from the norm then becoming subject to medicalization as a form of "correction" through pharmaceutical therapies. However, this instituting of a line of demarcation between the normal and the abnormal or pathological is not very easily accomplished but demands consent from a variety of research bodies, authorities, and, at the bottom line, the general public. Shostak and Conrad (2008) examine three cases where attempts at medicalizing conditions led to different outcomes depending on the success or failure to get a wider recognition for the operative hypotheses of the research work. They first speak about the concept of geneticization as "[t]he process by which 'differences between individuals are reduced to their DNA codes, with most disorders, behaviours, and physiological variations defined, at least in part, as genetic in origin" (Lippman, 19991; 19, cited in Shostak and Conrad, 2008: S288). In the recent interest for human genome mapping activities, there has been a close relation of unraveling connections between sequences of genes and specific medical disorders or conditions (Navon, 2011). In the first case discussed by Shostak and Conrad (2008), researchers studying depression were fairly successful in making connections between the genome and the incidence of the health condition. While the scientific evidence that certain gene sequences are associated with depression is rather imprecise and loose—"in theory . . . two-thirds of the population has a phenotype that is associated with a susceptibility to depression," Shostak and Conrad (2008: S306) note—there were no major concerns regarding these knowledge claims. No particular social group was stigmatized, and there were no immediate social consequences for any specific social community. Depression could therefore be conceived of as a medical disorder that could be connected to the genome without being overtly criticized: "That much depression is now seen as a genetically caused disease is the result of cultural definitions, institutional forces, and political and economic interests that arose decades ago. These earlier events ensure that genes associated with depression are understood to be causes of a disease condition," Shostak and Conrad (2008: S304–S305) argue. On the other hand, when scientists claimed that they had identified specific features in gay men's brains and when one American scientist eventually announced that he had isolated the "gay gene," the gay and lesbian community was enraged because of the underlying assumption that homosexuality is a form of abnormality that could be isolated like any disease. Shostak and Conrad (2008) thus emphasize the role of the social community and the mobilization of protests against a far-driven "gene-centric" understanding of human behavior. The gay and lesbian community actually played a key role in undermining the claims made by the "gay brain" and the "gay gene" research frameworks, not because these conjectures and hypotheses were of necessity invalid, but because the very legitimacy of such a research framework was put into question as being socially and culturally legitimate. The gay and lesbian community therefore not only "criticized" the research frameworks but accomplished what Hacking (2002: 55) calls an "undoing," that is, undermining the original propositions as legitimate candidates for truth or falsehood. Expressed differently, the gay and lesbian community put into the question whether the research framework aiming at identifying genes allegedly associated with homosexuality was socially legitimate at all. Instead of engaging in scientific pursuits leading to a pathologization of homosexuality, the sciences should engage in more pressing concerns, critics contend. As a consequence, the "gay brain/gene" research framework was widely rejected by both the scientific community and the broader public as being mistaken and an example of science going in the wrong direction. Say Shostak and Conrad (2008):

> The case of homosexuality vividly demonstrates how social movement activism can reinforce a critical juncture, especially by shifting regimes of credibility . . . That is, in contrast to the case of depression, in which there is a very little redundancy in events preceding and following the critical juncture, in the case of homosexuality, social movement organization, mobilization, and institutionalization are woven throughout the sequence in which genetics research is embedded. (Shostak and Conrad, 2008: S307)

In the third case, where it was found that specific ethnic communities and some phenotypes (e.g., Afro-American soldiers in Vietnam) where more sensitive to the exposure of certain chemicals, the connection between the genome of these groups and medicalization was not further explored. In their conclusion, Shostak and Conrad (2008: S310) suggests that there are in fact no clear, unambiguous and determinate connections between geneticization and medicalization: "[G]enetic information does not always lead to geneticization, nor does geneticization invariably lead to medicalization. Rather, there is a lack of consistent fit among genetics, geneticization, and medicalization. Examining this lack of consistent fit reveals that genetic information takes its meaning from its embeddedness in different moment in sequence of events and their social structural consequences." Social conditions, interests, and institutions mediate the role of the genome and the possibilities for medicalizing certain disorders or conditions. For instance, while depression is widely accepted as the outcome from or associated with biological processes (but still with some social implications), homosexuality is widely accepted (outside more orthodox circles) as a being part of the human condition and must not be treated as what is subject to "correction" through medicalization. While such ideas may have gained a foothold in the nineteenth century where, e.g., criminality was seen by some authorities as being innate rather than the outcome or effects of unfavorable social and economic conditions, the hypothesis that there is such a thing as a "gay gene" is today widely regarded as some kind of curiosity acquiring little serious attention. In summary then, it is neither the major pharmaceutical companies, nor any other individual institution that may determine if specific conditions should be subject to medicalization, but only a variety of social actors and interest groups in collaboration may enact such research frameworks. Truth, then, in the form of the capacity of articulating legitimate research hypotheses, is by no means for the few to determine. Truth is, as Nietzsche and later on Foucault suggested, what is produced on the basis of knowledge and power, but such resources are rarely located in single places. The history of medicine is full of examples of medical conditions that have either been widely endorsed during periods of time, or been surrounded by controversy (the debated medical condition of fibromyalgia, for example), indicating that even in the community of experts, there are few opportunities for enacting legitimate realities detached from broader social interests and concerns.

If the demand for financial performance is the principal driver of biomedicalization, the emergence of new genomics and so-called post-genomic therapies may open up new research programs and platforms where pharmaceutical companies are capable of producing new blockbuster drugs that are both life saving and life enhancing. In the next section, the uses of new technologies on the molecular level are addressed, and some new possibilities and challenges of the industry are sketched.

PRACTICES AND TECHNOLOGIES: FROM
GENOMICS TO THE POST-GENOMICS ERA

During last fifteen years or so, the single most important shift in focus in the development of new drugs has been the increased interest in the human genome and the accompanying genomics technologies. In 2001, the Boston Consulting Group issued a report announcing that "by applying genomics technology, companies could on average realize savings of nearly $300 million and two years per drug, largely as a result of efficiency gains. That represents a 35 percent cost and 15 percent time savings" (cited in Kahn, 2008: 741). This report is indicative of the various promises and beliefs inscribed in the new technoscientific methods being developed in the biopharmaceutical industry. New technologies and methods are in many ways helpful in advancing the life sciences, but they do not come for free and they demand significant investment in human capital to be effectively operated. Consequently, in a short-term perspective, it may be that new technologies and methods increase rather than lower the costs for developing new therapies. In addition, during the first decades of the new millennium, the relative disappointment regarding the ability to translate know-how about the human genome into therapies has turned attention toward the so-called post-genomic technologies and approaches.

In both these two shifts in focus away from the traditional small molecules in vivo research framework, the development of various biocomputational approaches plays a significant role. Thacker (2006: xi) points at the tripartite view of the DNA as the "actual" DNA of the patient, the "wet" DNA in the test tube, and the "dry" DNA in the computer database. In genomics research, all these three understandings of the concept are drawn on at the same time; the DNA is simultaneously present in all these different materializations or "biomedia." "DNA's mobility across the in vivo, in vitro, and in silico contexts enables exchanges across media, a condition I have previously called *biomedia*," Thacker (2006: 10) writes. However, as genomics have been increasingly institutionalized in the life sciences and the biopharmaceutical industry, the very idea of know-how of sequences of DNA, e.g., "Expressed Sequence Tags" (ESTs) of DNA, as "intellectual properties" has gained a foothold, but this idea is of necessity accompanied by an infrastructure that organizes DNA into "data strings, computer files, and informational visualization" (Thacker, 2006: 17). In other words, in order to become intellectual property, the DNA must first be subject to inscription into biomedia. Biomedia are in turn based on two separate but increasingly entangled scientific trajectories, that of mathematics enabling computation and computer science developing the technologies for the computation practice. In Thacker's (2006: 26) view, the future of the life sciences and the biopharmaceutical industry is thus largely a matter of continuing the path of *informaticism*, that is, continuing to translate biological systems and their properties into information possible to examine through biomedia and biocomputation approaches. This is a provocative point made by Thacker, overturning the *raison d'être* and role of the biopharmaceutical industry:

> [T]he main challenge put forth to the pharmaceutical industry is not how to develop sustainable and effective treatments, but rather *how to transform material products continually into the long-term generation of information*. What generates economic value, from this standpoint, is an infrastructure for the production of information, yet without ever completely severing the link to the patient's biological body. (Thacker, 2006: 80–81)

This shift in focus from "wet lab biology" to a biocomputational approach will imply among many things that the life sciences are taking the step from studying life as a biological material substratum to the study of "biodata" as a set of information to be examined. One such approach that has been discussed in the literature is systems biology, a biocomputational approach operating on the basis of mathematical algorithms and biomedia. For Fujimura (2005: 195), systems biology is "too new a subfield of biology to have had an impact on the daily practices of genetics, but fast it is gaining attention." In the post-genomic era, the belief in a linear association between genes or gene sequences such as SNPs and diseases has, if not been abandoned, lost its status as the uncomplicated and straightforward road to new therapies. "Today, we are told that the age of the genome is past, that the genome no longer provides all the answers, that we have instead Rnomics (for RNA, proteomics, systeomics, and physiomics," Fujimura (2005: 197) notes. For Fujimura, systems biology is a buzzword similar to that of genomics in the 1990s, but what it seeks to accomplish is to examine and integrate large data sets provided in clinical trials in so-called global scale analyses, i.e., where the totality of the data will be examined at the same time. Fujimura (2005) explains:

> In contrast to reductionist genetics, one could argue that systems biology is attempting to model biological complexities is as organized systems in order to understand them. Systems biology seeks to explain how organisms function by using information on DNA, RNA, and proteins to develop systematic models of biological activities. It wants to connect networks, pathways, parts, and environments into functional processes and systems. The focus is on functioning organisms and less on environments, but systems biology does attempt to incorporate environments into its models. (Fujimura, 2005: 198)

The role of systems biology is thus to examine the functions of a biological system in an integrated and coherent framework rather than isolating biological pathways and examining them one by one and hoping to construct meaningful models of the biological systems as patchworks of separate systems (Konrad, 2004: 155). Walkenhauer (2001: 258. Emphasis in the original) argues that systems biology is "an emerging field of biological research that aims at a systems-level understanding of genetic or metabolic pathways by investigating *interrelationships* (organization or structure) and *interactions* (dynamics or behaviours) or genes, proteins, and metabolites." What is key here is to examine a biological system as an integrated and interdependent complex structure:

> Crossing several scale-layers from molecules to organisms, we find that organisms, cells, genes, and proteins are defined as complex structures of *interdependent* and subordinate *components* whose relationships as properties are largely determined by their function in the whole. This definition coincides with the more general definition of systems as a set of components or objects and relations among them. (Walkenhauer, 2001: 258. Emphasis in the original)

Systems biology thus hopes to outline the complex biological pathways of biological systems without reducing them to single systems, that is, to examine biological systems as "self-regulating, adaptive, and anticipatory systems" (Walkenhauer, 2001: 259). Burbeck and Jordan (2006: 529) suggest that systems biology is a rather wide term involving two basic components, *modeling* and *simulation*. Modeling is the construction of images of the interrelated biological pathways on the basis of the data examined, and simulation is the next step in which the model can be used to examine how the biological system is responding to various changes in the environment or various forms of manipulations. Vemuri and Nielsen (2008), proponents of systems biology, underline the prediction as one of the key merits of the systems biology approach, arguing that "the ultimate goal of biology is to describe biological systems in sufficient details to enable quantitative prediction of factors such as their behavior and the effects of external factors" (Vemuri and Nielsen, 2008: 178). One of the fields they point to is that of "metabolic engineering" where, for instance, yeast cells can provide an understanding of how metabolic processes take place, a key to both many metabolic health disorders such as type 2 diabetes and obesity and of importance in bioengineering where yeast cells are used in many biotechnological processes.

Even though the proponents of biocomputation and bioinformatics approaches such as systems biology mention the potential learning in shifting focus from the one-by-one analysis of genomics ("the gene sequence XYZ causes the disease ABC") to examining the biological system en bloc, to integrate all the genes, proteins, enzymes, and so forth involved, the perspective is nevertheless anchored in a cybernetic framework of analysis in the tradition of Norbert Wiener (1948, 1950), suggesting that the human body is primarily to be examined as "not so much bone and blood, nerve and synapse, as they are patterns of organization" (Hayles, 1999: 104. See also Pickering, 2010): that is, an organization that at the bottom is a structure of information capable of reproducing itself over time. "He [Wiener] points out that over the course of a lifetime, the cell composing a human being change many times over, identity cannot therefore consist in physical continuity . . . Consequently, to understand humans, one needs to understand how the patterns of information they embody is created, organized, stored, and retrieved," Hayles (1999: 104) writes. In this overarching cybernetics framework of analysis, information plays a key role. Biological systems are material, but the essence of life is informational (Kay, 2000). For Fujimura (2005), this perspective, translating biological systems into information thereby rendering the biological data subject to computation and mathematical analysis, is strongly indebted to an engineering science tradition; Systems biology is influenced by "artificial intelligence, robotics, computer science, mathematics, control theory, and chemical engineering" (Fujimura, 2005: 219–220). Torgersen (2009: 82) goes even further and suggests that systems biology represents an "almost taylorist procedure of knowledge accumulation." No matter how subtle such analytical frameworks are, they are still anchored in the regime of computation:

> Systems biology aims to represent gene networks, cells, organs, and organisms as systems interacting with each other and with their environments. It employs complex sets of biological networks to abstractly model these interactions. Molecular networks include protein-protein interactions, enzymatic pathways, signaling pathways, and genereglatory pathways. Calls are now envisioned as elements in a cell-signaling pathway and in a cellular computing system. (Fujimura, 2005: 219)

However, as Fujimura (2005) admits, it is too early to determine whether this approach will be able to make any worthwhile contributions to the life sciences and to the development of new registered drugs. At the same time, there are some indications of controversies between the "old school" tradition of new drug development centered on small molecules, pharmacology know-how, and in vivo studies, and the new biocomputational and bioinformatics framework. In one of the few empirical studies of systems biology, Torgersen (2009) shows that there is some skepticism among the proponents of systems biology regarding the *ancient régime* of research:

> Systems biology intruded into a field previously dominated by qualitative experiments and introduced a new understanding not only pertaining to the way knowledge is acquired but also to how uncertainty is treated. Although systems biology is no longer new, it is still seems to be underestimated with respect to its potential disruptive power with regard to the conceptual understanding of modern biology. (Torgersen, 2009: 78)

Proponents of systems biology claim to build on a more "context-based and process-oriented view" compared to traditional experimental molecular biology studying "one or a few proteins, RNAs or DNA sequences through cleverly designed experiments" (Torgersen, 2009: 78). For proponents of the new biocomputation approach, emphasizing the need for "standardized methods to generate hypotheses on the basis of computational skills in a non-personalized way" (Torgersen, 2009: 79), the traditional approach is dismissed as being "anecdotal": "Systems supporters perceive *wet lab* biologists as doing merely *anecdotal* research, fractional and sporadic analyses of tiny parts of a problem determined by the incidental availability of certain tests and reagents. Finding the right assay to test a particular mechanism is considered a matter of sheer luck at best" (Torgersen, 2009: 79). On the other hand, proponents of the traditional approach claims that biological systems are too complicated and demonstrate emergent properties that make the idea of being able to construct models of biological systems such as cells a futile pursuit. Having empirical data collected at specific periods of time will only enable a relatively static and atemporal understanding of the biological system. In order to understand how a biological systems works, there is a need for well developed animal models of in vivo studies, where not only biological and biochemical data are acquired but also where behavioral data are subject to analyses. In research on the central nervous systems (CNS), for instance, animal models are used to collect information regarding how the animal (rat or mouse) behaves after medication. In this perspective, Wiener's idea of conceiving the human or any other biological organism in informational terms and assuming that access to sophisticated mathematical algorithms and computer science know-how would enable an understanding of the biological systems "from the bottom up," on the basis of collected but essentially non-situated and non-contextualized information is a form of scientism, a belief in the superior possibilities of rational analysis. The biological system demonstrates immensely more complex patterns and possibilities for emergence than such a cybernetic system presumes.

In summary, there is some debate over whether, in the biopharmaceutical industry, the traditional, "pre-genomics" pharmacological approach, genomics, or post-genomics processes (or combinations thereof) will dominate the life sciences and the industry more specifically in the future. However, there is no doubt that neither genomics nor post-genomics approaches have to date been able to fulfill the expectations that have been expressed on their part. For the pharmaceutical industry, the consequence is that there is a variety of new domains of expertise and technologies and tools that need to be attended to, raising the costs for R&D and even at times taking away attention from new drug development to the maintenance of increasingly specialized domains of expertise. Only the future will tell what technologies, tools, and domains of know-how will establish themselves into leading positions in the industry and in the life-science disciplines.

SUMMARY AND CONCLUSION

The biopharmaceutical industry grew out of small-scale but well-equipped pharmacies in the nineteenth century. Only later, when the university managed to overcome its instituted unwillingness to deal with practical matters, were scientific research and pharmaceutical research combined. Today, there is a close collaboration between (primarily) publically funded university research and research in the biopharmaceutical industry. The biopharmaceutical industry is regularly criticized for failing to produce drugs for diseases that cause death in the poorer regions of the world and for engaging in developing "lifestyle drugs" that are more financially lucrative. In addition, not only do biopharmaceutical companies claim to invest significant resources in marketing and promoting their drugs, they also aim to render certain medical or social conditions and predicaments amenable for therapies. Such a biomedicalization of, e.g., "female sexual dysfunctions" or mood swings is part of a strategy to not only fit the therapy to the illness but to connect desirable behaviors (e.g., being sexually active and happy) to certain drugs. In a regime of increased biomedicalization, more conditions are subject to pharmaceutical treatment, and drugs are increasingly defining medical conditions. The recent shift in focus from genomics, exploring the human genome sequence and opening up connections between gene sequences and certain medical conditions, to so-called post-genomic technologies may not change the product development strategies of biopharmaceutical companies, but it may provide instruments and methods enabling a more detailed understanding of more complex medical conditions such as neurodegenerative diseases or forms of cancer, so that the biopharmaceutical industry may be able to promote more life-enhancing or life-saving drugs at the expense of sexuo-pharmaceuticals and modified SSRI therapies.

4 The Tissue Economy

INTRODUCTION

In the last chapter of this volume, the pharmaceutical industry and the biotechnology industry were examined as emerging fields of expertise where the life sciences meet the market. The major multinational pharmaceutical industry has a major role in determining the future of the life sciences, both through the intervention into political and juridical practices and decision-making and through the more direct contributions to the life sciences, either through research work or through sponsoring contracts with research groups in universities. In comparison to the pharmaceutical industry, the biotechnology industry is still in its infancy and dependent on venture capital or state funding to maintain activities. Beside these two industries—one major astral body with a small moon circulating around it—there are various more or less institutionalized economic activities that also play a key role in the bioeconomy. This rather heterogeneous category includes activities such as organ donation, reproductive medicine such as in vitro fertilization, and what has been called the tissue economy, a variety of economic activities based on recent advancements such as tissue engineering and other forms of biotransformational medicine and engineering. In this chapter, these elements of the bioeconomy are examined and related to ongoing discussions in the industry regarding the possibilities for making money on the basis of life-science know-how.

One of the concerns regarding the bioeconomy is the colonialization of the life sphere (i.e., not only "everyday life" as such, but the functioning of the actual biological organism) of economic interests and logics. As was discussed in Chapter 1, this volume, there are always possibilities for the human body to be translated into what Samuel, Dirsmith, and McElroy (2005) call the "physico-fiscal body," where diseases and medical conditions are translated into monetary terms. The concern is, in other words, that there will be a reification of the body in the neoliberal economics doctrine of thinking where costs and income, supply and demand, and the principal parameters turn diseases into commodities and calculation procedures. Wilkinson (2006) identifies three ways to commercially exploit the human body (Table 4.1 below) where all three are of relevance in the bioeconomy.

Table 4.1 Ways of Commercializing the Body (adapted from Wilkinson, 2006: 3)

	Types of entity	Specific examples
Commercialization of physical objects	Body products	Paying blood and gamete 'donors'
	Body parts	Paying 'donors' of kidneys and other solid organs
Commercialization of abstract objects	Representations od the body	Commercial modeling and pornography
	Genetic information	DNA patenting, control/ ownership of personal genetic data
Commercialization of bodily services	Sexual services	Prostitution
	Reproductive services	Paid surrogacy
	Other services	Paying research subjects

Prostitution (Chapkis, 1997) and pornography (McNair, 2002) are commercial and controversial economic activities that have little to do with the advancement of the life sciences, but the possibilities for commercialization of physical objects, abstract objects such as genetic information, and bodily services have been further extended through the advancement of the life sciences. Therefore, five out of the seven "types of entity" listed in second column are of relevance in the bioeconomy.

Taylor (2005) emphasizes an additional tendency when commercializing the body and its capacities and parts, that of translating the actual bodies of patients into universal bodies that may be rendered open for inspection—a form of "liquidity of the body," in Carruthers and Stinchcombe's (1999) terms. This is what Taylor (2005) refers to as "materializing practices," which is of central importance for the bioeconomy. Making reference to feminist social theorist Judith Butler (1993) and her idea of the body as being performatively constituted, Taylor emphasizes a "processual view" of the body. In Butler's (1993: 9. Emphasis in the original) view, the body is to be conceived of as "not a site or surface, but as *a process of materializations that stabilizes over time to produce the effects of boundary, fixity, and surface we call matter.*" For Taylor (2005: 745), "the body, one might say, is not so much a thing as an–ing. That is, not simply the inert objects on which mind and culture perform their meaning making, bodies take shape and take place through practices of all sorts: feeding, legislating, training, cutting, explaining, beating, loving, diagnosing, buying, selling, dressing, and healing, among others." The body is what is *produced* or *performed* through various activities.

In addition, from the perspective of the life sciences, the produced or performed body is also the *enacted* body (Mol, 2002; Mol and Law, 2007). The body that is being examined from a variety of specific regimes of knowledge cannot remain one single and unified model but instead appears as what Mol (2002) speaks of as "the body multiple," the body that is composed of isolated yet mutually constitutive and interrelated biological systems. The great French physician Xavier Bichat conceived of the human body as a set of interrelated biological systems in the early nineteenth century, and in Mol's (2002) view, the increasingly differentiated life sciences and health care sector have further decomposed the human body into a number of specialist domains. Seen in this way, it is relevant to speak of the body, as Taylor (2005: 747) does, as a "contingent configuration": the body is neither "an object" nor "a text," nor only "a locus of subjectivity," but rather "a contingent configuration, a surface that is made but never in a static or permanent form." In the bioeconomy, there is ample evidence of this kind of enactment of the body, human or otherwise, into different "contingent configurations." These configurations are, however, neither exclusively based on life-sciences categories, nor on market possibilities, but are a constant process where the human body is turned into different theoretical frameworks and practical possibilities, both shaped by instituted social and cultural beliefs. The body is in this view never, or almost never, a brute fact, an unambiguous biological system, but always changes in meaning and possibility depending on the activities undertaken. In the bioeconomy, the human body is a framework for techno-scientific advancements and economic action.

This chapter is structured as follows: First the practice and emerging trade derived from organ donation are examined. Second, the growth of reproduction technology such as in vitro fertilization is discussed as a growing sector in the bioeconomy. Third, the focus is shifted toward what has been called the tissue economy (used as the title for this chapter), namely, the totality of activities engaged in collecting, storing, and using tissues and biological specimens. Fourth and finally, the plastic or cosmetic surgery industry, only loosely coupled with the advancement of the life sciences but still drawing a substantial legitimacy from connections to and associations with the life sciences and medicine, is discussed as the widely known and familiar method for shaping biological systems. In other words, plastic and cosmetic surgery is justified as a topic of discussion in this setting in terms of being some kind of miracle work on display produced by the life sciences, in many cases promoted in popular culture such as in television shows such as "Extreme Makeover," where cosmetic surgery sculptures human (primarily female) bodies to comply with instituted beauty ideals.

ORGAN DONATION: THE AFTERLIFE OF THE BODY

Perhaps one of the most spectacular elements in the bioeconomy is the swift advancement of the possibilities for using human organs as *Ersatz* materials in human bodies. The ability to procure human organs and recreate biological functions has been one of the oldest ideas in the science literature, effectively portrayed in Mary Shelley's novel *Frankenstein* first published 1818, in which a scientist is capable of fabricating life on the basis of body parts and electricity. Even though Shelley conceived of life as what could be created "from the top down," from the constitutive elements, rather than "from the bottom up" (as in today's culturing of cell lines from diseased human beings, see Terranova, 2004: 101), the very idea that larger biological systems such as organs can be transplanted into a patient's body has been a source for both fascination and abhorrence. Although this new scientific contribution opens up many possibilities, it also causes a lot of concern regarding how to organize the trade of organs in an ethically, politically, and socially sustainable manner. Today, there is an endemic shortage of organs globally: In the U.S. alone, 76,000 people were waiting for transplants in 2000 (up from 18,000 in 1989), but there were only 6,000 donated organs. The figures indicate that 5 percent of Americans need a transplant at some point in their lives, and half of these die while on the waiting list, Wilkinson (2006: 116) reports. In this situation, where demand for organs vastly outnumbers supply, there are strong economic incentives for being in the position to control the access to and circulation of organs. Consequently, there is a relatively rich flora of stories—fortunately most of them not verified by evidence—about organ theft in the poorer parts of the world, especially in the sprawling slums of the metropolitan areas of the third world (Sharp, 2003; Dickenson, 2008). As anthropologists have pointed out, even though there is little truth in these horror stories, it is indicative of poorer people's view of the Western world and the financially endowed and how we may think of the Third World as a repository of organs. At the same time, China has been strongly criticized by human rights organizations for selling organs from executed prisoners, a conspicuous violation of international agreements (Wilkinson, 2006; Dickenson, 2008).

The more day-to-day work with organ donations is a less spectacular engagement with minute control systems and the matching of organs and recipients. Still, the very act of procuring the organs is always a matter of making quick but informed decisions, and therefore the very act of procuring organs is a most unnerving moment for the layperson. Lock (2002) provides a first-hand account in her ethnographic study of organ donation, including the arrival of a dying patient to an emergency care unit, the death of the patient, the donation of the organ to another patient on the waiting list, and finally an interview with the recipient months after the dramatic events. For the layperson, this intriguing sequence of events clearly demonstrates the scope of the decision that is made. There is relatively little time for contemplating the alternatives, and even though there are firm procedures, there is also space for individual interpretations of idiosyncratic events.

Lock (2002) dedicates a significant amount of space to discussing the ethical and cultural implications derived from the new possibilities for organ donation. For instance, she is particularly concerned about the enactment of a new definition of death, namely, brain death, in contrast to the conventional "lung death" (Lock, 2002: 109), first articulated at the end of the 1960s and widely endorsed by the medical community by the early 1980s. For Lock (2002), there is a risk that the medical possibilities and the economic and "biological" value of the organs of a brain-dead patient/cadaver influence the very definition of death. That is, rather than being a religious or cultural construct embedded in tradition and beliefs, death is becoming a by-product of what is economically and socially feasible. Das (2000: 269) clearly states her position: "The classical definitions of death even in the clinical context were based upon permanent cessation of the flow of vital fluids. But as the perceived need for more organs and tissues arose, the classical definition was sought to be redefined to meet this need."[1] Just as the definition of man, as suggested by Foucault (1972), is the outcome of predominant sources of knowing structured into discourses, so too is death. Death is a form of enactment or agreement, defined on the basis of biomedical possibilities (and costs, some would say) rather than a theological or cultural construct. Lock (2002) describes a particularly interesting situation from her empirical work in a Canadian hospital, which clearly indicates the problem about where draw the line between life and death:

> As the orderly maneuvered the patient into the assigned space, an intern picked up the patient charts. 'Looks like this is going to be a good donor,' he said. 'Should we call the transplant coordinator?' A senior intensivist, on the phone at the time, overheard this comment and immediately said, 'Not so fast now. Slow down.' After hanging up, the internist looked at the chart himself and briefly observed the busy nurses as they set to work checking the lines and tubes sustaining the patient. He turned to the intern and repeated once again, 'Not so fast.' When I left the unit an hour or two later, the patient was stable, but the condition of his brain remained in doubt. A week later I was told that this man was out of the ICU [Intensive Care Unit] and in an ordinary ward where he was breathing on his own and doing well. A full recovery was expected. (Lock, 2002: 101)

How can we, Lock (2002) asks, balance the care of individual patients and the economic and social interests in the organs among all the patients on the waiting lists for organs, the hospitals, research groups, interest organizations, and other relevant stakeholders, in a society where organs are always in short supply? Isn't there always a concern that the patient, costly to care for over periods of time (many potential organ donors are in a coma for long periods), carries organs that have substantial economic value and that would give other patients better and happier lives or life at all? "Once transplants were routinized, vital organs rapidly became of immense value to other interested parties: physicians, transplant coordinating organizations, dying patients and their families. But for an organ to be of worth in this way, it must be first made into an object, a thing-in-itself, entirely differentiated from the individual from which it is procured," Lock (2002: 48) remarks. The key to this discussion is actually the concept of death itself. While it is generally believed that a brain-dead patient is no more than a "living cadaver"—at least that is the image promoted by what Sharp (2003: 47) calls the "transplant ideology"—Lock (2002) claims that the concept of brain death is more complex:

> Brain-dead patients will, we know for certain, 'die' as soon as they are removed from the ventilator. We take comfort from this knowledge when proclaiming them dead even though they look alive. But patients in cerebral death are rarely on ventilators and can usually breathe without assistance. All they need is assistance with feeding—as do a great number of patients who are obviously fully alive. (Lock, 2002: 120)

Even though the authorities in the field of medicine and health care have been careful to outline policies and regulations for how to determine the death of a potential donor, there are still some disturbing practices that interfere with the definition of brain death. Sharp (2003) points out that during the procurement of the organs from brain-dead patients, the organ donor is anesthetized during the surgery. Sharp thus poses the inevitable question: If the patient who is defined as dead is subject to anesthesia, i.e., if the organ donor is dead, why take care to undertake this procedure (Sharp, 2003: 87)? The answer from responsible authorities is that this procedure is intended to make the work less cumbersome for the physicians and nurses doing the procurement, and that the use of anesthesia is in fact of little importance for the organ donor. Still, the question remains whether medical expertise can be 100 percent sure if the organ donor remains conscious. The question whether brain death is a "death proper" or not remains disputed.

No matter what one thinks about the definition of brain death, there is a shortage of organs and donors globally. Sharp (2003) argues that the criteria for qualifying as a donor have gradually been lowered as the supply fails to meet the demand, and today the use of less healthy donors is often practiced.

> We've changes the criteria in the last year [There's] no [upper] age [limit, for example] . . . as more and more people are added to the list and more and more people are dying every day, because of the lack of organs, the transplant surgeons are getting more and more liberal with the criteria they will accept . . . [for us today the] only contraindication is HIV/AIDS. (Organ Transplantation Coordinator, cited in Sharp, 2003: 64)

Even though the organ trade is surrounded by regulations, ethical standards, and policy statements, maintaining that organ donation is a highly controlled and monitored activity, there are, after all, strong economic incentives for engaging in the trade: "Although veiled in a complex array of euphemistic constructions, organ transfer and in turn, the donor body are sites of lucrative medical practices sustained by an ever-expanding demand for technological expertise" Sharp (2003: 26) notes. The possibilities of medical practice are moving ahead faster than our willingness to donate organs. Lock (2002: 19) emphasizes that as soon as a patient is declared dead, the patient is instantly transformed into a "container that must be handled with care" (see Roach [2003, chapter 3] for a first-hand account of the procedure). Commonly used expressions, such as "procurement of organs," "organ harvesting," and, the more recently used term, Roach (2003) suggests, "organ recovery," propose a rational handling of organs in the event of organ donation. However, such a vocabulary and other accompanying practices emphasizing the "rational" handling of patients and organs are nevertheless based upon the capacity to change the focus from caring for a patient to procuring organs for the benefit of other patients more or less momentarily at the event of the death of the organ donor. Hogle (1995) suggests that it is easier said than done to transform the focus from one activity to the other:

> Clinical protocols and standards, derived from those used for living patients, are nevertheless intended to treat the body and its materials as straightforward, organic, exchangeable materials. The bodies, however, have an ambiguous status; they are a source of materials represented by collected laboratory data and placed within predetermined categories, but they are also persons with histories and families. (Hogle, 1995: 495)

She continues: "Although human materials are translated into useable objects, old cultural meanings and categories remain. Moreover, new meanings are inscribed back on these bodies and their materials, using the very means that were intended to detach them from their human attributes" (Hogle, 1995: 496). For instance, during her participant observation during an organ procurement operation, Lock (2002: 22) is particularly disturbed by the procurement of the eyes of the organ donor: "For me it seems, removal of the eyes represents more of a violation than does procurement of internal organs," she admits. In the Western tradition of thinking, the eyes and vision play a central role both as a source of knowing and also as the location of personality and humanity (Blumenberg, 1993). Therefore, removing a liver from an organ donor to pass it on to some patient in need of it may be relatively easier to accept than thinking about the eyes including the retina and a number of different tissues as "spare parts" that are transferred to another human being. In medical terms, such concerns have little relevance, but culturally speaking there is apparently a difference between internal organs and, for instance, the eyes. Another culturally permeated domain of anxieties regarding life, humanity, and the human body is the field of so-called *transgenic organs*, i.e., organs that are grown by and procured from animals such as pigs. Human beings and pigs have significant biological similarities, and there are today possibilities to use organs from transgenic pigs. However, cultural concerns regarding the mixing of humans and animals cause much anxiety. Says Sharp (2003: 221): "Transgenic pigs are simultaneously wondrous and monstrous creatures because they bear the promise of an unending supply of transplantable parts while also undermining the safety associated with species integrity."

In summary, possibilities for organ transplantation are one of the relatively recent challenges for humanity. Humankind is today in a position to repair and recreate vital human organs but there is an excess of demand for organs that will easily lead to a situation where poorer populations are "more worth dead than alive" (Sharp, 2000: 296), leading to ethical concerns and trade-offs. For instance, much organ donation work benefits from, e.g., gang-related violence in metropolitan areas. On the one hand, there is a disturbing reliance on criminality in disenfranchised social strata for the supply of organs; on the other hand, a death of, say, a young street gang member is not entirely meaningless when a range of vital organs are passed on. Family members of such organ donors may take comfort in knowing that their relatives made a contribution to the community and to society. Waldby (2000) discusses the so-called *Visual Human Project*, an Internet site where the body of the former criminal Joseph Paul Jernigan, of Waco, Texas, is put on display for the benefit of, e.g., medical students. Jernigan was convicted for burglary and murder in 1981, and in August 1993, he was executed by an injection of a lethal dose of potassium chloride. Prior to his execution, Jernigan decided to donate his body to the Visible Human Project. During his life, Jernigan was described as a "cruel and murderous drunk" and a "mad dog," but after his death his donation was appreciated, and he was described as an "Internet angel" in *Chronicle of Higher Education* (cited in Waldby, 2000: 54). "In his life he took a life, in his death he may end up saving a few," the article continued. It is complicated to examine such events in both ethical and practical terms. Jernigan was apparently a violent and dangerous man, and to some extent his decision to donate his body made a contribution to a greater good, but there is still lingering concern that social outcasts, criminals, the physically sick, and the psychologically disoriented are little more than repositories and source materials for the health care sector, which can benefit more financially endowed social strata. In the bioeconomy, where tissues and organs acquire an economic value, there are also ethical and practical concerns accompanying the emerging possibilities. Gang-related deadly violence is, for instance, then no longer simply a waste of human life, but the death of young men becomes part of an economic circulation of human organs. Organ donation as practice and as business is then a terrain beset with ethical concerns and practical trade-offs.

REPRODUCTION TECHNOLOGIES AND THE BABY BUSINESS

While the field of reproductive medicine is a more "positive case" than that of organ donation, there are still ethical issues to be addressed. In the Western world, in Europe and in North America, men and women tend to become parents at an increasingly higher age. Especially in the middle class, younger people tend to study for longer periods of time, to spend time traveling and exploring the world, and to engage in careers, prior to even thinking about becoming parents. A significant number of couples or single women may then make the unpleasant discovery that they cannot very easily conceive a baby. Today, it is estimated that about 10 percent of the American population suffers from infertility problems (Almeling, 2007). While prior generations had to live with this predicament or adopt a child, today there are advanced technoscientific procedures in place to help childless couples and single women become parents. Needless to say, undergoing in vitro fertilization (IVF) treatment is by no means an entirely joyful experience, but demands, especially for women, much effort. Clarke (1998: 30–52) provides an overview of the emergence of reproductive medicine in the twentieth century and points out the advancement in endocrinology, agriculture, and what she calls "the new biology" (i.e., genomics, proteomics. See also Franklin and Roberts, 2006; Thompson, 2005). Even though the field of reproductive medicine was articulated from the early twentieth century as an opportunity for women to take control over their "reproductive capacities" (Clarke, 1990: 34) through the use of developing contraceptive drugs, it was not until the mid 1960s that the pharmaceutical companies and American federal funds started to invest in reproductive medicine: "After 1965, both federal and industry (largely pharmaceutical) support rose dramatically . . . Funding jumped from under \$38 million for 1960–1965 to \$332 million in 1969–1974" (Clarke, 1990: 28). Today, there is a great stock of know-how in the field of reproductive medicine, and infertility clinics are present throughout the world. "Effectively . . . the process of reproduction has been deregulated, privatised and made available for investment and speculative development," Waldby and Cooper (2007: 58) remark. The day-to-day work in the field of IVF reveals some strong undercurrents of culture, and the field is both thoroughly gendered and interesting to examine from a postcolonial theory perspective as poorer parts of the world increasingly supply, for instance, surrogate mothers for wealthy Westerners.

ASSISTED FERTILIZATION

The single most important input resource in IVF are oöcytes, unfertilized human eggs. These eggs are either donated by younger women in the West (e.g., students in need of money) or procured from, e.g., Ukraine or other former Soviet Union republics, and end up in so-called fertility clinics in, e.g., Cyprus and Belize or North America (Waldby and Cooper, 2007: 61). Clients pay between £8,000 and £12,000 per treatment, and the outcome is always uncertain. Normally, the more IVF treatments one endures the higher the chance of conception. For the egg donor, the very procedure is by no means uncomplicated, but the donor is participating in what Waldby and Cooper (2007: 59) call "clinical labour"[2] and Clarke, Shim, Shostak and Nelson (2009: 22) call "biolabour." Already here, in the very early stages of the process, there is a distinction made between Caucasian women serving as egg donors for Caucasian recipient couples and "poor, uneducated, dark-skinned [women] restricted to their role as surrogate mother in the reproductive market" (Waldby and Cooper, 2007: 63). In addition to the apparent operative distinction between ethnical and race groups in the international IVF market, Waldby and Cooper (2007: 64) suggest that there is a fluid line of demarcation between the "reproductive economy" and related fields such as "sexual and domestic labour"; working in one field may easily lead to a "migration" in the other. The common denominator may be poverty: women without economic resources may use their bodies in manifold ways to make a living and to support their children (Dickenson 2008).

However, the IVF industry is careful not to mingle with, for instance, the sex industry and invests many resources in positioning itself as a legitimate business operating on the basis of the reciprocal "gift of life." The gift of life is still not easily passed around but is carefully regulated by various institutionalized procedure and routines. Almeling's (2007) study of an egg agency and a sperm bank offers some insight into the degree of control of egg donors. Even though the very egg per se plays a relatively marginal role in determining the biography of the child who is eventually born, egg agencies are careful to recruit "suitable" donors. The criteria for being a donor include being physically attractive, showing evidence of high intelligence (in terms of, e.g., SAT performance), and being healthy, as in the case of university students, or having several (healthy) children, i.e., having an adequate "track record" in the field of reproduction (Almeling, 2007: 327). Sperm donors, on the other hand, are generally expected to "be tall and college educated with consistent high sperm count." Women are naturally paid a much larger amount of money than the sperm donors are, and, Almeling (2007: 328) says, are "perceived as more closely connected to their eggs than men are to their sperm." Egg agencies are pay close attention to the process of recruitment of egg donors and insist on creating what Titmuss (1970) speaks of as a "gift relationship" (in the case of blood donation) between the egg donor and the recipients. Here the egg agency staff faces a paradox in terms of maintaining the ideology of the "gift of life" at the same time as there are financial compensations involved in the transaction. "[E]gg agencies structure the exchange not only as a legalistic economic transaction, but also the beginning of a caring gift cycle, which the staff foster by expressing appreciation to the donors, both on behalf of the agency and the agency's clients," Almeling (2007: 333) argues. At the same time, the egg agencies tell potential donors to think of the donation "like a job" that nevertheless leads to the amazing task of helping childless couples or single women become parents. At the same time, egg agency staff frown at women seeking to "make a career" as egg donors since such a thoroughly professional view of the trade would threaten the "gift relationship" ideology so central to the industry: "[W]omen who attempted to make a career of selling eggs provoke disgust among staff, in part because they violate the altruistic framing of donation" (Almeling, 2007: 334). Most egg agencies therefore allow no more than three donations from each donor.

In addition to the formal economic transactions between the recipients, the egg agency, and the egg donor—based on a "strictly business" agreement—it is relatively common that the recipients give flowers, jewelry, and additional financial "gifts" to the egg donors. Such practices are allowed by the egg agencies, Almeling (2007: 334) suggests, because they are "upholding the constructed vision of egg donation as reciprocal gift-giving, in which egg donors help recipients and recipients help donors."[3] The tripartite relationship between egg agencies, egg donors, and egg recipients thus rests on a heterogeneous body of institutions including that of reciprocal gift relationships, economic interest, and a serious engagement in the donation activity that must not be turned into a truly professional attitude to the assignment. Almeling (2007) shows that egg donors are disciplined to think of themselves in altruistic terms at the same time as they must be aware of the scope of the economic transaction. In a gender perspective, the egg agencies thus reproduce the conventional view of women as careful guardians of their reproductive resources while men are expected to be happy get a bit of cash for their semen—for "getting paid for what they are doing anyway," as the joke goes. Women to some extent *are* their eggs—otherwise the ideology the gift relationship would not make sense—while sperm is what can be easily spared. The trick of the egg agencies is thus to effectively balance what Hirschman (1977) in an entirely different setting spoke of as "the passions" and "the interests." A careful balancing of altruism and economic benefit is prescribed and encouraged by the egg agencies. As Zelizer (2005: 27) has demonstrated, the domains of "intimacy"—to which human reproduction certainly belongs—and economic concerns are not combined without much legitimizing work and investment in new institutional logics: "[M]oney and intimacy represent contradictory principles whose intersection generates conflict, confusion, and corruption. Thus people debate passionately the propriety of compensated egg donations, sale of blood and human organs, purchases of child care or elder care, and wages for housewives." As a consequence, egg agencies need to balancing seemingly opposing demands and interests.

The work in the IVF clinics, where the fertilization process is assisted, unfolds as a series of events wherein the individual organs and the gametes (egg, sperm) are treated as individual, freestanding entities or events,

Cussins (1998, 1996) suggests: "The organs become a focus of repair and therapy, with all the qualities of the classic specimen of study. The uterus and ovaries and tubes are represented *sui generis*, as it were, on the monitor, floating apart from the context of the rest of the body, and of the whole person" (Cussins, 1996: 586). The entire process can be separated into a series of stages, including the egg retrieval from the woman, the fertilization of the egg in the laboratory, the growth of the embryo in various media containing the nutrition needed during the first days after the fertilization, embryo selection through visual inspection, and transfer to the woman's uterus. The assisted fertilization process thus unfolds as two parallel series of activities, one in the interface between the couple or single woman seeking assistance, the totality of investigation, information and counseling activities taking place in the front office and also the clinical work of egg retrieval and embryo transfer, and one set of activities including the fertilization, the embryo growth, and the embryo selection conducted in the laboratory setting, the back office of the clinic. The front-office activities are primarily handled by physicians, gynecologists, midwives, and nurses, while the laboratory is primarily populated by embryologists, biochemical analysts, microbiologists, and other scientific professions. Much of the assisted fertilization work is thus separated from the patient. Franklin (1998) suggests that the epistemic culture of assisted fertilization is, in her mind, somewhat misleading, enacting infertility (or, in many cases, "subfertility") as being a matter of minor clinical intervention, making very little, almost nothing to affect the biological reproductive system:

> The tantalizing feature of IVF is the idea that there *is* just a minor adjustment to be made, just a small gap to be bridged, just a little push in the right direction, just the need for a 'helping hand,' as the technique is often described. More often than not, several adjustments are needed, and consequently there is a significant component of trial and error in identifying them. (Franklin, 1998: 109)

Despite such collective beliefs, statistics reveal that about half, at best 60 percent, of couples undergoing one, two, or three cycles of assisted fertilization are successful in becoming pregnant. This relatively low success rate leads to a strong statistical orientation of the field:

> The whole 'epistemic culture' of the unit is based on the production of statistics. By this I mean that what it is for a procedure to work and be an indicated therapy is expressed statistically, rather than say, as a matter of experiments, or a matter of fact. Fertility clinics, particularly private ones, are increasingly in competition for patients. Reputation draws patients, and these are built primarily on successfully initiating pregnancies. A patient calling an infertility unit has a right to, and often will, ask what the center's success rates are. (Cussins, 1998: 85)

As a consequence, "much energy," Cussins (1998: 85) says, goes into "compiling the statistics and generating success rates." Competitors' rates are examined with interest and at times with suspicion, and the possibilities for comparing statistics are debated. Cussins (1996) examines some of the activities wherein the patient undergoing the therapy is transformed into a set of resources that are explored and exploited in the pursuit of accomplishing a pregnancy, The organs, gametes, and processes involved in fertilization and conception—two terms closely associated but separated in time, wherein fertilization is the fusion of gametes and conception is "the process of genetic combination, which occurs over the succeeding thirty-six hours" (Franklin, 1998: 104)—thus need to be analytically separated while they are part of an integrated biological process. This ability to keep biological entities apart while still integrating them is referred to as a form of "ontological choreography" by Cussins (1996: 600), a construction of an assemblage or a "functional zone of compatibility" composed of elements that are both interrelated, yet to be examined as individual entities or processes:

> The objectified body must not lose its metonymic relation to the whole person, and neither must the instruments lose their acquired properties of personhood in virtue of which they fix, by-pass or stand in for stages in the woman becoming pregnant. I called this processes of forging a functional zone of compatibility that maintains referential power between things of different kinds *ontological choreography*. (Cussins, 1996: 600)

Cussins (1998) argues that the work in assisted fertilization clinics is formally based on strictly medical expertise but in fact ideas about normality and naturalness, i.e., socially and culturally embedded beliefs, influence and determine how decisions are made. For instance, the highly specialized procedure of visually inspecting and selecting what embryos to transfer to the uterus after a few days of growth is determined both by both clinical evidence in the form of statistics but also by certain aesthetic preferences regarding symmetry and geometries: "The evenness of the cells, the similarity of cell size, and the presence of 'blebs' are also recorded. The embryos are given a 'grade' to reflect how 'pretty' they are. Round evenly developing embryos are good, and uneven, 'misshapen' embryos with blebs and not good. The 'not good' embryos are routinely referred to collectively as 'crud'" (Cussins, 1998: 93).

In summary, the work in assisted fertilization clinics is based on the ability to effectively handle a set of biological entities and processes and on the social and emotional responses and needs on the part of the patients. The clinics are thus a meeting point between the social world where childlessness is a stigma and an emotionally stressful situation and the biological world wherein the "natural" process of fertilization and conception is not properly functioning and thus needs to be given "a helping hand" on its way.

ADOPTION AND SURROGACY

In addition to the more widespread IVF treatment (it is estimated that about 3 percent of all children born have been assisted in their fertilization), there is also a thriving "baby business" (Spar's [2006] provocative term) including adoption agencies and, perhaps more controversial, surrogate mothers. Adoption agencies have been part of society for centuries or even millennia and are widely regarded as a legitimate business. This domain of baby business specializes in handling the "stock" of available children. In popular culture as well as in real life, there are numerous heartbreaking stories about what it feels like for children not to be selected by potential parents, and all aspects of the "selection" of a child must be a disheartening event. There is also a competition between healthy children and sick or even deformed children where the latter categories regularly pull the shortest straw, normally ending up spending most of their childhood in institutions. Despite the unnerving treatment of human beings like goods to be traded, the adoption industry helps many children get a home and pursue lives that are better than in the institutions.

The use of surrogate mothers, banned in many countries of the world but legal in, for instance India, is a more controversial approach to becoming a parent (Pande, 2009; Markens, 2007; Goslinga-Roy, 2000). Terms like "reproductive outsourcing" and "reproductive tourism" clearly indicate that this may be a widespread activity in parts of the world (Twine, 2011). Wilkinson (2006: 137) distinguishes between *partial* or *straight* surrogacy "where the surrogate mother is the genetic mother," and *full* or *host* surrogacy where the "surrogate provides only gestational services and the gametes are provided by others (often, but not necessarily, the commissioning parents)." Both these forms of surrogacy are riddled with controversies and juridical concerns (Markens, 2007). Wilkinson (2006: 116) says that there are at least three principal objections to surrogacy: "*harm* to surrogates of children; the *commodification* of surrogates, children, or (more generally) reproduction; or the *exploitation* of women especially those who are poor or vulnerable in some other way." Thomas Frank (2008), combining at least the latter two objections, argues that surrogacy is the end point of the neoliberal tradition of thinking where even motherhood could become subject to economic transactions and market-based activities. For Frank (2008), this is a deplorable change in perspective where virtually everything may be bought and sold. For some feminists and postcolonial theorists, the use of Third World women as surrogate mothers is a puzzling and alarming tendency to institute new forms of neocolonialist practice. "Gestational surrogacy is embedded in a transnational capitalist market that is structured by racial, ethnic, and class inequalities and by competing nation-state regulatory regimes," Twine (2011: 3) argues. The young and poor women serving as surrogate mothers have been reported to be stigmatized in their community and must spend the pregnancy period in isolation in health care institutions. Some commentators, such as the American feminist writer Andrea Dworkin (cited in Wilkinson 2006: 136), even make a clear connection between surrogacy and prostitution as two forms of female exploitation:

> Motherhood is becoming a new branch of female prostitution with the help of the scientists who want access to the womb for experimentation and power . . . Women can sell reproductive capacities the same way old-timer prostitutes sold sexual ones but without the stigma of whoring because there is no penile intrusion; it is the womb, not the vagina, that is being bought. (Andrea Dworkin, 1983)

However, notwithstanding this in many cases harsh critique, there are examples of couples becoming parents through the labor of surrogate mothers. Cohen and Athavaley (2009) report about the Arizona couple Rhonda and Gerry Wile, who became parents in August 2009. The price paid for the surrogacy is in the range of US$2,000–10,000, a massive amount of money for many Indian women. Read alongside Frank's (2008) critique, Cohen and Athavaley (2009) tell another story where surrogacy gets a human face and is anchored in actual biographies and experiences. While Frank (2008) speaks about the broader neoliberal setting and the economic hegemony of the wealthy Manhattanites capable of paying for everything they want—true, economic freedom in Milton Friedman's (2002) use of the term—Cohen and Athavaley (2009) add some flesh and blood to the narrative. No matter how many heartwarming stories about the joys of parenting are told, surrogacy practice is by no means uncomplicated. Wilkinson's (2006) careful analysis, based on an analytical philosophy tradition of thinking, of a number of different arguments against surrogacy however leads him to the conclusion that there are few watertight arguments embedded in empirical data against surrogacy beyond the sheer belief in universal norms prohibiting the commercialization of reproduction as such. Still, being perhaps in its early stages, there is a need for more elaborate institutional control in this domain. As Spar (2006) emphasizes, there is a relatively low "price elasticity" in the baby business—aspiring parents are virtually willing to spend their last penny to get a child of their own—and therefore there is a need for international standards, agreements, and regulations.

THE MARKET FOR TISSUES

The market for tissues is here used as a relatively broad term denoting all kinds of economic transactions where organs and tissues acquire an economic or financial value which renders them subject to economic circulation, i.e., they are bought and sold on the "tissue market." Waldby and Mitchell (2006: 6–7) propose the term tissue economy to capture the changes during the last few decades:

> Solid organ transplantation has been practiced since the late 1950s and commonplace since the late 1970s, as the refinement of tissue typing, surgical techniques, and immunological suppression has allowed organ donors to be matched with compatible recipients . . . Skin, bones, heart valves, and corneas can now be banked and used in surgery . . . Reproductive tissue—sperm, ova, and embryos—can be donated and transplanted. (Waldby and Mitchell, 2006: 6–7)

Waldby and Mitchell (2006) emphasize that the key term in understanding the tissue economy is *technicity*. This is a rather broad and complex term, used by the French technology theorist Jacques Ellul (1964) capturing the ability to "procure, potentiate, store and distribute" tissues (Waldby and Mitchell, 2006: 32). That is, rather than being strictly biological materials, the tissues must be able to function as "components" in biological systems that have a durability and immunological specificity. In order to trade tissues, they must serve the role of exchangeable elements in a broader biological system in analogy with the technical elements in a technical system. In the tissue economy, the tissues and other biological components are parts of a "biomachine," the aggregated biological system such as the human organism. One example of the scope of the tissue economy is that today, there are more "than 282 million archived and identifiable pathological specimens from more than 176 million individuals are currently being stored in the United States repositories" (Andrews and Nelkin, 2001: 4–5, cited by Waldby and Mitchell, 2006: 6–7). Each year, at least 20 million specimens are added to the stock of tissues, and today, "virtually everyone has his or her tissue 'on file' somewhere."

Richard Titmuss's (1970) study of blood donation in the U.K. and the U.S is a classic work on the economic value of biological resources. In Titmuss's (1970) view, drawing on the work of the anthropologist Marcel Mauss (1954) on the function of reciprocal gifts in human societies, blood is not effectively distributed on the basis of market mechanisms but is embedded in what Titmuss refers to as "gift relationships," an ethos of reciprocity where people give away blood for free to receive blood themselves if and when needed. In his careful, empirically grounded analysis, Titmuss provides several arguments against market transactions: "The first is that a private market in blood entails much greater risks to the recipient of disease, chronic disability and death. Second, a private market in blood is potentially more dangerous to the health of donors. Third, a private market in blood produces, in the long run, greater shortages of blood" (Titmuss, 1970: 157). That is, on all criteria—economic efficiency, administrative efficiency, price, and "purity, potency and safety"—the "commercialized blood market fails" (Titmuss, 1970: 205). As a consequence, Titmuss proposes a

Gemeinsschaft-type of relation in a society where blood is not economized (Titmuss, 1970: 209–246). Needless to say, this idea of blood being given away for free is at odds with the neoliberal idea about the need for property rights, self-interested economic agents, and so forth. More recent studies of the storing and circulation of tissues suggest that the idea of giving is not very fashionable for the time being. Today, there are instead a variety of services based on economic compensation. However, a few large-scale research projects still rely on the informed consent of participants. Lock (2001) examines the international Human Genome Diversity Project, widely referred to as the "vampire project" since blood samples were collected from a variety of ethnic groups all over the world. Lock (2001: 69) is critical about the research project and claims that it leads to a "fetishism" of the human DNA (see also Keller, 2000; Lewontin, 2000; Oyama, 2000; Griffith, 2001; LeBreton, 2004; Rosoff, 2010)[4]: "Because blood is a renewable resource and simple to donate, it is all too easy for scientists and other outsiders to objectify and fetishize human DNA." This critique is related to the concerns regarding the DNA as being the "book of life," an idea—which Francis Crick dubbed "the central dogma" of genetics—that is increasingly abandoned. Says Lock (2007: 62) "Metaphors associated with the mapping of the human genome—the Book of Life, the Code of Codes, the Holy Grail, and so on—are entirely outmoded ... DNA is, after all, a blueprint for the organism" (Jeremy Rifkin's [1998] *The Biotech Century* would be a fine illustration to this enthusiastic embracing of the concept of gene.) The large numbers of samples of blood are thus collected without any clear idea of what to do with them and what kind of theories to advance. In Lock's (2001) view, the Human Genome Diversity Project represents a form of neocolonialist approach seemingly caring for "endangered peoples" while in fact being couched in mistaken ideas about what the human genome is potentially capable of revealing or explaining.

STEM CELL POTENTIALS AND THE STORING OF BIOLOGICAL SPECIMENS

Another interesting case in the tissue economy, addressed in a number of places in the literature, is the cultured cell lines derived from human beings, at times not even alive today. One of the most widely used cell lines, the HeLa cell line, derives from the Afro-American woman Henrietta Lacks who died in 1951 from an unusually aggressive form of cervical cancer but whose cells are still used in much research work. "There is more of her [Henrietta Lacks] now, in terms of biomass, than there ever was when she was alive," Enright (2000: 8, cited in Lock, 2001: 74) notes. The cell samples from Mrs. Lacks were collected without the informed consent of family members, and it was not until 1973, more than 20 years after Henrietta Lacks's death on October 4, 1951, that Bobbette Lacks, the daughter-in-law of Mrs. Lacks, learned from her friend's brother-in-law working at the National Cancer Institute that there was a so-called HeLa cell line widely use in the life-science community (Skloot, 2010: 179–181. See also Dickenson, 2008: 22). The Lacks family tried to sue the hospital making the sample but failed to gain control over the biological specimens. The HeLa cell line is a form of immortality of the donor—whose photo can be found on the Internet—a peculiar afterlife in biochemistry laboratories and in Petri dishes. In other cases, tissues were not used as input material in the research work but instead were what are stored in, e.g., cryobanks. In the recent interest for stem cell research, holding the promise to enculture or engineer new organs or tissues on the basis of stem cells, undifferentiated "master cells" that may be developed into all human organs, there is a growing (but still small) market for the storage of stem cells. Stem cells are for instance to be found in umbilical cord blood. Andrews and Nelkin (2001: 32) estimate that the likelihood that a newborn infant will ever need her umbilical cord blood is "fewer than one in 20,000." Smith (2009) refers to this practice as "modern day alchemy," indicating the speculative nature of the pursuit. Still, Brown and Kraft (2006: 322) cite an advertisement for an American cryobank offering the service of storing blood samples: "By storing your baby's umbilical cord blood with California Cryobank Stem Cell Services, you are safeguarding the future health of your child by providing your baby with a lifetime of insurance needed to take advantage of today's medical breakthroughs and tomorrow's discoveries" (Web Advertising—Cryobank Inc.). While this kind of advertisement envisages the storing of umbilical cord blood as an option to take advantage of the future advancement of the life sciences, critics claim that the collection of blood during the delivery of the baby implies risks for both the child and the mother because midwives and obstetricians need to take care of one additional assignment. For mothers in particular, there is always a risk of postpartum hemorrhage during the third phase of the delivery (Dickenson, 2008: 47). These practical concerns are rarely addressed in the promotion of cryobank services.

For some, stem cell research[5] holds a great potential for future generations to take advantage of the advancement of the sciences whose future possibilities can only be vaguely imaged (Smith, 2009), while for others this is a shameless exploitation of gullible parents wanting to give their children the best health care they can offer. In general the entire research framework based on stem cells is one of the most heavily debated and morally charged areas of the bioeconomy. For researchers, the stem cell research agenda and the debate about its merits and dangers are excellent examples of how science and society need to be co-aligned, indeed *co-produced* in Jasanoff's (2004) phrase (Hoeyer, Nexoe, Hartlev, and Koch, 2009; Kent, Faulkner, Geesink, and Fitzpatrick, 2006). "The stem cell wars provide a powerful demonstration of the ways in which science and society are co-produced, always mutually influencing and constituting each other, rather than developing independently," Prainsack, Gesink, and Franklin (2008: 352–353) argue. They continue: "[S]tem cell science has a powerful symbolic currency of the remaking of human life and the manipulation of human origins. This science stands in for diverse social, religious and historical agendas—from the debates concerning abortion, to the legacies of the Second World War." Waldby (2002), on her part, conceives of stem cells as yet another "biological actor" being introduced along with other entities such as genes:

> Stem cells are one . . . new biological actors, recently taking their place along genes as potent icons of promised control over biology and health. The term 'stem cell' refers to any cell that can renew tissue in the body. The type most prominent in the media is 'pluripotent,' undifferentiated cells that have the capacity to develop into almost all of the body's tissue types. (Waldby, 2002: 306)

As in the case of genes, in the mid and late 1990s stem cells were widely described as the "book of life" or the "key to life," that is, as an underlying master code capable of explaining, when properly decoded, virtually all secrets and wonders of life. In Waldby's (2002) view, stem cells are the most recent of these potential openings into the very texture of life. While enthusiasm and engagement are key resources in any scientific endeavor, Waldby nevertheless points at some of the challenges for the stem cell research program. First, the collection of blood from umbilical cords may easily lead to controversies with the influential "pro-life activists" (see, e.g., Simonds, 1996) who generally reject the use of such biological tissues. Second, the general concern regarding cloning and the intervention into hereditary material and its association with the stem cell research program may easily lead to an undermining of the legitimacy of the research Waldby, 2002: 306). Taken together, stem cell research remains one of the most recent fields where much hope is granted to what potentially may be accomplished. At the same time, all research work that seeks to "grow life" (organs, tissues) is easily compromised as being some kind of Frankensteinian research project.

FABRICATING LABORATORY ANIMALS

The production and use of genetically modified laboratory animals is another field in the tissue economy that is highly controversial and that has led to sharp criticism among, for instance, animal liberation activists. Being perhaps one of the most widely used and therefore paradigmatic practices and accomplishments in the bioeconomy, genetically modified animals are on the borderland between nature and culture, biology and technology (Kohler, 1994). For instance, a laboratory mouse (Rader, 2004), designed to develop a terminal disease within a few weeks, is a form of teratological creature (Braidotti, 2006: 101), a "monster" in the original sense of the term as being in a permanent state of liminality between brute nature and fabricated reality:

> [M]ice, and cells of biological research are altered by humans environmentally or physically to do 'unnatural things,' but they are not literally machines. They occupy a form of 'edge habitat,' where organisms with their own natural histories come into contact with and are shaped by the technological, industrial environment of human beings. Living technologies such as flies, mice, and cultured cells are part of the attempt to stabilize the innate flux and variation of living things as well as to simplify and standardize the objects of research as much as possible . . . Genetically and physically reshaped living matter plays an infrastructural role in making biology the same over time and space (Landecker, 2007: 25–26)

"Humans' technological capacities to modify elementary components of life itself" (Franklin and Lock, 2001: 3) thus extend into actual, living animals. Well-known fabricated species of nature such as the Harvard University patented Onco-Mouse (Murray, 2010; Kevles, 2002; Haraway, 1997), the world's first patented genetically modified animal, and Dolly the Sheep (Franklin, 2007), the first publically demonstrated cloned animal, brought into being at the Roslin Institute in Scotland in the mid-1990s, are thus accomplishments that are part of everyday life science. While Dolly was controversial because the very idea of cloning humans caused a stir among the wider public, the genetically modified mice are today widely accepted and used in run-of-the-mill research. The century-long distinction between nature and culture and the separation between natural and un-natural is increasingly ceasing to play an actual role but remains, by and large, an ideological reminiscence from a period where technoscience played only a marginal role. Therefore, rather than gazing at the life sciences in sheer wonder or thinking of them as an appalling uprooting of Mother Nature herself, one may follow Parry (2004a) in thinking of biotechnology as a form of production in analogy with ship wharves or automobile plants:

> The biotechnology of the life-science industry also produces important commodities, but they are not the familiar products that are associated with manufacturing of old such as ships, steel, or textiles. They are products that are quite alien to us—transgenic organisms, cloned animals, and artificially generated bio-chemical compounds that have no parallel in nature—entities that are, in effect, a fusion of the organic and the technical. (Parry, 2004a: 3)

Just as technologies have gradually—at times momentarily—changed the content and form of human lives, so the life sciences may in the future enable new forms of humanity. Proponents of "transhuman" or "post-human" ideologies uncritically praise all such advancement as if there were no ethical, economic, or social trade-offs or costs involved, but a more moderate position would be to at least not reject the advancement of the life sciences and to recognize the possibilities that may follow from a more elaborate and sophisticated framework for "fusing the organic and the technological." That is, between the enthusiastic embrace of new scientific advancement and its staunch rejection, there is a space for more tempered stances. Hacking (2007) for instance claims that the eye surgery that helped him see clearly again implies no anxieties on his part even though he knows that there is a plastic chip inserted in his eyes. More than anything else, Hacking claims to feel gratitude for regaining his eyesight. Even though there is a need for a systematic critique of the life sciences and the bioeconomy at large, in many if not most cases, there is a clear benefit for many humans that the sciences can accomplish based on collective accomplishments.

"LIFE IS WHAT YOU MAKE IT": COSMETIC SURGERY AND THE SHAPING OF THE BODY

> "In the physiognomies of Rembrandt's portraits we feel very clearly that the course of a life, heaping fate on fate, creates this present image. It elevates us, as it were, to a certain height from which we can view the ascending path toward that point, even though none of the content of its past could be naturalistically stated in the way that portraits with a psychological slant might seek to suggest . . . Miraculously, Rembrandt transposes into the fixed uniqueness of the gaze all the movements of the life that led up to it: the formal rhythm, mode, and coloring of fate, as it were, of the vital process." (Simmel, 2005: 9–10)

George Simmel praises Rembrandt van Rijn's art as capable of capturing the full existence and course of life of the individuals being portrayed. For Simmel, life is a process of becoming and, e.g., Renaissance art, despite all its merits, failed to captures the *durée* of the subject. In Rembrandt's art, on the contrary, the totality of lived time is incised onto the faces of the subject; the passing of time leaves a mark, and Rembrandt's portraits display a full, lived existence including all the sorrows, joy, boredom, and curiosity experienced in human life. For Simmel (2005: 11), then, "[t]he richest and most moving portraits of Rembrandt are those of old people, since in them we can see a maximum of lived life." In Simmel's essay on Rembrandt, the great Dutch master is celebrated for being able to apprehend and accommodate lived time in his art. No single moment of human existence escapes Rembrandt's gaze, Simmel suggests; it is all there, testifying to the conditions of human life. Rembrandt thus both apprehends life and preserves it.

The portraits of the Dutch bourgeoisie and the aristocracy and their subordinates—the merchants and bishops, housewives and chancellors, maids and servants—once and for all freeze the totality of seventeenth-century life in continental northern Europe.

In contrast to Rembrandt's art, cosmetic surgery seeks to accomplish something entirely different, that is, to erase and eliminate the marks of lived time, duration, from the flesh of the human body. What Rembrandt wants to put on display as a form of homage to human existence and our capacity to stand the ordeal of everyday life, the cosmetic surgeon silently makes go away, producing a human body devoid of temporality. Like a Renaissance artist, the cosmetic surgeon creates a beauty that is "timeless," denying the duration of human existence. If death is the ultimate scandal and "humiliation" of modern Western reason, as suggested by Margaret Lock (2002: 201), then cosmetic surgeons are modern in terms of deferring lived time until the very moment of death. Death and signs of it, ageing in its various forms, then need to be kept at a distance. If ageing is the gradual dying of the organism, a being-toward-death, the cosmetic surgeon serves as the guardian of youthfulness and the suspension of temporality. In the ontology of cosmetic surgery, temporality is never the linear and ceaseless flow of moments of time leading to the other, but temporality can be transcended as its visual manifestations are eliminated.

One of the most widely discussed and debated changes in the bioeconomy is the emergence of a mass market for plastic or cosmetic surgery (Gimlin, 2010; Jones, 2008; Pitts-Taylor, 2007; Blum, 2005; Fraser, 2003; Negrin, 2002; Gilman, 1999). In comparison to the other fields of the bioeconomy, more or less entangled with, or the outgrowth from, the life sciences and contemporary technoscience, cosmetic surgery is perhaps not as closely connected to the state-of-the-art research but is still undoubtedly a scientific discipline in its own right. Cosmetic surgery "owns virtually nothing to recent 'revolutions' in biomedical knowledge," Atkinson, Glasner and Lock (2009: 8) say.[6] At the same time, cosmetic surgery has arguably "more impact [than, e.g., tissue engineering] on culturally shared beliefs and practices surrounding the body and personal identities, and has a direct impact on a collective perception of the body's plasticity" (Atkinson, Glasner, and Lock, 2009: 4). As a consequence, cosmetic surgery play a key role in institutionalizing new images of the human body not so much as an endowed physical structure to be kept in balance as a construction site, a domain where "continuous improvements" may be carried out similar to what architectural theorist Rem Koolhaas calls a "junkspace" (Koolhaas, 2002; Jones, 2008). However, cosmetic surgery is of necessity dependent on recent advances in surgery more broadly and should not be dismissed as some kind of fad or craze that will eventually disappear. Instead, one may think of cosmetic surgery as in the intersection between the life sciences, surgery, mass markets, and popular culture (e.g., what has been called the "celebrity culture" and its emphasis on attractive physical appearance and what Jones [2008] calls "makeover culture"). In 2005, the industry was today between $13 and $15 billion, and growth is estimated at 11.2 percent annually (Dickenson, 2008: 135). In the same year, 2005, 2 million cosmetic surgery operations were conducted in the U.S. alone, a fourfold increase since 1984 (Pitts-Taylor, 2007: 3). In addition to the surgery, approximately 6 million non-surgery procedures like Botox injections were conducted in 2005. In only one year, between 2004 and 2005, the cosmetic surgery industry grew by 44 percent. Today, the cosmetic surgery industry is promoting what is called "cosmetic wellness," a concept that clearly associates relatively advanced surgical procedures with health and well-being more generally (Pitts-Taylor, 2007: 25). Originally, cosmetic surgery or aesthetic surgery was developed from the end of the eighteenth century to restore the faces and noses of syphilis patients or soldiers returning from war with bodily deformations (Gilman, 1999). Cosmetic surgery may not easily side with other bioeconomic activities such as the fabrication of genetically modified laboratory rats or reproductive medicine, but a shared stock of know-how produced in the life sciences is a common denominator that makes cosmetic surgery a key component in the bioeconomy. If nothing else, cosmetic surgery is at the forefront in terms of marketing of bioeconomic services and expertise and may thus give some indications of how bioeconomic futures may appear.

Needless to say, cosmetic surgery is a disputed and heterogeneous practice. There is little criticism regarding the restoration of the skin of patients with burn injuries or the correction of physical deformities that inhibit individuals from living normal lives, but when it comes to recent procedures such as liposuction and breast augmentation there is a widespread concern, for instance among feminist writers, that women are exploited in terms of succumbing to misogynic ideologies portraying womanhood in terms of mere physical attractiveness or resting on a general fear of ageing. While such criticism is relevant for understanding the massive growth of cosmetic surgery and the overrepresentation of women—89 percent of cosmetic surgery patients are women (Blum, 2005)—there is a need for broadening the focus on the cosmetic surgery phenomenon to fully understand the social production of demand for costly and painful modifications of the (primarily female) body. For instance, a popular belief when it comes to cosmetic surgery is that women of 40 and above are a majority of the clients, trying to maintain their youth allegedly to "compete" with younger women. Hogle (2005: 705) suggests that there are both lower income groups and younger women in this category: "The majority of procedures are purchased by those individuals with annual incomes less than $50,000, and 20% are purchased by individuals younger than 34 years of age, including a growing number of teenagers having liposuction and breast augmentations." Hogle (2005), just like Blum (2003), emphasizes that cosmetic surgery is a social practice that needs to be explained on the basis of a number of explanatory frameworks: "Identity politics, consumer culture, perceived competition for jobs or partners, institutionalized contexts, and technology all contribute to the demand for aesthetic body enhancements," Hogle (2005: 705) suggests. The concept of surgery comes from Greek *cheir* (hand) and *ergon* (work), and surgery is thus "the work of the hand" (Prentice, 2005: 838). However, as Hirschauer (1991: 313) emphasizes, surgery is always a matter of enacting an idealized image of the human body that is being reconstructed. That is, surgery may be accomplished by the help of what Prentice (2005: 857) calls "somato-conceptual intelligence" of the surgeon, the capacity of combining practical, embodied skills and formal medical know-how, but the accomplishment of the work is inevitably social and cultural in character, based on instituted preferences for what is beautiful and what is not.

In Blum's (2005) ethnographic work on the "culture of cosmetic surgery," she strongly emphasizing the surgeons' view of themselves as "miracle workers" helping their patients become what they truly are and eliminate physical features that veil their "natural" beauty, or, in the case of middle-age and elderly women, restoring their waning youthful appearance, a form of *automorphism*—a reconstuction of the self. While it is obvious that cosmetic surgeons are not working on the basis of altruism alone, they express a sense of *noblesse oblige*, a willingness to help clients handle their perceived "difficulties" with their looks. Perhaps such narratives are primarily attempts at establishing oneself as an ethical subject on the basis of contributions to the community. Blum makes an intriguing comparison with Susan Bordo's analysis of men's use of pornography not as a form—as the common criticism suggests—of objectification of women, but rather as a form of turning women into subjects gratifying and affirming the male. Similarly, Blum (2005) suggests that for the surgeon, the (primarily female) patient needs to be constituted qua individual subject because she alone can articulate a firsthand account of the work provided by the cosmetic surgeon:

> It is not that they [cosmetic surgeons] are just objectifying my body (and those of their patients) as so much meat for their transformational miracles. There also needs to be an appreciative subject of the surgery who can afterward look at the mirror and recognize the surgeon's skill. While surgeons may be objectifying the body, they depend on the living subject who can evaluate outcome, insist upon revision, go to another surgeon . . . then praise the 'greater' surgeon to all friends and family as miracle workers. (Blum, 2005: 26)

In Blum's (2053) view, there is a dialectical and sophisticated social mechanism regulating the surgeon and the patient's relation, wherein the two parts mutually produce the subject position of the other. The surgeon takes an affirmative view of the concerns, even the suffering, of the patient regarding perceived faults in her body and offers an opportunity to handle perhaps life-long traumas derived from perceived "defects." The patient, on the other hand, recognizes the enacted role of the surgeon as a professional capable of producing not only reshaped bodies but also, *ipso facto*, new biographies and life chances. Cosmetic surgeons are aware that there is a delicate balance between expectations and outcomes and realities, and therefore they do not accept patients who have recently experienced a significant trauma, say, a divorce or a loss of a child. This category of patients may develop expectations that are not possible to fulfill, and the consequences may be devastating for both parties. Following this line of argument, Victoria Pitts-Taylor (2007) argues that the cosmetic surgery industry is not promoted in terms of producing beauty, but rather the discourse is steeped in psychological ideas about the "inner self" and "becoming what you truly are," or, in the case of middle age or older women—Pitts-Taylor (2007) says relatively little about male cosmetic surgery patients—to "rejuvenate oneself." Says Pitts-Taylor (2007: 35): "[T]he dominant logics of contemporary cosmetic surgery now reach significantly beyond beauty ideals. Such logics depend upon essentialist notions of authentic inner selves. They require an understanding of the body and its surface as a signifier of authentic inner meaning. They recruit psychiatric strategies—or alternatively, political or consumerist ones—to decode the meanings they find." In the same vein, Brooks (2004: 227) argues that while cosmetic surgery operates on the surface of the material body, promoting it as "a site of creative self-formation and re-formation, malleable material through which new identities are forged," cosmetic surgery is ultimately grounded in the idea of "an inner self apart from, or superior to, the body" (Brooks, 2004: 231). That is, the "become what you are" ideology of cosmetic surgery conceives of the self as a non-material, even transcendental category, existing beyond embodied matter, and cosmetic surgery is the practice of shaping the physical, enfleshed matter we refer to as our bodies to the stage where they are in harmony with our inner selves. Brooks here makes reference to the concept of "a foundational fantasy," "a symptom of Western, Protestant, liberal, humanistic, capitalist, patriarchal dominance, [that] invokes an egoistic, individual subject, a subject 'without ties, dependent on no-one' who objectifies and denies the agency of nature (the body)" (Brooks, 2004: 232). In contemporary society, man masters nature even to the point where human bodies become "malleable materials" that we as consumers can choose to sculpture in any way we want.

Even though Pitts-Taylor is not uncritical of cosmetic surgery, she is skeptical regarding certain feminist analyses claiming that any person paying for cosmetic surgery is being duped, leading to a loss of agency on the part of this category of patient. Instead, the patients she met in cosmetic surgery clinics during her fieldwork "[d]id not seem to be the crazy junkies that one might expect from media accounts, nor did they seem to be the self-hating victims depicted in some of the most high-handed feminist descriptions" (Pitts-Taylor, 2007: 165). Blum (2005) suggests that the intimate connection between cosmetic surgeon and patient is widely overlooked in the critique of the industry. She points at what can be compared to medicalization in the case of pharmaceuticals, namely, the active construction of the demand for surgery through the colonialization of the body. Blum (2005) herself raises a number of issues regarding cosmetic surgery, women's position in society, and celebrity culture, and Heyes (2009: 79) speaks even more explicitly about the "colonialization of surgery possibility" where increasingly numbers of body parts are turned into domains where cosmetic surgery can be legitimately used (e.g., the case of genital labia promising "vaginal rejuvenation"). Other new "products" in cosmetic surgery include umbilicoplasty ("navel enhancement"), breast nipple enlargement, and toe shortening (Dickenson, 2008: 135). That is, an increasing number of body parts are becoming subject to cosmetic surgery.

In the final chapter of her ethnography, Pitts-Taylor accounts for her own experience from rhinoplasty surgery. Rather than having a life-long trauma with her nose, Pitts-Taylor says that she thought of her nose as being "unremarkable," but still she admits that even though she was initially "motivated by a desire to put myself into the role of patient," she was also "attracted to the idea that I could be more beautiful, my deep training in critiques of heteronormativity notwithstanding" (Pitts-Taylor, 2007: 165). However, as suggested by Blum (2005), Pitts-Taylor was disturbed that her, in her mind, relatively normal and unspectacular nose—"not perfect, but hardly terrible" (Pitts-Taylor, 2007: 168)—was "pathologized" by all but one of the five cosmetic surgeons she consulted: "Despite the fact that I had offered my face up for scrutiny, they hurt my feelings," Pitts-Taylor (2007: 169) writes. Having the authority to pass judgment on beauty and thus to draw the line of demarcation between the normal and the pathological, four out of five cosmetic surgeons did not hesitate to portray Pitts-Taylor's nose as qualified for rhinoplasty. For Pitts-Taylor, this encounter with the cosmetic surgery authorities of necessity locates the candidate patient in a position where she (at times he) suffers from some disorder that needs to be corrected: "Generally, the responses to my desire for rhinoplasty can be categorized in one of the two ways: either I was psychologically normal and my nose was flawed, or my nose was normal and I was psychologically or morally unwell" (Pitts-Taylor, 2007: 170). Eventually, Pitts-Taylor underwent the surgery and after a week of massive pain and suffering[7]— inevitable effects of cosmetic surgery that are generally overlooked in the makeover culture—she found herself happy with her new nose. Being a dedicated feminist, some of her friends were aghast over her submission to cosmetic surgery, thinking of her as a traitor to the cause. Apparently, good feminists don't submit to cosmetic surgery.

In Heyes's (2009) view, cosmetic surgeons are instituting an increasingly shrinking zone for normality—an "aesthetic conformity" according to Brooks (2004: 225)—where the surrounding domains outside this narrow field are "abnormal" deviancies that may be surgically corrected. Heyes (2009) thus suggests that the potential client is "educated into the visual lexicon of bodily defects" by the cosmetic surgeon. Cosmetic surgeons are thus actively involved in, if not portraying, bodily features as being overtly abnormal, at least envisioning, say, the nose of a consulting client as something that may be "improved" through surgery. As Heyes (2009: 81) notices, "it takes a tough-minded individual to walk out of a consultation having refused a procedure that an 'expert' on bodily aesthetics thinks is warranted, without any further psychological consequences." What is a concern is that the cosmetic surgery literature reviewed by Heyes (2009: 87) includes recommendations on how "pathologize the dissatisfied patient." Patients who have "almost any negative emotional reaction to surgery" are here conceived of as being mentally disordered and suffering from what has been called Body Dysmorphic Disorder (BDD) (Pitts-Taylor, 2007: 19). Thus, cosmetic surgery is not only a matter of "sculpturing the body" but equally a matter of managing expectations and desires, making the client/patient aware of the possibilities enabled by cosmetic surgery. What the cosmetic surgeon does to the body must be accompanied by the expectations of the client. The mind is in a very immediate sense embodied.

Given this alignment of hopes, beliefs, and embodiment, the slogan of the American Society of Plastic Surgeons, "Life Is What You Make It," is indicative of an ideology that grants a key role to agency, not entirely different from the neoliberal doctrine of the *homo oeconomicus*, the calculating and enterprising human being. A nose or a pair of breasts that does not correspond to my perceived image of myself or the general norms of beauty is not a matter of being fortunate or not, but is a matter of enterprising capabilities and willingness to create and manage one's own life—the life one may think one deserves. Blum (2005: 51) rightly points out that the very term "buying" is a verb that paradoxically combines agency (as in "one chooses to buy something") and victimization ("one 'buys into' as a form of submission"). Like perhaps no other form of consumption, the buying of cosmetic surgery is closely connected to the latter sense of the term, that is, women or men choosing to modify their bodies are at times treated as if they are unhappy or in general disoriented. The perhaps most widely known case of "cosmetic surgery going wrong" in the public mindset, is that of Michael Jackson (see, e.g., Pitts-Taylor, 2007: 17). Mr. Jackson's increasingly bizarre looks were generally treated as the surfacing of the traumas and despair of a human being in a state of distress and psychological instability. In Blum's (2005) study, the celebrity culture and its insistence on physical attraction as an index for social and economic success and the enterprising culture of the neoliberal economic regime in combination with the improved capacities and routines for delivering safe cosmetic surgery with good results are some of the key factors when explaining the steady growth of the industry. Dickenson (2008: 152) argues that a general disappointment with the loss of shared social beliefs and norms has paved the way for an enterprising ideology where one invests in the body rather than in the community: "Disappointment in social ideals means that we turn inwards. In the absence of a belief in eternal life, everything becomes invested in this life, in this body. Long life is our ferocious desire, eternal youth our supposed right and the myth of the body without origin or limits our crusading new religion." In the case of cosmetic surgery, enterprising ideologies are materialized in the very body, the female body refusing to age but constantly being rejuvenated through surgery and the injection of chemical substances such as Botox. Margaret Lock (2002: 201) points out that in the modern Western tradition of rational thinking, "death becomes a scandal, 'the ultimate humiliation of reason'" (Lock, 2002: 201). Cosmetic surgery is one form of struggle against death, a Promethean endeavor to resist death.

As an element in the bioeconomic regime, cosmetic surgery may appear an odd practice, but it is nevertheless part of a wider enactment of the human body and other biological systems that are open for precise manipulations and active engagements in reshaping not only the hereditary biological materials and other elementary processes but also the very surface of the organism. If nothing else, there are significant ethical concerns derived from the advancement of cosmetic surgery that feminist scholars and postcolonial theorists, for instance, have pointed out. Women consume cosmetic surgery to look more physically attractive; for instance, in Asia it is common to modify the eyelid to produce a more Caucasian "look." The beauty ideal hegemony of the blond and slim Hollywood actress is a global standard for how women should look that generates a demand for bodily modifications. Cosmetic surgery may operate on the surface, but the know-how it relies on is biological and medicinal in nature, and the underlying ideologies run deep into the flesh.

SUMMARY AND CONCLUSION

This chapter brings together a diverse set of activities and practices, ranging from the beginning of life (in vitro fertilization) to the afterlife of human tissues such as retinas or major organs such as livers or kidneys. Some of the practices are closely connected to the advancement of the life sciences, while others have little scientific credibility or relevance (e.g., the storage of umbilical cord blood) or are only loosely coupled or indirectly associated with the life sciences (cosmetic surgery). However, all these activities operate in the intersection between life-science know-how and expertise and economic interests. Even though cosmetic surgery is highly debated and frowned on in certain quarters, it remains a quickly growing industry with a substantial turnover. The emerging possibilities for developing stem cell technologies and growing new organs on the basis of stem cells (such as the case of artificial retinas, grown from collagen, a protein existing in, e.g., hair) are very likely to open up new economic ventures placing the public in new situations where individuals have to evaluate the potential of various investments offered by bioeconomic entrepreneurs. If such prospects are intimidating or holding great promise for a healthier and happier life, they inevitably translate life-science know-how into a broader range of possibilities and choices for individuals, and as such possibilities emerge, concepts such as health, well-being, and beauty are likely to be renegotiated and modified, ultimately drawing a new line of demarcation between the normal and the pathological.

5   Living in and Managing the
     Bioeconomy

INTRODUCTION

In this final chapter of this book, a number of social and organizational consequences of the bioeconomy will be addressed. This book is intended to serve as an introductory text for the field of organization theory and management studies, and consequently this chapter will be oriented toward the questions of work, organization, and management, that is, the practical aspects of the bioeconomy rather than, say, the ethical or cultural consequences. However, this does not mean that organization theory and management are entirely removed from discussions and debates that pertain to the economization and commercialization of life-science know-how and research. Therefore, in this chapter feminist theories of life and the critique of the industrialization of women's reproductive capacities will be addressed, and issues pertaining to the postcolonial or neo-colonial economic regime of the bioeconomy will be discussed. In the latter half of the chapter, some practical research questions and research agendas are examined, which may show the way to a more detailed understanding of the new economic regime based on the economization of the life sciences.

The chapter is organized into two parts. The first part presents two critical view of the emerging bioeconomy, namely a feminist and a postcolonial view of how biological systems are increasingly located at the center of economic pursuits. The second part addresses a number of issues related to the management of the bioeconomy, an economic regime where the life sciences play a central role. First, the concept of professionalization as a key term in the organization theory vocabulary is addressed. Second, the concept of clinical labor is introduced in some detail. Thereafter, the issues of marketing and consumption in the bioeconomy are discussed. Fourth, the future relationship between university and industry in the field of the life sciences will be addressed as representing a new form of hybridity where the boundary between private and public is no longer as decisive as the two terms suggest. Fifth, the concept of technology is examined in terms of what is no longer of necessity used to denote a large-scale mechanical system but may increasingly designate biomaterials that intervene with the human body on various levels. The chapter ends with a summary of the key arguments.

CRITICAL PERSPECTIVES ON THE BIOECOMONY

Feminist Thinking and the Question of Life

Like perhaps no other theoretical framework, feminist and gender theory has contributed to reestablishing the body and its materiality at the centre of analysis in social theory (Jeacle, 2003; Witz, 2000; Kaufert, 2000; Broadhurst, 1999; Cartwright, 1995; Longino, 1992; Dallery, 1989; Jordanova, 1989). With the pervasive and all-encompassing influence of the so-called linguistic turn in the social sciences, concepts such as discourse, narrative, story, text, and so forth have wielded an enormous influence in the analysis of social practice. This comprehensive influence of the language and the linguistic is derived from a heterogeneous body of texts including analytical philosophy (e.g., the later Wittgenstein and the work of Austin), literature theory (e.g., Mikhail Bakhtin), structuralist theory (e.g., de Saussure's semiotics), and post-structuralist theory (most noteworthy the works of Derrida and Foucault). Karen Barad (2007) is explicit about her impatience with this perspective:

> Language has been granted too much power. The linguistic turn, the semiotic turn, the interpretative turn, the cultural turn. It seems that at every turn lately every 'thing'—even materiality—is turned into a matter of language or some other form of cultural representation . . . Language matters. Discourse matters. Culture matters. There is an important sense in which the only thing that does not matter anymore is matter. (Barad, 2007: 132)

In post-structuralist feminist theory and in the queer theory developed by Judith Butler (1993, 1999), the very materiality of the body[1] and of other practices is affirmed in a manner that breaks with the tradition of the linguistic turn. This does not, however, imply that this corpus of texts returns to a naïve realist view of the body as an immutable totality of brute matter. Instead, materiality is understood on the basis of social beliefs and conventions, and, similarly, the social is always of necessity material in terms of norms and rules manifested in material artifacts and entities (Suchman, 2007; Orlikowski, 2010, 2007; Orlikowski and Scott, 2008). Rosi Braidotti (1994: 4), for instance, suggests that "the body, or the embodiment, of the subject is to be understood as neither a biological nor a sociological category but rather as a point of overlapping between physical, the symbolic, and the sociological." Elizabeth Grosz (1994: 18), making a distinction between *the material* and *the lived* body, a distinction present in, e.g.,

German (*Lieb* and *Körper*), suggests that the "[t]he lived body is neither brute nor passive but is interwoven with and constitutive of systems of meaning, signification, and representation." Given that the human body is not to be examined as brute materiality, a thing as such, but as a surface of inscription where social beliefs and ideologies are played out, there is a need for understanding how the body as well as other forms of materiality plays a constitutive role in assembling society and its organizations. Elsewhere, Grosz (2004: 3) says, "[w]e need to understand the body, not as an organism or entity in itself, but as a system, or a series of open-ended systems, functioning within other huge systems it cannot control, through which it can access and acquire its abilities and capacities." In this theoretical recuperation of the body, making it a hybrid construct in the intersection between nature and culture, the individual and the collective, there is a clearly articulated interest in feminist circles for the more thorough theoretical *Durcharbeitung* of the Western tradition leading up to the present situation where the female body plays a number of different roles and takes on different symbolisms. In her more recent works, Grosz (2005: 7) has discussed the very idea of nature in the Western tradition. According to Grosz, nature has here been understood in terms of "[d]ynamic forces, fields of transformation and upheaval, rather than as a static fixity, passively worked over, transformed and dynamized only by culture, a view prevalent in social, political, and cultural theory." Such Cartesian dualism—mind *versus* body, nature *versus* culture—has been one of the standing epistemological axioms in the Western tradition (Gatens, 1996). In the modernist tradition of thinking, in the tradition of Charles Darwin in the middle and end of the nineteenth century and of Henri Bergson in the first decades of the twentieth century, life is portrayed as a "mode of self-organization" that "overcomes itself," ceaselessly diverging from itself and evolving into new configurations. In such a vitalist view of nature as a relentless flow, life is "always be in the process of becoming, something other than it was" (Grosz, 2005: 8). Tim Ingold (1986) eloquently captures this view of life, central to Bergson's work, as being regulated by a dynamic impetus:

> Bergson, for his part, rejected the idea of absolute individuality in the organic world. 'The living being,' he argued, 'is above all a thoroughfare,' along which all the impulsion of life is transmitted. And as each individual, like a relay runner, takes up this impulsion and passes it on, as each generation must lean over and touch the next, so how can we tell exactly where one individual begins and another begins? (Ingold, 1986: 107).

In this view, individuality is nothing but a short transition point in the evolution, the flow of life across generations. Referencing and discussing Darwin's work, Grosz (2005: 26) says that this evolution is a "[f]undamentally open-ended system which pushes towards the future with no real direction, no promise of any particular result, no guarantee of progress or improvement, but with every indication of inherent proliferation and transformation." That is, Darwin's great contribution to Western epistemology, Grosz (2005: 30) suggests, is that rather than conceiving of nature as being a "linear or progressive development," Darwin's discoveries were characterized by "a force of spatial and temporal dispersion"—a vital force with no inherent teleology of goal. With the help of Darwin's path-breaking work, nature, that is, the totality of organisms including humans and related biological systems, can no longer be seen as having inherent meanings, but such ideas are of necessity created "from the outside." That is, ideas about humans and corporeality are always social in nature, aiming at capturing and regulating the biological matter that constitutes human life.

Returning to the issue of the bioeconomy, feminist theorists such as Rosi Braidotti and Elizabeth Grosz suggest that in order to understand the present regime about life and biology, there is a need for de-familiarizing or de-naturalizing taken-for-granted beliefs about what the body is and to think in new or at least complementary terms. For instance, in the bioeconomy, the economic regime where the human body and biological systems gain economic value since they have become increasingly valuable input resources in a variety of practices, embodied matter becomes something entirely different from its status in previous economic regimes. For instance, stem cell research (Ikemoto, 2009; Rubin, 2008; Salter and Salter, 2007; Franklin , 2005; Waldby, 2002), the latest breakthrough in the life sciences generating hope for identifying therapies for a range of terminal diseases, is dependent upon stem cells derived from human fetuses. According to national and international regulations, such cells may be donated by parents through "informed consent." Cell lines may grow for decades after the physical death of the person donating the original cells. These are two examples how the boundary between life and death, central to common sense thinking, is transgressed in the new regime of the bioeconomy. As suggested by Ingold (1986), in a process-based view of matter and life, the individual is a mere transition point, a bifurcation of life where the vitalist flow aggregates for a period of time. The HeLa cell line lives on decades after Henrietta Lacks has ceased to live. Life is no longer truly a matter of being a sharply demarcated terrain where death begins but is instead enacted on the basis of knowledge and truth-claims dependent on certain technoscientific life-science procedures. "Death does not destroy things so completely that it annihilates the constituent elements: it merely dissolves their union," Lucretius pointed out in his *De Rerum Natura* (Lucretius, 2001: 60).

Speaking about more concrete and less theoretical implications and perspectives, feminist theorists have also made important contributions in terms of addressing implications from the life sciences when it comes to reproductive medicine and technologies, that is, the industrialization and economization of life per se (for instance, Waldby and Cooper [2007] speaks of "post-Fordist biotechnology and women's clinical labour." See also Longino [1992]). While for instance in vitro fertilization (IVF) has helped thousands of childless couples to become parents, there is a concern about the growth in expertise regarding reproduction in terms of turning it into an economic commodity (Dickenson, 2008). Clarke (1998) has sketched the heterogeneous changes in a number of scientific disciplines leading to today's situation where the distinction between "born" and "made" is becoming increasingly complicated to sort out (Franklin and Roberts, 2006). Reproductive medicine was, like most other domains of expertise, by no means a linear development, but occurred as a number of different domains of expertise (e.g., endocrinology, agriculture, and microbiology) combined their accumulated know-how and transformed this into a new field of medicine. For feminist theorists, reproductive medicine is not a concern in itself but becomes so when the seemingly inevitable processes of economization puts a price tag not only on the services provided but also on the input materials and various social practices that the new opportunities will lead to. "Effectively . . . the process of reproduction has been deregulated, privatised and made available for investment and speculative development," Waldby and Cooper (2007: 58) write. Waldby and Cooper (2007) are critical about the trade of, e.g., oöcytes, unfertilized human eggs procured from women in, e.g., Ukraine and other former republics of the Soviet Union. This is, in Waldby and Cooper's (2007) view, a new form of work that they term clinical labor, which opens up a new territory for the exploitation of women in economically disadvantaged positions. In addition, since primarily white, middle-class couples in the Western hemisphere tend to favor white children, the role of women of color in, e.g., India is restricted to the role of surrogate mothers. Ukrainian and Russian women, generally representing a Caucasian phenotype, are entitled to deliver the oöcytes, but women unable to provide such resources are assigned other roles in the increasingly globalized "baby business" (Spar, 2006; Dickenson, 2008). Waldby and Cooper (2007) are concerned that reproductive medicine, no matter how positively charged the rhetoric of the "gift of life" may appear, potentially opens up new forms of exploitation of the poor and disenfranchised, a form of "neocolonialism with a human face" where life giving is becoming the new domain for exploitation.

Sharp (2011) has addressed gender issues in the field of biomaterials, a professional domain of expertise including a variety of research areas such as *tissue engineering*, the growing of new organs *ex vivo* from cell cultures, *xenotransplantation*, the transfer of organs from so-called transgenetic animals (e.g., pigs) to humans, and "[e]fforts among bioengineers to design what they refer to as 'artificial' organs" (Sharp, 2011: 2). In Sharp's (2011: 7) view, this field, which constitutes what she speaks of as "body tinkering," is still very much in an "anticipatory discipline" because, first, "[m]any devices remain in the experimental phase "and second, "[t]he endpoint is never stable because of a strong professional ethos that asserts that one can always improve on the present model" (Sharp, 2011: 8). The human body is here enacted as a form of biomachine wherein the "body's beauty lies in its seamless integration with the machine" (Sharp, 2011: 24), constituting a bio-mechanical hybrid. In Sharp's perspective, such an image of the human body is gendered as it draws on a "steadfast, masculinist imagery" of the body:" "Most often . . . images [in, e.g., promotion materials] portray robust and sometimes even militarized, muscular males," Sharp (2011: 13) remarks. In this specific regime of body tinkering, the role of bioengineers is to "[f]oresee mechanical glitches, prevent device malfunction, refine a product's design to a point of elegance, and perhaps even surpass the capabilities of messy, fleshy organs" (Sharp, 2011: 9). The predominant scientific ideology is then to conceive of the human body as what is always ready to be supported and assisted by mechanical devices or biologically produced tissues that not only restore bodily functions but are also capable of expanding embodied capacities. The imagery is not primarily targeting elderly, fragile bodies, bodies in physical decline and in need of support to uphold elementary bodily functions, but instead the human body is advanced as a masculine, muscular, and even militarized body in its prime. Sharp's study demonstrates that gendered beliefs and norms are key elements in the scientific ideologies that propel the field of bioengineering. Bioengineering is a gendered professional field.

In summary, feminist theory may help criticize the recent advancement of the bioeconomy and the life sciences into a more deep-seated critique of nature and humanity. In addition, feminist theory calls for attention to the concerns about commercializing economic processes.

POSTCOLONIALISM AND THE BIOECONOMY

Postcolonial theory is another scholarly field that has demonstrated an interest in debating the consequences of the bioeconomy (Sunder Rajan, 2006; Shah, 2006; Petryna, 2009). Postcolonial theory is commonly portrayed as a theoretical Creole, a mixture of all kinds of theoretical frameworks and methodological approaches used in a variety of disciplines such as literature theory, anthropology, political science, and organization theory (Ashcroft, Griffiths, and Tiffin, 1995; Castle, 2001; Young, 2001; Parry, 2004b). The principal concepts in postcolonial theory are terms such as colonialism, neo-colonialism, de-colonialization, race, and ethnicity. Just as gender plays a central role in feminist theory, for postcolonial theorists race and ethnicity are categories that have been used to structure and organize a variety of colonial and neo-colonial practices and political projects (Spivak, 1987, 1990; Bhabha, 1994). For instance, in the widely known postcolonial work, Edward Said's *Orientalism* (1979), the idea of the Orient is thought to be a fabrication of the West, emphasizing the differences between rational and modern occidental Europe and the traditional and irrational Orient, characterized by mysticism and exoticism, and being of necessity a backward and conservative part of the world. Such inscriptions of (unfavorable) values and qualities have been observed throughout history and are today being articulated into new forms, for instance, the inability of certain national economies in South America and Africa to comply with the neoliberal economic doctrines prescribed by the World Bank, the International Monetary Fund (IMF), and other international institutions advising or regulating decision-makers in developing countries (see, e.g., Chwieroth, 2010; Griffin, 2009). The postcolonial critique has its origin in the 1940s and 1950s when primarily French intellectuals, such as Aimé Cesaire (1950) and Franz Fanon (1963, 1986), with their roots in the French colonies, started to theorize about the colonialism experience and the constitution of the "colonial subject" on the basis of the encounter with Europeans. However, prior to these more scholarly and existential reflections and discussions, literature had portrayed the consequences of colonialism in not very flattering terms. For instance, the novels of the Polish-British author Joseph Conrad (e.g., *An Outcast on the Islands, The Heart of Darkness* and *Almayer's Folly*) describe the rampant colonialist economy of the late nineteenth century when brute exploitation of the peoples in the colonies was accompanied by the development of race ideologies that ultimately culminated in the holocaust during World War II. In Conrad's literature, not only the colonialized people suffered but also many Europeans or individuals of European ancestry were subsumed by highly racialized theories regarding the alleged differences between different ethnic groups. Even the European lowest in status (e.g., Almayer in *Almayer's Folly*) could pride themselves at least on being white, which granted them certain privileges in the colonialist regime (see, e.g., Stinchcombe, 1995).

While common sense thinking may suggest that colonialism has gradually ended as former colonies have acquired independence in the post–World War II period (especially in the early 1960s), postcolonial theorists claim that colonialist ideologies and modes of thinking live on in new forms (see, e.g., Banerjee and Linstead, 2004; Cooke, 2003). In addition, economic policy and international trade agreements continue to disadvantage developing countries, still relying on much financial support from the industrialized world and suffering from weakly developed institutions manifested in, for instance, in the degree of corruption that continues to be a major concern in the developing world. Postcolonial theory thus continually critically reviews and evaluates initiatives taken to "modernize" and otherwise develop the so-called Third World. In addition, postcolonial theory makes a contribution in analyzing the relationships between ethnic groups in different parts of the world. Recent managerial ideas such as "diversity management" (Konrad, Prasad, and Pringle, 2006; Janssens and Zanoni, 2005) can be effectively examined on the basis of a postcolonial theory framework (Mir, Mir, and Wong, 2006).

As suggested in previous chapters, the bioeconomy operates on the basis of the economization and financialization of biological resources, either as "wetware" such as tissues, organs, or renewable biological substances such as blood or semen, or as clinical data derived from clinical studies (as in the form of "wet," "dry," and "embodied DNA," discussed by Thacker, 2006: xi). In the bioeconomy, biovalue is transformed into biocapital, further translated into financial resources. There is evidence of less economically developed countries hoping to establish themselves as centers of the emerging bioeconomy. For instance, Baradwaj and Glasner (2009) is accounting for how India is aiming at establishing itself as a global hub for stem cell research, thus taking India one step further than being the center *par préférence* for the outsourcing of software development activities. Sunder Rajan (2006) similarly examines the growing biotechnology in India, with the hope of making India a leading center for the life sciences. In these two studies, the widespread use of English, the high standard of higher education, and the access to skilled scientists are some of the assets that India is promoting. In these cases, "New India" is not restrained by its colonial past but on the contrary takes advantage of the elitist education systems instituted in the period of British governance.

In addition, India is today becoming a leader in providing surrogacy, and the term "reproductive outsourcing" captures the very content of this trade. "Surrogacy is estimated to be a $445 million business in India . . . The Confederation of Indian Industry predicts that medical tourism, including surrogacy, could generate $2,3 billion in annual revenue by 2012. Gestational surrogacy is an important gendered niche in the global medical market," Twine (2011: 17) reports. For many, Indian acceptance for surrogacy is an alarming example of a gendered, neo-colonial practice: "Surrogacy upsets the traditional moral framework in which reproduction is regarded as a 'natural fact' grounded in love, marriage and sexual intercourse . . . replacing it with a commodification of bodies, feelings, and values," Pande (2009: 391) summarizes. At the same time, for many Indian women this emerging industry makes them significant amounts of money in a relatively short time. In the city of Anand, in Gujarat province, a national center for surrogacy, the median income is Rs. 2,500 (U.S.$60) per month. One surrogacy may generate U. .S$3,000–5,000, a sum equivalent to "nearly ten years of family income" (Pande, 2009: 383). In addition, women in Anand who recruit new surrogate mothers earn about Rs.10,000 (U.S.$300) (Pande, 2009: 387). While it is easy to dismiss the surrogacy industry as the ultimate stage of the "commodification of everything" process and the conspicuous exploitation of Third World women through new ideologies and practices (see, e.g., Frank, 2008), it is also, from the horizon of the community of surrogate mothers in Anand, Gujarat, a form of clinical labor that is well paid in comparison to other forms of labor.[2] This does not of necessity make this trade either legitimate or desirable, and the confusion regarding the status of surrogate mothers is well represented in the presence or lack of legislation in different parts of the world. For instance, Brazil, Israel, and the U.K. have banned surrogacy; no regulation at all exists in India, Finland, Belgium, and Greece (Pande, 2009: 381). These two groups of countries are thus relatively heterogeneous in terms of which ones accept or refuse surrogacy. As Spar (2006) has argued, when it comes to getting a child of one's own, there is relatively low "price elasticity," and childless couples are willing to spend a significant amount of their accumulated or future economic resources to get their beloved child. Without any firm regulations and legislation in this domain, there are risks that undesirable opportunistic behavior and even a black market for surrogacy may be developed.

Other studies more or less explicitly drawing on a postcolonial frame of reference point at the exploitation of biological resources in the developing or less economically privileged regions and parts of the world. Petryna (2006) notes that the higher approval rates for new chemical substances, an outcome of a more efficient approval procedure from the U.S. Food and Drug Administration (FDA), have led to a shortage of clinical subjects— patients participating in clinical trials:

> [T]he available pool of human subjects in the United States is shrinking. The relatively affluent U.S. population is using too much drugs ... 'Treatment saturation' is making Americans increasingly unusable from the drug-testing standpoint, as our pharmaceutical bodies produce too many drug-drug interactions providing less and less capacity to show drug effectiveness and making drug tests results statistically invalid. (Petryna, 2006: 37)

Second, the access to such patients is reduced in the U.S. and part of the Western world as patients tend to consume more and more pharmaceuticals, which potentially biases the clinical data. "People live on pills in the West. You have the fifty-year-old who takes four or five different medications. Someone living in Eastern Europe may be on one medication for high blood pressure or whatever, but certainly not four or five," one clinical trial researcher (cited in Petryna, 2009: 21) claimed. Third, as pharmaceutical companies increasingly develop more sophisticated molecules for more complex disorders and illnesses (e.g., neurodegenerate disorders), the early filtering of useful molecules in animal models less effectively sorts out promising compounds, and therefore the number of clinical trials in humans has increased significantly. That is, animal models are less capable of predicting what compounds have a good efficacy in humans. Previously, about 90 percent of compounds were filtered out in animal models, but now the figure is as low as 50 percent (Petryna, 2009: 20). To handle this new situation, pharmaceutical companies increasingly conduct their clinical trials outside their home markets, in Eastern Europe or in Latin America: "The number of people participating in and required for pharmaceutical clinical trials has grown enormously since the early 1990s. The number of clinical trial investigators conducting multinational drug research in low-income settings increased sixteenfold, and the average annual growth rate of privately funded U.S. clinical trials recruiting subjects is projected to double in 2007" (Petryna, 2006: 33). In Eastern Europe or in Latin America, the population has a similar phenotype as in North America and Western Europe, and these regions are particularly attractive, Petryna (2006: 41) emphasizes, because of the so-called *treatment naivité:* "Treatment-naïve populations are considered 'incredibly valuable' because they do not have any background medication (medications present in the patient's body at the time of the trial), or any medication, for that matter, that might confuse the results of the trial." That is, populations not having the economic resources to consume very many drugs are still valuable for serving as testing populations for new medicine. Since approximately 40 percent is spent on clinical trials (Petryna, 2009: 11–12), a total cost of $17.8 billion in 2007, the economic and scientific incentives to conduct clinical trials outside core markets are substantial. However, as clinical trial costs are soaring, the pharmaceutical industry and the clinical research organizations need to be aware of the thin red line between effective new drug development and exploitation, both in practice and in corporate rhetoric. For instance, in Petryna's (2009) ethnography of clinical trial work, many interviewees express their enthusiasm over the possibilities for conducting clinical trials in, e.g., Eastern Europe. One of the scientists addresses the effects of air pollution in parts of Russia and explains how that could be explored in clinical trials:

> Different pollution profiles, different ways of regulating (or not regulating) air pollution, and high rates of lung cancer and respiratory diseases mean shorter life spans. There you have people getting cancer who are a lot younger. Younger people are desirable from the perspective of trials because they are a better bet to be responsive to therapy. And we have better data up-front for different age groups, which is good for approval. (Scientists, cited in Petryna, 2009: 22)

In addition, the costs for each patient participating in clinical trials in Russia was estimated to be about 40–50 percent lower than in the US. Petryna also reported that she learned from the study that even though there are international standards for good clinical practice and regulatory bodies, some of these standards are, as one interviewee put is, "workable," i.e., possible to negotiate with the hospitals and clinicians, that is, "CROs [Clinical Research Organizations] have different standards and operating procedures with respect to accepting and implementing risky protocols and different levels of toleration for potential liabilities" (Petryna, 2009: 26). There is apparently a political economy of clinical truths at work in the domain of clinical trials.

Another perhaps even more alarming role of developing economies is to either serve as repositories for organs and other biological tissues, or—at the other end of the "production chain"—as the last site for dumping the specimens of biological leftovers not finding their buyers/receivers in the industrialized world. As Sharp (2000: 296) notes, while the subaltern groups may accumulate relatively little economic resources during the course of their lives, in many cases living in acute poverty, their organs—up to fifty organs may be procured from one single individual human body today—may have an economic value that exceeds the resources acquired during a lifetime. This may result in a situation where the poor become repositories of organs. One does not need to be a thick-skinned cynic to foresee what kind of opportunistic behaviors may derive from such "medical marketplaces" valuing organs and tissues highly and being able to connect an economic and monetary value—a price tag, in short—to a kidney or a liver. China has been criticized by international human rights organizations for selling organs from executed prisoners (Dickenson, 2008), a clear violation of the regulatory framework. Needless to say, organ procurement and trade need to be carefully regulated and controlled by national and international bodies and institutions, and any violations against the agreements must be carefully investigated.

In the latter case, dumping low-quality organs in less economically developed markets, no matter how shocking and incredible this may sound some studies suggest that such practices have been observed. Scheper-Hughes's (2000: 199) ethnographic study of organ donation and the international circulation of organs and tissues provides a few examples from both Brazil and South Africa:

He [a Brazilian doctor] complained of the U.S.-based program which routinely sent surplus corneas to his center. 'Obviously,' he said, 'these are not the best corneas. The Americans will only send us what they have already rejected for themselves.' In Cape Town, Mrs. R., the director of her country's largest eye bank [an independent foundation], normally keeps a dozen or more 'post-dated' cadaver eyes in her organization's refrigerator. These poor-quality 'corneas' would not be used, she said, for transplantation in South Africa, but they might be sent to less fortunate neighboring countries that requested them. (Scheper-Hughes, 2000: 199)

Not only are developing countries expected to serve as the laboratory for the development of drugs that they are less likely to consume in relation to consumers in the North and West, but they are also expected to accept the corneas that have been rejected in North-America and Europe. The philosopher Georgio Agamben's (1998) writing on the *homo sacer*, the man in Roman law who can be can be killed by anyone but cannot be sacrificed in rituals, has been used to understand this relative lack of respect for the lives of the poor multitude. In this view, the poor play the role of *homo sacer*, a life not having any specific value in itself but one that may be used for other purposes, e.g., displaying the human body on the Internet as in the case of the visible human project (Waldby, 2000) or acting as a repository of organs. Agamben's concept of *homo sacer* is commanding attention for the widespread use of practices that demand thorough discussions and clear ethical guidelines without mindlessly exploiting the biological resources.

The triumph of liberalism and neoliberal economic policies is not the "end of history" as suggested by Francis Fukuyama in terms of historical traditions and entrenched beliefs being once and for all abandoned. Instead, both gendered and racial assumptions and beliefs are reproduced and maintained in the new economic regime. Both gender and race are important analytical categories when examining how life-science know-how is translated into commodities and service offerings. More important, these analytical categories may be used to articulate a critique of the bioeconomy, an analysis of where the boundary between legitimate and illegitimate practices is to be transgressed. Needless to say, no theoretical framework can provide any definite answers regarding, for instance, whether surrogacy is ethical or not, but may merely point at some opening of discussion. Is allowing surrogacy a feminist stance, helping women in the developing world take on entrepreneurial identities and support themselves, or is it merely a new form of overt exploitation of women? For infertile couples taking advantage of surrogacy services, what are their roles and responsibilities in the globalized bioeconomy? Are they legitimate clients, villains, or even victims themselves? Organization theory does not provide very many answers to these complicated questions but at least it can point out some of the traits and characteristics of this new bioeconomic regime, strongly emphasizing the economization of virtually all forms of biological life and specimens.

LIVING IN AND MANAGING THE BIOECONOMY

No matter how the future evolves, there are a few organizational aspects of the bioeconomy that have implications for the understanding of key organization theory terms such as professionalization, work, and consumption. In this section, some of the potential implications for how the life sciences may be organized and managed in the future are discussed.

Professionalization and Clinical Labor

The concept of profession is a central entry in the sociology of work and organization theory. The term denotes a specific category of skilled and specialized workers who are sheltered by entry-barriers and who maintain direct control over the domain of work (Leicht and Fennell, 2001). Professions are in general privileged groups in the economy, and to qualify as a professional one needs to demonstrate academic credentials and work experience in a professional field. Examples of professionals are medical doctors, lawyers, engineers, and scientists. The professions are closely associated with institutions. First, a profession is an institution in its own right, regulating and controlling the entrance of newcomers to a specific field of expertise. Second, professions are in the position of serving as "institutional actors" (Scott, 2004) and establishing new institutions, which maintain the domain of jurisdiction and the status of the profession. "[P]rofessionalism is a set of institutions which permits the members of an occupational community to make a living while controlling their own work," Freidson, (2001: 17) summarizes. While some of the most prestigious professions— the fields of medicine and law are the examples *per préférence* in the literature—may appear to be eternal and having little history, the concept of profession in fact suggests a dynamic trajectory. There are many examples of successful and failed attempts at professionalizing a domain of expertise, and each professional field is filled with struggle over authority and the prerogative to define the field. Famous examples are between obstetricians and midwives, or between mainstream medicine and so-called alternative medicine. In all these cases, there is a perceived zero-sum game where one profession's loss is the (aspiring) profession's win or vice versa. Most professions are therefore characterized by a fierce competition over resources or authority (Abbott, 1988; Halpern, 1992). There is also evidence of de-professionalization, for instance, in the case of totalitarian regimes where careerist dilettantes may be given the authority to influence various fields. In Nazi Germany, architects with little talent could be given large responsibilities because they pledged allegiance to party doctrines, and consequently clumsy and un-elegant buildings—potentially in line with the perceived preferences of Nazi leaders—were erected in the interwar period in Germany (Freidson, 2001: 129). In the study of Soviet science, the term Lysenkoism is used to denote party-controlled and ideologically correct science where political doctrines rather than scientific professionalism regulate the sciences (Babkin and Mirskaya, 2003). In the regime of Lysenkoism, genetics was declared "a bourgeois pseudo-science," and leading geneticists were imprisoned and research institutes closed down. Outside such totalitarian societies certain professions may lose their status and authority as new economic conditions emerge. In the West, architects have been seen as members of a profession that has lost some of its authority over the entire building process, as the construction industry increasingly relies on large-scale projects orchestrated by major construction companies, where the architect play a restricted role as a consultant in the design phase that precedes the production phase in the project.

In general, the professions continue to play a central role in the knowledge society and the knowledge economy, but they are increasingly brought under the authority of various managerialist practices including auditing and enterprising ideologies. Freidson (2001: 131) distinguishes between "social trustee professionalism" or "civic professionalism," where professionals serve the public interest, and "expert professionalism" (Brint, 1994), where the professions are taking on a new identity, that of the expert being hired by individual clients in the form of contracting in a market economy. Brint (1994) believes this change in perspective is indicative of how the neoliberal emphasis on market-based activities is colonializing the professions. While the professions acquired their status and prestige on the basis of the contributions they were making to society, today the gold standard for evaluating the professions is their market value. For instance, while classically trained musicians were part of a bourgeoisie culture until at least the mid-twentieth century (Kramer, 1995: 9), the role of classic music and the consumption thereof (attending concerts and operas) have been dramatically reduced during the last decades. Rather than being state-funded, musicians are increasingly expected to "sell their expertise" in the marketplace. The same tendency is observable in all domains of art, and artists are today expected to take on enterprising and entrepreneurial ideologies to support themselves and justify their activities (García, 2004; Belfiore, 2002). A similar tendency is apparent in most of the professions where various forms of auditing and quality control are imposed on academic researchers, doctors, and other specialized professional groups. Brint (1994) explicates his position:

> The shift from social trustee professionalism to expert professionalism has led to a splintering of the professional stratum in relation to the market value of different forms of 'expert knowledge.' There is the real possibility in this split for the eventual consolidation of the professional stratum into a more exclusive status category, since 'formal knowledge' implies gradations in the value, efficacy, and validity of different forms of knowledge . . . In this process of splitting, the technical and moral aspirations of professionalism have tended to separate and to become associated, respectively, with the 'core' and the 'periphery' of the stratum. (Brint, 1994: 11)

Brint (1994: 16) suggests that the professions have served an important role in the emerging modern society as being what is neither democratic nor capitalist, that is, not under the full authority of political decision-makers or dependent on the fickle movements of the market, but as a "stabilizing force" in periods of political or economic turmoil. While the professions have arguably aimed at advancing their own positions, such position has in many cases been beneficial for the general public (as in the obvious case of medicine). In the neoliberal regime of governance, there is really no room for such intermediary position between the market and the hierarchy of the political bodies and institutions, but the professions are inevitably drawn to the market side of the continuum, This is a fate shared with the political institution as the neoliberal state serves to pave the way for corporations in all domains of previously state-governed activities such as military defense and penal institutions (Davis, 2009b). It is noteworthy that Brint (1994) locates this decline of social trustee professionalism not in the late 1970s and the neoliberal revolution but to the early 1960s (in the case of the U.S.): "Beginning in the 1960s, social trustee professionalism fell increasingly under attack for its apparent lack of correspondence to the organizational realities of professional life" (Brint, 1994: 39). The new economic order at the height of the Fordist regime of accumulation, running of out steam in the early 1970s and leading to a full-blown economic crisis in the middle and end of the decade, apparently demanded professional expertise that was not out of joint with the times. "Expert professionalism" was thus based on market transactions and open competition between members of the professional community.

In the contemporary neoliberal regime of economic activities, professionals are controlled and monitored by both authorities and political bodies and various forms of consumer control in the form of customer satisfaction indexes and other means for making professional work transparent and open for evaluation and judgment. Of necessity, there is an apparent lack of information on the side of the client or consumer—it is not simply a matter of "choosing your own cardiologist"—but this is compensated for by a number of auditing practices and accreditations that help guiding the consumer/client/patient. In most domains of professional work, the last decades have been strongly oriented toward translating underlying professional expertise into figures, ratios, statistics, and other representations signaling the status and expertise provided (Sauder and Espeland, 2009). In the field of university education, a rich variety of rankings, lists, and reviews arguably help students make their choice of Alma Mater. The average SAT scores demanded to enter the university and the financial endowment of different universities are on public display as indexes of the standards of the both the faculty and the students, determining the status of the university (Washburn 2005; Bok, 2002). In short, in the neoliberal regime of governance, professional expertise may not be wholly transparent for the layman, but the status and economic effects derived from such expertise are carefully inscribed and mathematized into formal documentation.

In the bioeconomy, professionals will maintain a key position in terms of being the main organization mechanism for knowledge-intensive work. Just because the professions are increasingly turned into "expert"—a concept having connotations that make it a poor candidate for serving as a synonym for professional—and their work is rendered transparent through monitoring and auditing practices, this does not make the professions less influential. In the bioeconomy, expertise in the life sciences and the capacity to translate this expertise into commodities and marketable offerings are domains where we may see many new professional groups establishing themselves as new fields of know-how are developed. For instance, in the case of "upstream activities" (to use an industrial metaphor), in the field of the life sciences, characterized by a relentless development of new scientific frameworks and methods, and most recently a variety of post-genomic research methods, new fields of knowledge are being instituted as potentially leading to breakthroughs in therapies. The emergence of computer science, mathematics, and biochemistry into biocomputation and bioinformatics is one example of a new field of know-how that produces its own cadre of professionals. Computation chemistry is one such professional community where chemists no longer spend their working lives in laboratories tinkering with test tubes, fluids, and biological species but instead operate on the basis of large-scale data sets collected in clinical trials and computer software analysis. Computation chemists are thus not dealing with the "wetware" of biological systems, but seek to construct solid theoretical models of biological systems based on "dry" data. Another example of a new professional community intimately connected to post-genomic research methods is the protein crystallographers studied by Myers (2008). In the post-genomic era, dealing with the disappointment regarding the relatively limited human genome (limited to some 25,000–30,000 gene sequences and where 95–97 percent of the genome is "junk DNA" (Kay, 2000: 2, seemingly inactive genes not transcribing any proteins), the millions of proteins produced are conceived of as being a new pathway to understanding the "inner workings of life" that the human genome mapping programs (HUGO) once promised to reveal. Proteins are cumbersome microbiological entities, as it is complicated to predict their shape or their interaction with, e.g., receptors in cells, and therefore there is a need for constructing images of the proteins to give a sense of how the protein moves and enfolds in space (Myers, 2008)—the protein crystallographer's professional domain of expertise. Computation chemists and protein crystallographers are two domains of professional expertise whose future is yet to be determined. Similar to the early proponents of visualization techniques such as the x-ray, such new professions may encounter a bright future as a standard operation procedure technique in the life sciences or may be widely treated as interesting but not very helpful technical curiosities. No matter what fate such new life-science professions are moving toward, they are still examples of the dynamics and movement of both the life sciences and the profession, capable of instituting new domains of expertise as technological and scientific knowledge unfolds.

Downstream in the bioeconomy, there is a similar example of new professional groups. One new category of professional that Sunder Rajan (2006) is studying is the "bioethicist," the expert in framing and discussing ethical and moral problems derived from the new opportunities derived from the life sciences. For instance, in the field of reproductive medicine, there are the possibility of what critics have called "designer babies," where foetuses with defects or disease may be aborted, leading to a variety of ethical problems that need to be addressed. Bioethicists are a relatively new professional group claiming jurisdiction over issues of ethics and morals pertaining to the uses of the life sciences (Salter and Salter, 207). Sunder

Rajan (2006) tends to conceive of this new profession as a form of Marxist *Überbau*, complementing and justifying the material accomplishments of the life sciences. That is, rather than being part of the advancement of the life sciences from the outset, bioethicists are constructed as a professional category after the *fait accompli* of the life sciences. Rather than having a say in whether reproductive medicine is the right way to go in the first place, bioethicists are expected to deal with the anxieties and concerns that are a by-product of these advancements. There are also other professions being created such as the organ donation coordinators interviewed by Sharp (2003), who serve to direct organs to patients as they appear, seemingly haphazard accidents of gang-related violence; such events lead to a supply of a much-awaited liver or heart or any other vital organ that a patient have been anticipating for perhaps years. Also further downstream there are new professional groups connecting clients and consumers with the life sciences, for instance, in the field of marketing cosmetic surgery or IVF clinics. The work of these professional groups is widely understudied but may provide important insight into the "commodification practices" in the intersection between the life sciences and the markets. Of necessity being a terrain beset by ethical concerns and regulations, these professional groups need to pay minute attention to what is institutionally legitimate and what are the lines of demarcation between what is ethically correct and what is a violation of such rules. In summary, then, the bioeconomy is likely to provide a fertile soil for the establishment of new professional groups, serving as "expert professionals" operating in market-based economies where consumer choice and audit-based control are central principles for the operations.

If the professions have traditionally denoted privileged groups in society, sheltered by academic credentials and institutional boundaries, the bioeconomy may also produce new opportunities for other forms of labor not of necessity being protected by such resources. Besides the more immediate supply of traditional work assignments in bioeconomic organizations (e.g., as secretaries in cosmetic surgeons' offices or as janitors in life-science research institutes) there may be opportunities for new forms of clinical labor (Waldby and Cooper, 2007: 59). One such example is the surrogacy mothering work conducted by the Indian women studied by Pande (2009), making quite large sums of money by giving birth to another woman's baby. Another case is egg donation labor studied by Almeling (2007). Although Almeling (2007) strongly emphasizes the ideology of the "gift relationship" woman to woman, such ideologies primarily function to conceal the clinical labor connected with the donating women and to ward off potential criticism regarding the "commercial egg factory business" the egg agencies pursued. During the 2008 economic recession (widely addressed as a "financial crisis" in the media), there was an increase of this form of clinical labor reported from, e.g., the U.S. where, for instance, female students engaged in this business to make a living (Beck, 2008). Even donators of semen may be treated as clinical laborers, though their contribution is less valued economically as semen seems to be not in short supply in the market for reproductive medicine. However, this market price may change radically because sperm quality (operationalized as the "density" and "motility" of the sperms) is increasingly reduced in male populations. Today, sperm donations are more part of a "gift relationship" than a full-blown form of clinical labor.

Also in the domain of clinical trial work, there may be opportunities for developing new routines for being part of large-scale clinical studies, especially in the less economically developed regions in the world. As clinical trials are increasingly moved to parts of the world where drug naïve populations are to be found, this may be an opportunity for such groups to make a living. In the advertisement of an Indian CRO examined by Prasad (2009), discussed in Chapter 1, this volume, the size and scope of the patient groups in India were envisaged as assets to be exploited. Potentially, these groups of patients may be given some share of the economic value generated by successfully developed therapies.

MARKETING AND CONSUMPTION IN THE BIOECONOMY

A third area where one may see changes in the future are the marketing and bundling of goods and services derived from life-science know-how. Already there are advertisements for Botox facial treatments and cosmetic surgery in women's magazines and the popular press, and in the future we may see examples of how "experiences" and life-science treatment may be bundled into "plastic surgery retreats" or "IVF holidays" (Dickenson, 2008). Spar (2006) indicates that the location of IVF clinics in Belize or in Cyprus suggests an awareness of the opportunities derived from the combination of tourism and health care. Again, like most commodities, services, and offerings based on life-science know-how, there is a delicate matter of balancing the "fun part" and the seriousness of the treatment. However, this industry is still in its infancy, and therefore there will potentially be a slow and gradual advancement of new practices. Some of these commodifications and products will naturally rest upon expectations on the life sciences that may never be fulfilled, as in the case of the cryobank advertisement reported by Brown and Kraft (2006), promising to store the umbilical cord blood of a newborn baby, to enable the exploitation of stem cell research therapies in the future. Stem cell research is undoubtedly one of the most promising domains of research in the field of the life sciences, holding a promise to repair organs on the cellular level as stem cells differentiate into new organs, but no one can claim that storing blood today will ensure the materials for repairing bodily organs in the future. Such bright futures may be the case, but this kind of advertisement balances on a thin line to exploit the goodwill of parents who want to provide the best for their newborn child. As a consequence, marketing services based on life sciences is always a delicate matter, and experiences from, e.g., cosmetic surgery—one of the most "public" of the life-science contributions—is that this kind of expertise is to be marketed and executed with care and with a great deal of trained judgment.

Another field that is relatively unexplored is the practice of branding. Branding plays a key role in contemporary consumer society as indexes of desirable qualities (Schultz, Hatch, and Larsen, 2000), and the life sciences (e.g., health care and pharmaceuticals) have traditionally relied on either social trustee professionalism and state-governance (in the case of health care) or on international agreements and standards (as in the case of new drug development), and there has been relatively little branding work done in the public arena. However, pharmaceutical companies early on recognized the key role played by medical doctors such as general practitioners and used the "detail man" (Greene, 2004) to "inform" the decision-makers about new drugs being launched. This kind of marketing was, Greene (2004) argued, a delicate balancing of different objectives and was never promoted as "marketing," as such a term would violate the professional ideologies of the medical professions: "'Detailing' here refers to the unique performances, half sales pitch and half educational service, with which pharmaceutical sales representatives present physicians with prescribing information, or 'details,' concerning new medications" (Greene, 2004: 271–272). In addition to the "detail man," the pharmaceutical industry's sponsoring of medical conventions and conferences is widespread in the industry (Brody, 2007), which tries to find new ways to market their products while veiling such interests under the banner of a general interest in the advancement of the sciences. During the last few years, more liberal regulations regarding the marketing of non-prescription drugs have led to a sharp increase in, e.g., television commercials advocating specific medicines (including the notorious declaration of all the potential and alarming side effects at the end of the often highly evocative commercials portraying the beauty of a life devoid of pain and suffering enabled by the drug in question). To date, such promotion and branding have been relatively restricted to the market for drugs, but one may easily see how a de-regulated market for, e.g., health care services may lead to larger budgets for marketing in this sector. One frequently addressed question is then whether it is in the public interest that such organizations re-allocate time and resources from core activities (e.g., R&D) to marketing. In the case of the pharmaceutical industry, several critics have remarked that the costs for marketing, sales, and administration are commonly higher than the costs for R&D in major multinational pharmaceutical companies. As Angell (2004: 73) points out, the pharmaceutical industry takes pride in being a "research-based industry" but is better thought of in terms of being "an idea-licensing, pharmaceutical formulating and manufacturing, clinical testing, patenting, and marketing industry" where basic research plays a relatively minor role. At the same time, it would be unfair to criticize actors in the bioeconomy for failing to act in accordance with instituted and enacted beliefs in neoliberal economies; working in a market-based economy means by definition competition, and competition leads to a need for the promotion and marketing of the products offered (Greene, 2007). The question then is of course to what extent market-based activities are beneficial for the greater good in research-based industries. The concept of "market-failure," central to economic theory and denoting investment with large fixed costs and long-term payback times, making such investments unattractive for private investors, potentially plays a role here.

In addition to television commercials, the Internet plays a larger role in constructing "bio-social" communities (Rabinow, 1992) around certain medical conditions. In Åsberg and Johnson's (2009) study of the promotion of the erectile dysfunction therapy Viagra, the Swedish Pfizer homepage promoting Viagra constructs an image of "ideal-typical" male qualities, including being sexually and physically active, and makes connections between this image and the Viagra brand (see also Mamo and Fishman, 2001). On the homepage, operating on a complex semiotics of gender, images of healthy looking and attractive middle-aged men engaging in stereotypical male activities such as changing tires on a car are posted, thereby making a connection, Åsberg and Johnson (2009) suggest, between the capacity for sexual activity and masculinity more broadly and the capacity to use tools and materials: healthy, well-functioning men are capable of tinkering with their cars and having sexual intercourse as well. The homepage is tinted in the deep blue color (of the pills) that is associated with Viagra in all marketing activities, and euphemistic terms such as "erectile quality" are used to avoid more anxiety-provoking terms. Åsberg and Johnson (2009) demonstrate that in order to promote drugs like Viagra, marketers cannot strictly rely on medical data but need to create evocative and appealing images of men and maleness. This easily leads to a stereotypical enactment of maleness where the field of possibilities for legitimate and "normal" male behavior is narrowed down to a few legitimate scripted roles. Just as women are exposed to images and narratives where they are expected to critically evaluate their bodies and their physical appearance, so too are men. Being able to perform with adequate "erectile quality" is thus not a matter of personal conditions but is part of a "normal" and "healthy" life for a man. Unable to comply with these standards, individual men are asked to think again about their "erectile quality." Åsberg and Johnson's (2009) study demonstrates that the Internet is a key medium for creating a long-standing relationship to actual and potential consumers and, perhaps more important, for gradually establishing new images of certain medical conditions, both creating a demand for certain therapies and legitimizing the medicalization of medical conditions. In the future, life-science products and service marketing will very likely take place on the Internet.

In summary, marketing and branding are two fields where one may observe significant changes and new practices that may demand some scholarly attention and critical reflection. Being a delicate balancing of information and promotion, marketers need to learn from, e.g., the pharmaceutical industry how to make the offerings Trojan horses being sneaked in under the auspices of information (Greene, 2004), or exposed as a general concern for public health and well-being. Not even cosmetic surgery, in many cases propelled by celebrity culture and the cult of youth and beauty, is in the position to market its own services as a conspicuous "rejuvenation" of one's body, but must use more subtle means for promoting its expertise.

UNIVERSITY-INDUSTRY COLLABORATIONS
IN THE LIFE SCIENCES

Another domain where the there may be some development is in industry and university collaborations (Bercovitz and Feldman, 2008; Boardman and Corley, 2008; Rafferty, 2008; Anderson, 2008; Croissant and Smith-Doerr, 2008; Boardman and Ponomariov, 2007; Rothaermel, Agung, and Jiang, 2007; Vestergaard, 2007; Nerkar and Shane, 2007; Stuart and Ding, 2006; Jong, 2006; Smith and Bagni-sen, 2006; Youtie, Libaers, and Bozeman, 2006; Powell et al., 2005; Bozeman and Boardman, 2004; Etzkowitz, 2003, 1998; Zucker, Darby, and Armstrong, 2002; Murray, 2002; Louis, Blumenthal, Gluck, and Stoto, 1989). The goods and services offered by companies in the bioeconomy are based on life-science expertise, and as new commercial opportunities emerge there is likely to be a less strong emphasis on separating "basic" and "applied" research and the "context of discovery" and the "context of application." Sternizke (2010: 811) suggests that "[a]bout 20% of drugs could only be developed with substantial help from recent academic research" (see also Nerkar and Shane, 2007). He continues: "[P]harmaceutical industry . . . is, much more than other industries, dependent on scientific advances as well as work done in the public sector. Such work, particularly of a scientific kind, is equally important for all types of drug innovation" (Sternizke, 2010: 819). In the case of biotechnology, the entire industry is a spin-off from university research, initially publically funded. While the capacity to fully exploit investment in intellectual capital and know-how is credible on paper, in practice a range of concerns need to be addressed: for instance, how to avoid free-rider problems derived from publically funded research. One of the key areas of criticism when Stanford University patented Boyer and Cohn's recombinant DNA in the 1970s was that publically funded research should not be protected by intellectual property rights, and there is a widespread concern that public funding will benefit private interests, being a kind of reallocation of resources from the public to the private sector. An accompanying problem addressed by, e.g., Washburn (2005) is that the free circulation of knowledge is impaired by the overarching tendency to impose intellectual property rights on any piece of new know-how. In Washburn's (2005) view, the university system, rooted in the medieval cloisters and monasteries, has been a remarkably effective institution in terms of establishing routines and systems of credentials enabling a global circulation and peer-based control of know-how (see also Shapin, 1994, 2008). In neoliberal regimes of control, where virtually any know-how may be subject to economization and financialization, there is a concern regarding the sharing of know-how; such know-how may be translated into money and other economic resources. For Washburn (2005), there is a need for an extended public debate regarding the role and purpose of universities in contemporary society; should they operate in the service of humankind at large or should they be given a more restricted role as the collaborator of a few private firms to develop know-how that can be further purified into products and services?

On the other hand, there is a stream of criticism claiming that the roles of universities and university professors and privately owned companies on the other hand are too unregulated. Healy's (2004, 2006) and Brody's (2007) discussions of the widespread use of ghostwriting in promoting specific substances or therapies suggests that scientific credibility and the status of individual researchers are too easily exploited in unethical ways. These kinds of concerns are not easily handled by individual professional ideologies and codes of conducts, as researchers in the life sciences are expected to take part in public discussions, but there is potentially a need for a more thorough institutional framework guiding and directing both researchers and companies. It is not very likely that major pharmaceutical companies are willing to break laws or violate good business practice, but at the same time they make use of the resources at hand. These concerns demand the enactment of transparent policies and the institutionalization of monitoring organizations. By and large, in the extensive body of texts (e.g., Boardman and Corley, 2008; Boardman and Ponomariov, 2007; Smith and Bagni-sen, 2006; Zucker, Darby, and Armstrong, 2002) that addresses the increased collaborative efforts across industry-university boundaries, the majority is activity encouraging more extensive collaborative efforts. Perhaps there is a need for more reflexive and self-critical evaluations and discussions to further advance a university sector that is not only operating in the interest of a smaller and economically favored minority but benefitting humankind more broadly. In the bioeconomy, opening up new possibilities to manipulate life per se, this issue becomes even more acute as a totally unrestricted bioeconomy could easily lead to a form of necrocapitalism (Banerjee, 2008) where biopiracy is gradually tolerated and the respect for human and other life erodes.

RETHINKING HUMANITY: THE HUMAN AS
BIO-TECHNOLOGICAL ASSEMBLAGE

In the bioeconomy to come, it may be that the human biological organism is increasingly complemented by new technological devices. In the social science literature, there are many reflections about the implications of the merging of man and machine, the mingling of organic materials and technological artifacts (Sharp, 2011). The term cyborg (*cyb*ernetic *org*anism) has been a standing reference in the literature since Donna Haraway (1991) introduced the term in her feminist epistemology (see, e.g., Thomas, 1995; Hayles, 2006; Lenoir, 2007). More recently, the discourse on nanotechnology has called attention to the vision wherein technologies on the nanoscale (or more likely, the microscale) may be capable of repairing or maintaining the human body from within (Jones, 2004; Berube, 2006; Bensaude-Vincent, 2007; Milburn, 2008; Choi and Mody, 2009). In general, a substantial body of texts discusses the transhuman or posthuman condition, a new world order wherein the human body is open for a variety of technological integrations and manipulations. In many cases, such accounts are polarized into either presenting bleak scenarios wherein the human body may be easily colonialized by political or economic interests (Armitage, 1999: 49), or an overtly positive outlook where humans are capable of living longer, happier, and healthier lives on the basis of technological devices and prostheses (Selin, 2007; Berube, 2006). Such images of the future are often a form of science-fiction writing, but in fact there are already today a number of examples of how the human body is recreated on the basis of medical technologies. In the field of surgery, there are a number of examples of how parts of the human bodies may be substituted by technologies; joints may be replaced by metal objects, and cardiac surgery replaces parts of the heart with biomaterials. Pacemakers keep the heart beating for perhaps decades after initial health concerns are diagnosed. In the field of cosmetic surgery, various chemical substances (Botox, silicon, etc.) are used to augment the human body. In this view, the human body is already a terrain where technologies are being located and brought into function. The human body is then no longer a closed territory but is instead a domain where biological and mechanical or technological resources meet and integrate. One of the implications is that the careful separation between life and non-life cannot be simply inscribed into the biology-technology matrix. That is, while life is traditionally associated with biological systems and organisms, there is reason to recognize that technologies are an extension of the vital force of the biological system.

Georges Canguilhem (1992) suggests that the operating of a machine testifies to an inherent vitalist force similar to that of biological life. The machine operates on the basis of strictly linear functions and mechanisms: "[I]n the case of the machine there is a strict adherence to rational, economical rules. The whole is rigorously the sum of the parts. The final effect depends on the ordering of causes" (Canguilhem, 1992: 56). As a consequence, there is no element of *emergence* in machines, no room for "monstrosities":

Life is experience, meaning improvisation, acting as circumstances permit; life is tentative in every respect. Hence the overwhelming but often misunderstood fact that life permits monstrosities. There are no monstrous machines . . . Whereas monsters are still living things, there is no way to distinguish the normal and the pathological in physics and mechanics. Only among living beings is there a distinction between the normal and the pathological. (Canguilhem, 1992: 58)

Machines operate on the basis of technological and scientific principles and cannot deviate from them; yet, Canguilhem (1992) suggests, such machines are capable of sustaining life when being co-located with biological systems. Canguilhem's thinking thus recognizes a vitalist capacity that cuts through the all-too-Cartesian separation between organic and non-organic systems, life and non-life. Hacking (1998: 207) emphasizes this shift in focus in Canguilhem's work: "Even if in the end we resist the notion that machines are extensions of the body—just because they are too far from the body—*they are an extension of life, of vitality, of living force*; or, to repeat another word used above, a projection of life." Hacking (1998: 207) thus underlines that Canguilhem is helping us to look at the world with a gaze that "cut across the mechanisms that has been thrust upon us ever since Descartes." Canguilhem thus opens up a view of the human body not as an exclusively biological arrangement but as a field where vitalist forces are maintained by all means. The human body may be part biological, part technological, but what matters is the capacity to maintain the vital force that, in Xavier Bichat's famous formulation, "resists death." The line of demarcation between organic and non-organic life then ceases to play a key role in the bioeconomic regime. Given this shift in perspective, from the biological *qua* substance to biology as an ensemble of functions, there is a need for a new operative theoretical framework capable of accommodating such post-Cartesian images of the human body. Gilbert Simondon, a French technology philosopher and Canguilhem's contemporary and a student of Maurice Merleau-Ponty, introduced the term *transduction* to denote the gradual "individuation" of a biological system: "The term [transduction] denotes a process—be it physical, biological, mental or social—in which an activity gradually sets itself in motion, propagating within a given area, through the structuration of the different zones of the area over which it operates," Simondon (1992: 313) writes. Simondon suggests that all processes of individuation are the outcome of the dynamic responses to information in the organism's milieu. The individuation of the organism, its transduction, is then by no means an Aristotelian hylemorphism inasmuch as the organism realizes its "potentiality" that resides within—the chestnut has the capacity of becoming a full-grown tree, etc.—but is a thoroughly open-ended process of responses to external conditions. "This is the contribution that Gilbert Simondon makes to the body: he liberates it from the presupposition of a form, demonstrating how a body is always across lives. The body's individuation is its force for becoming, not its endpoint," Manning (2010: 118) remarks. Simondon is useful because he uses the term transduction to denote the constitution of technological artifacts and ensembles, thereby drawing no firm line of demarcation between the organic and non-organic, the biological and the technological (Simondon, 1992; Dumochel, 1995; Harvey, Popowski, and Sullivan, 2008). Just like the biological organism, "the technical object is a unit of becoming" (Simondon, 1980: 12). He continues: "the technical being evolves by convergence and by adaption to itself; it is unified from within according to a principle of internal resonance" (Simondon, 1980: 13). We "do not know what a body can do," Spinoza (1994: 72) famously claimed in his *Ethics*. This would be an apt slogan for Simondon's (1992, 1980) work, if we add that "we do not know what a technology can become" and "we do not know the ways in which bodies and technologies may co-mingle." Simondon suggests that the processes of individuation, concretization (in the case of technology), and transduction are generic principles in the constitution of entities and matter. As a consequence, his philosophy of transduction as a form of process of individuation is helpful to understand and examine the position of the human body in the bioeconomy as what is increasingly an ensemble of biological and technological components. Says Hansen (2007: 95), addressing the work of Simondon: "Because human embodiment no longer coincides with the boundaries of the human body, a disembodiment of the body forms the condition of possibility for a collective (re)embodiment through technics. The human today is embodied in and through technics."

In summary, the work of Canguilhem and Simondon open up a new perspective on the relationship between biological organisms and technology, no longer stuck with the Cartesian doctrine carefully separating the biological from the technological. Rather than maintaining this separation, both biological and technological systems are capable of upholding vitalist forces that resist death or otherwise improve the quality of life in terms of maintaining physical and intellectual capacities of the body. In the bioeconomic regime, the human body is manipulated and transformed in various ways ,but terms like *biomachine* (Paul Virilio, cited by Der Derian, 1998: 20) impose a too mechanical image on humans—more that of a robot than a biological system. Consequently, the bioeconomy does not promise to produce entirely transhuman or posthuman species as the critics may claim, but are rather to re-create the human body as a zone where technoscientific and mechanical entities are brought into the vital system of the human body (Thacker, 2003; Hayles, 1999). Thacker (2004) emphasizes this dual image of the body where biological and mechanical systems are integrated:

Nanomedicine—and nanotechnology generally—is . . . predicated on a view of the body that is open to the intenventions of medical design and engineering at the molecular level. In this approach, the 'body' is understood as 'matter' on two coexistent levels: First, the body is taken as natural matter, as the biological, living body that interacts constantly with nonbiological, nonliving objects—this would constitute the body as the object for nanomedicinal intervention. But, the body is also taken as technical matter, in a reductionist move that states that, at bottom, both living and nonliving, biological and nonbiological entities are essentially matter. (Thacker, 2004: 122)

Returning to Bichat's paradigmatic definition of life, such ensembles of biological, biochemical, and technological entities and devices are then brought together, capable of resisting death and enhancing the longevity of human beings. The modernist fear of the technological colonialization of the human body (a theme recurring in popular culture in, e.g., the European and Hollywood cinemas ranging from *Metropolis* to *The Stepford Wives*) is thus possibly replaced by an affirmation of the possibilities derived from the individuation of the technoscientifically mediated human body. We are not, with Paul Virilio's term, on the "verge of the biomachine" (cited in Der Derian, 1998: 20) in the technology-skepticist tradition of thinking, but are instead moving to a position where the technosciences and the life sciences more specifically are in the position to influence the human body without reducing it to inert technological matter. This shift in focus demands a proper biophilosophical framework that recognizes the blurred boundaries between the human body and its outside. As a consequence, the work of Georges Canguilhem and Gilbert Simondon is of interest for understanding technology in the new millennium.

THE SHAPE OF THINGS TO COME: HUMAN LIFE REINVENTED ON THE BASIS OF THE LIFE SCIENCES?

Late modern society is fundamentally shaped and influenced by neoliberal enterprising ideologies and norms, suggesting that as members of this society we are expected to care for ourselves and make sure that we are capable of making a contribution to society. In addition, late modern society is embedded in technoscientific advancements, and all the technologies, practices, and possibilities derived from the sciences constitute modern life. In the consumerist society, new possibilities for consumption are easily instituted as another option for acquiring new consumer goods or taking advantage of service offerings. When the population is ageing or is in general dissatisfied with the health status or physical appearance (as in the case of cosmetic surgery) and has the economic resources demanded, there is a shared ground for consumerist ethos and the technosciences. The life sciences have brought a great number of new possibilities to the table, and there is today a range of possibilities for intervening into the human body, both on the level of the organs and tissues and on the microbiological and cellular levels. In the view taken in this book, science is neither the motor of society nor existing on the outside, but is on the contrary what is co-produced with society. Members of society legitimize and endorse scientific practices and projects, and the outcome from such work may become products and services that are traded on the market. Even though the technosciences and society are co-produced, the impact and effects of scientific practices cannot be fully anticipated. For instance, we cannot really know if women donating their eggs will suffer from premature menopause until they reach the age of forty, or if cosmetic surgery will imply future costs in terms of unanticipated degradation of human tissue. Only then will we know if these interventions into the biological system were a good idea of not. Expressed differently, the life sciences provide many opportunities and possibilities, but their long-term consequences are not easily overlooked from the standpoint of the present period. Only after decades and perhaps centuries of experience, may the scope of the life-science revolution be fully understood.

As in most historical perspectives, neither the doomsday gloom nor the evangelical scenarios are likely to become true in the future. Human bodies, organs, and tissues are probably not going to be traded freely and without regulations, and the life sciences may demonstrate a great deal of progress in curing forms of cancer and mediating neurodegenerate diseases, but the human body may not be totally rehabilitated on the basis of scientific skills and know-how. However, the life sciences may be expected to increasingly serve as the foundation for a range of product offerings, ranging from genomics analysis to cosmetic surgery and new and more effective forms of in vitro fertilization. It is this zone between the neoliberal nightmare of free exchange of body parts and tissues and the science fiction of the human body as an ensemble of technical and biological materials continuously modified and manipulated, that will deserve attention in the next decades, especially in the field of the social sciences. Already today, IVF therapies are bundled with holiday experiences, and this blending of life-science technology and therapies and everyday life experiences is not an entirely unlikely formula for how life sciences may be consumed in the future. What Foucault (1990) talked about as the "care of the self" (*souci de soi*) or "technologies of the self" in his three-volume work on the history of sexuality is perhaps an important underlying social norm or institution in late modern society of the coming decades. We only have our one single life and our one single body, and investing time, effort, and economic resources in enhancing well-being and the capacities of the body may become increasingly common in the future. The neoliberal doctrine and its emphasis on freedom of choice and de-regulation have helped produce significant (but unevenly distributed) wealth in late modern society; these times, when the consumption of consumers goods and services is either saturated or, in the face of environmentalism, facing a shift in consumer focus, may pave the way for consumption centered on the human body as a form of care of the self. If the case of cosmetic surgery is paradigmatic in this case, it is, as suggested by for instance Blum (2005) and Dickenson (2008), a form of investment based on the care for of the self. However, the issue in the case of cosmetic surgery is the gendered, racial, and cultural concerns derived from the manipulation of (primarily) women's sense of themselves and the psychological costs and emotional work involved in all bodily modification. However, when it comes to handling, say, the effects of Parkinson's disease or improving the chances of becoming parents, such objectives are more socially legitimate than correcting a nose that fails to comply with aesthetic norms. Being alive and healthy is widely recognized as a socially legitimate objective; filling one's lips with synthetic collagen to achieve the look of a Hollywood celebrity is quite another matter. Still, in both cases, the life sciences provide a number of opportunities and possibilities that, when translated into products and services, will constitute the bioeconomy—the economy based on the manipulation of life.

From an organization theory perspective, the organization of the bio-economy into professions, laboratories, technologies, firms, projects, networks, and other mechanisms constituting everyday practice is a rich research framework. Emerging professions, the constitution of laboratory practice, the formation of new companies, and so forth, are some examples of social practices wherein organization theory is capable of making an important contribution. While the ideology of the sciences imposes an image of scientific work as what is always already enclosed and terminated, blind to the untrained eye, a number of science and technology studies ethnographies demonstrate that the sciences are the outcome of detailed sociomaterial practices where abstract and intangible resources are mixed with materialities of all kinds, ranging from equipment and tools to bio-logical tissues and laboratory animals. Science is thus a form of tinker-ing or fabrication (Knorr Cetina, 1981; Pickering, 1995; Fujimura, 1996) that is constituted from the bottom up rather than the other way around. The bioeconomy is always of necessity what is in-the-making, in a process of becoming, brought to the markets and consumers by the capacity to assemble and coordinate a great range of resources and entities and pack-age them into socially legitimate products and services. That is, to draw on the case of cosmetic surgery—of great illustrative importance in terms of its relative purity—once again, it is not a miracle work produced strictly on the basis of the superior skills of the surgeon but relies on a long series of organized activities, symbolic as well as material, political, and behavioral, whose outcome is manifested in the "body work" executed on the patient's bare body. Cosmetic surgery is thus at the very intersection between sur-gical possibilities, laws and regulations, consumer choices, and economic interests; without the capacity of the cosmetic surgery institute or clinic to simultaneously mobilize and orchestrate all these heterogeneous resources, there would be no place for cosmetic surgery. Organization theory and management studies provide a highly heterogeneous box of tools (concepts, analytical frameworks, research approaches, etc.) that enables an under-standing of how bioeconomic practices are constituted and brought into existence. A human is killed in a car accident, and at the event of death a number of vital organs are procured from the cadaver and distributed to different locations where the organs are inserted into other patients' bodies, helping them live at times for decades. Such a series of events is needless to say not a trivial matter but is a manifold social practice wherein a variety of institutions, agreements, standards, technoscientific routines and practices, economic transactions, etc., are folded into one heterogeneous yet singular event.[3] Organization theory may inform the analysis of such a trajectory of a human liver or a pair of retinas based on the idiosyncratic theoretical framework that is capable of bridging the local and the global, the particular and the universal. In other words, rather than being the exclusive domain of research in the disciplines of anthropology, sociology, feminist studies, or science and technology studies, the bioeconomy is among many other things a field where a variety of organizations and practices of organizing co-exist and interact:

> The authority of science is not simply grounded in its texts, but rather in its organization. The important consequence is that science deserves no more and no different type of respect than other powerful organizations. People are willing to surrender to the experts because they are in awe of the privileged rationality of their science. So we, accept the experts telling us what to eat, who we are, how we should live, and how to raise our children. . . . Once we stop being too impressed by the experts and their science, and once we realize that their power is simply that of their organization, we can begin to loosen their tight grip on our lives. (Fuchs, 1992: 18)

For instance, stem cell researchers in, e.g., South Korea have been criticized by feminist organizations in the country for consuming large amounts of oöcytes (human eggs), human tissues collected from women and potentially affecting the menopause of the donor and ultimately her health (Dickenson, 2008). The life sciences are certainly not politics pursued by other means, but politics and interest are always present as constitutive and legitimizing elements in the sciences (Shostak and Conrad, 2008), and consequently there is a range of organizations affecting, e.g., stem cell research activities and initiatives. That is, in order to understand both the merits and potentials as well as the dangers and concerns of the bioeconomy, scholars and commentators need to pay attention to its organization. No matter what the shape of things to come will look like, it will in one way or another be organized along certain principles and routines.

CODA: ORGANIZING THE LIFE SCIENCES AND THE ROLE OF BUSINESS RESEARCH

As we can recall from the Introduction to this volume, organization researchers such as Zald and Lounsbury (2010) criticize the field of organization theory and management studies and institutional theory more specifically for the lack of social critique. More explicitly, they encourage scholars to "become more ambitious with their research aims" and to "more aggressively pursue more integrative theoretical approaches that cross narrow sub-disciplinary specialization." In comparison to Khurana's (2007) concern regarding the role of the business school, pointing at the hybridity of the institution as standing with one foot in scientific pursuits and the other in the domain of practical utility, Zald and Lounsbury (2010) have a straightforward message. They don't see the trade-off between "rigor and relevance," but rather want organization theorists and management scholars to make use of theories to understand the world and how it can be changed for the better. Speaking of the life sciences and their commercialization, one of the most significant social changes in the decades to come, some commentators have emphasized the need for thinking of such changes in interdisciplinary terms:

> In *empirical terms*, an analytics of biopolitics can bring together domains that are usually separated by administrative, disciplinary, and cognitive boundaries. The categorical divisions between the natural and the social sciences, body and mind, nature and culture lead to a blind alley in biopolitical issues. (Lemke, 2011: 121)

The business schools have a long tradition of hosting trans- and cross-disciplinary research, and they would be a fertile seedbed for the study of how the life sciences become commercialized and instituitionalized. The organization theory and management literature may here make many contributions to the study of the life sciences and the bioeconomy at large.

In pursuing such analyses, there is a need for new analytical perspectives to fully recognize the heterogeneity of the life sciences and their distribution over technological resources, theoretical framework, institutional arrangements, and other assets and resources being mobilized. Drawing on the epistemological writings of Karen Barad (2003, 2007), Wanda Orlikowski (2010: 128) calls for what she refers to as a ""relational ontology" contrasted with an "ontology of separateness," i.e., an "an ontology of separate things that need to be joined together," in Suchman's (2007: 3) formulation. A relational ontology "[p]rivileges neither humans nor technologies" "nor does it treat them as separate and distinct realities," Orlikowski (2010: 134) says. Thinking of the life sciences in such relational ontology terms means to seek to overcome the intuitive thinking enacting the world as a series of entities separated but yet interrelated; instead practices, technologies, artifacts, and other relevant analytical categories are conceived of as processes unfolding under determinate conditions. "[C]apacities for action are seen to be enacted in practice and the focus is on constitutive entanglement (e.g., configurations, networks, associations, mangles, assemblages, etc.) of humans and technologies," Orlikowski (2010: 135) proposes. The life sciences are then not so much organized as the autonomous production of epistemic objects such as molecules or proteins or biomaterials, but are instead part of broader arrangements wherein epistemic objects, technologies, tissues, human bodies, institutions are interacted and mutually constitutive. Orlikowski (2010) thus wants students of organizations and technologies to enact alternative analytical models enabling new perspectives and understandings of how, e.g., the life sciences serve society through their production of epistemic objects and interrelated know-how and expertise. Similarly, the political scientist Jane Bennett (2010: viii) speaks of the "vitality of matter, " meaning the "capacity of things—edibles, commodities, storms, metals—not only to impede or block the will and designs of humans but also to act as quasi agents or forces with trajectories, propensities, or tendencies of their own." Bennett (2010) here wants to promote a materialist tradition of thinking articulated along a series of thinkers including Democritus, Epicurus, Spinoza, and Deleuze, rather than along a Hegelian-Marxist axis of thinking. In this former tradition of thinking, materiality is never inert and "dead" but is instead characterized by its vitality and its capacity for interacting with other resources. "My aim is . . . to theorize a vitality intrinsic to materiality as such, and to detach materiality from the figures of passive, mechanistic, or divinely included substance," Bennett (2010: xiii) declares. Even though Bennett's (2010) ontology is more speculative and evocative than Orlikowski's (2010) relational ontology, they both draw on a materialist tradition of thinking and propose an analytical framework that would suit the study of the vital materialities, the "informed matter" (Barry, 2005) produced by the life sciences. The field of organization theory and management studies would be capable of hosting a range of research endeavors seeking to explore the processes wherein contributions made in the life sciences enter society in the form of commodities and the kinds of technological, social, economic, cultural, and juridical arrangements that need to be settled to co-align the social, material, and biological resources into functional practices.

Author Biography

Alexander Styhre, Ph.D (Lund University), is professor and chair of organization theory and management, School of Business, Economics and Law, University of Gothenburg. Alexander has published widely in the field of organization studies and his work has appeared in *Journal of Management Studies*, *Organization Studies*, *Human Relations*, and elsewhere. His most recent books include *Assembling Health Care Organizations* (co-authored with Kajsa Lindberg and Lars Walter, Palgrave, 2012), *Knowledge Sharing in Professions* (Gower, 2011), and *Visual Culture in Organizations* (Routledge, 2010). Alexander is the Editor-in-Chief of *Scandinavian Journal of Management*.

Notes

1. The term bioeconomy was first introduced in an OECD report published in 2006, "The Bioeconomy to 2030" (www.oecd.org/dataoecd/5/24/42837897. pdf), wherein biotechnology and other fields of the life sciences were pinpointed as key areas for future economic growth. Rose (2007) is thus further theorizing and discussing what was originally a politico-economic term rather than an analytical concept.

2. Monaghan, Hollands, and Pritchard (2010: 38) argue that the concept of obesity and the idea of an "obesity epidemic" (as announced by the WHO in 1998) are constituted and reproduced by what they name "obesity epidemic entrepreneurs," i.e., individuals sharing a concern for "constructing medicalized fatness as a social issue or crisis." Monaghan, Hollands, and Pritchard (2010) suggest that obesity is discursively produced from a variety of perspectives and that at least six categories of obesity epidemic entrepreneurs are discernable in this discourse: *creators* (defining the medical condition, i.e., scientists and clinicians), *amplifiers/moralizers* (media), *legitimators* (government), *supporters* (various groups having an interest in advancing obesity as a social problem), *enforcers/administrators* (health professionals setting "objective standards" for obesity and prescribing actions), and *entrepreneurial self* (individuals relating to various decisions and enunciations regarding obesity). Vrecko (2011: 558) speaks about the "the pharmaceutical management of obesity" (Vrecko, 2011: 556) as "the work of accommodating and reproducing contemporary consumer culture and associated forms of industry and capital" into a "productive assemblage," that is, an "arrangement of interconnected parts that have led to one another toward particular states of affairs that previously did not exist" (Vrecko, 2011: 559). For instance, the obesity drug *Acomplia* developed by Sanofi Aventis was not only praised in the press on the basis of its therapeutic effects but also because it had "[t]he potential to become the sort of blockbuster that appears once in a decade, like *Prozac* in the 1990s" (Vrecko, 2011: 563). In this view, the concept of obesity is by no means uncomplicated but is on the contrary brought into discussions and established as a "fact" through an intricate network of articulations and material arrangements and relations stabilized into productive assemblages constituting obesity both as a health condition and as a financial possibility.

3. There is a literature suggesting that the social sciences (e.g., sociology) are poorly equipped to address nature and biological systems (Newton, 2003; Goldman and Shurman, 2000). Goldman and Shurman (2000) speak of

"the great divide" between mainstream classic sociology and the sciences inasmuch as the sociology canon says relatively little about nature, biology, and the sciences exploring these domains. However, as many studies of the sciences suggest (see, e.g., Cambrosio, Keating, and Mogoutov, 2004; Haraway, 1989) nature and society are constantly folded into another in scientific research work. Still, the sciences and their area of investigations remain relatively underexplored in both the sociology and organization theory literature.

4. The concept of managerialism is a debated and complex term. Deetz (1992: 222) speaks of managerialism as a "discursive genre," "a way of conceptualizing, reasoning through, and discussing events that can be distinguished from potential competitive manners." In Kuhn's (2009: 685–686) view, "managerialism is a mode of thought and action based on a desire to control, enhance efficiency, normalize and suppress conflict and promote the universalization of sectional managerial interests." In addition, Costea, Crump, and Amiridis (2008) associate the term with three interrelated processes: "(a) Managerialism has produced wide-ranging series of *audit* techniques and vocabularies . . . (b) there has been a significant proliferation of *surveillance technologies*, especially in the 1990s . . . and (c) there has also been a growth in concepts and techniques that focus upon specifically *human attributes* of working subjects such as 'culture,' 'performativity,' 'knowledge,' or 'wellness.'" Managerialism thus operates on the basis of both technical arrangements and more intangible resources such as ideologies and collectively enacted beliefs.

NOTES TO CHAPTER 1

1. The strict, calculative aspects of "IVF investment" have been addressed in the organization theory and management literature by, e.g., Schmittlein and Morrison (2006) and Kaplan, Hershlag, and DeChercerney (1992). These papers do, however, say relatively little about the choices and preferences of the couples and single women enrolling in the IVF treatments but primarily examine the pricing strategies and calculated choices between different payment options.

2. Aristotle's *De Anima* is "one of the first, formalized attempts to think of an ontology of life" (Thacker, 2010: 8), advancing the concept of *psukhē* as being a principle of life, the *archē* of *zoē* and *bios*. *Psukhē* is thus a philosophical term that seeks to explain both the quasi-ontological notion of Life (the force or principle immanent in all life) and the naturalistic notion of the living (individual manifestations of Life). Thacker (2010: 17) explicates this important distinction: "Aristotle bifurcates the concept of *psukhē* into *psukhē*-as-principle and *psukhē*-as-manifestation. Put in different terms, we can say that Aristotle splits his ontology of life into *that-by-which-the-living-is–living* and *that-which-is–living*." This makes *De Anima*—commonly translated into *On the Soul* in English, a title testifying to the scholastic and theological reading of the text in the medieval period—a text split between being a biological and a metaphysical treatise. Says Thacker (2010: 11): "[W]hile Aristotle-the-biologist observes a set of characteristics unique to what he calls life, Aristotle-the-metaphysician struggles to articulate a coherent concept to encompass all these heterogeneous characteristics of life." However, the very idea that organisms are animated by some kind of life force or instinct is of ancient origin and appears in different conceptual frameworks in the history of biology.

3. In a review of recent conceptualizations of the organism, Shaviro (2010) suggests that rather than being portrayed as what is inherently changeable and adaptable, change is imposed on biological systems such as organisms and is essentially "forced adaptive reactions" to emerging conditions: "[L]ife is essentially conservative, organized for the purpose of self-preservation and self-reproduction. Organisms strive to maintain homeostatic equilibrium in relation to their environment and to perpetuate themselves through reproduction. Innovation and change are not primarily processes, but are forced adaptive reactions to environmental pressures. Life is not a vitalistic outpouring; it is better described as an inescapable compulsion . . . It would seem that organic beings only innovate when they are absolutely compelled to, and as if it were in spite of themselves" (Shaviro, 2010: 141).

NOTES TO CHAPTER 2

1. One key term in Foucault's work is *dispositif*, often translated into *apparatus* in English. For Agamben (2009: 2–3), a *dispositif* is the relations between a "heterogeneous set" of elements including "discourses, institutions, buildings, laws, police measures, philosophical propositions, and so on," that in one way or another regulate individuals and groups of individuals. Second, the *dispositif*, the apparatus, "always has a concrete strategic function and is always located in a power relation"; i.e., it never emerges or is constructed in isolation from broader social contexts. As a consequence, the apparatus "appears at the intersection of power relations and relations of knowledge." The apparatus is thus the totality of abstract principles that integrate heterogeneous elements and that therefore serve as the infrastructure of power and knowledge and, consequently, what constitutes the subject. Says Agamben (2009: 14): "I shall call an apparatus literally anything that has in some way the capacity to capture, orient, determine, intercept, model, control, or secure the gestures, behaviours, opinions, or discourses of living beings." These "living beings," humans in a specific society, are turned into subjects within a specific apparatus, i. e, are inscribed with qualities, aspirations, and so forth: "I shall call subjects that which results from the relentless fight between living beings and apparatuses" (Agamben, 2009: 14). The concept of *dispositif* is thus central to what Foucault (2003) talks of as biopolitics and eventually as *biopower* (Foucault, 2007).
2. Willse (2010) argues that the "biopoliticization of homelessness" is based on a transformation of social programs, central to the "Keynesian welfare social state," into "economic programmes." These economic programs dealing with "chronic homelessness" are, Willse (2010: 173), argues, part of neoliberal economies and thus "[t]hey enable rather than challenge the very conditions and systems that produce housing insecurity and deprivation." In other words, economic interests rather than social needs propel housing programs in what Jaques Donzelot has called the contemporary "social investment state." Similarly, Ericson, Barry, and Doyle (2000) claim that a deregulated insurance market leads to increased "moral hazards," i.e., the risk that any actor will act on the basis of self-interest and thus increase the risk of others, leading to more regulatory control at a higher cost. Both these two studies indicate that there are inconsistencies and ineffectiveness in deregulated markets that increase social costs and/or redistribute and concentrate financial resources.
3. In Karl Marx's *The Poverty of Philosophy*, economists are compared to theologicians in terms of separating between "natural" (e.g., markets) and

"artificial" (state-regulation) institutions, just as theologians distinguished between other religions as being "human inventions" while their own religion is "an emanation from God." (Karl Marx, *The Poverty of Philosophy*, chapter 2, "Seventh and last observation," cited in Žižek, 2009: 21). Following Marx, Žižek (2009) is talking about the "the utopian core of liberalism" as being a form of theology: "The way the market fundamentalists react to the destructive realities of implementing their recipes is typical of utopian 'totalitarians': they blame all failure on the compromises of those who realized their schemes (there will still be too much state intervention, etc), and demanded nothing less than an even more radical implementation of their doctrines" (Žižek, 2009: 19). At the same time, paradoxically, this "theology" of radical capitalism, Žižek (2009) suggests, is operating through the "de-totalization of meaning," as being what is *not* providing any unified and comprehensive worldview: "[C]apitalism is effectively not a civilization of its own, with a specific way of rendering life meaningful. Capitalism the first socio-economic order which *de-totalizes meaning:* it is not global at the level of meaning (there is no 'global capitalist world view,' no 'capitalist civilization' proper; the fundamental lesson of globalization is precisely that capitalism can accommodate itself to all civilizations, from Christian to Hindu and Buddhist)" (Žižek, 2009: 25). In other words, the "theology" of neoliberalism is a syncretic and loosely coupled system of beliefs, emphasizing a few central principles.

4. In what is called economic sociology or new economic sociology, this idea of markets as being inherently rational ignores all the work done to make the markets operate in the first place, prior to large scale action (Fligstein, 2001: 9). "Economies are not created *ex nihilo*, rather, they are composed of patchworks of heterogeneous forces. The locus of great interest then is the series of compromises that needs to be made for an economy to exist," Lépinay (2007: 88) says. Therefore, rather than assuming, in some kind of Panglossian manner that what is capable of surviving in economic markets is by definition rational, economic sociology suggests that such a far-reaching assumption must not be made without adequate proofs. Efficiency is then a social accomplishment and not an initial condition. Carruthers and Stinchcombe (1999) examine how well-functioning markets are dependent upon liquidity, i.e., how commodities are becoming standardized and open for economic transactions (see, e.g., Garcia-Parpet's [2007] study of the spot-price market for strawberries in France). "The sociologically interesting process concerns how heterogeneous claims on income streams associated with different sorts of assets get turned into homogeneous commodities that buyers and sells can understand," Carruthers and Stinchcome (1999: 354) write. The liquidity of an asset is thus closely entangled with the knowledge about the asset, enabling shared routines among many sellers and buyers in the market to evaluate the asset. If there is no such shared knowledge, then "market prices would be unstable, bid and ask prices would diverge markedly, the entrepreneurial use of information would create insiders with secret information, or delay for appraisal of value would slow the market" (Carruthers and Stinchcome, 1999: 354). In this perspective, the liquidity of an asset is aimed a reducing the transaction costs for trading the asset in large volumes. Carruthers and Stinchcombe (1999) show how "market makers" such as large investment banks and financial traders serve to accommodate the risks involved in establishing the liquidity of a specific asset. As opposed to the *laissex-faire* policies of neoliberal economic theory, Carruthers and Stinchcome (1999) do not assume that such a transparent regime of liquidity is produced all by itself:

Liquidity depends on 'know-ability.' An asset with transparent economic value, whose features can be credibly communicated to a large enough audience, will enjoy greater liquidity. Such an asset can be 'taken for granted.' This type of social transparency depends, in many situations, on prior organizational work to simplify, stratify, homogenize, and standardize the asset. Minting work creates social knowledge about exchangeable things, built on a foundation of commitments, certifications, guarantees, endorsements, and other risk-reducing and epistemologically simplifying mechanisms. Solid organizational commitments help to produce liquidity. In a similar fashion, the double-entry book-keeping method functioned as a cognitive framework and category system through which the assets and liabilities of a firm became perceptible and commensurable. (Carruthers and Stinchcome, 1999: 378)

This critique of neoliberal economic doctrines is quite articulated: "Since government rules, regulations, and institutions frequently get blamed for making markets imperfect (by 'interfering' with 'natural' market processes), it is tempting to conclude that liquidity arises out of an economic 'state of nature.' In fact, however, liquidity depends very much on elaborate institutional investments, market rules, and sometimes government regulations. There is nothing 'natural' about it" (Carruthers and Stinchcome, 1999: 379). In general, economic sociology points to the very practices and socially enacted norms and beliefs creating the possibilities for markets and economic action more broadly (see, e.g., Zelizer, 2007) that economists tend to take for granted once markets are in place.

5. In his review of the popular organization culture literature, Weeks (2004: 52) notices that all national culture traits—South Korean, French, Finnish, and so forth—are portrayed as being detrimental to organizational performance and longevity. The only culture that is legitimate is, at least according to the British and American press, an American competitive culture, but companies should not be "*too* American." In other words, American norms and value have a close to hegemonic influence in the organization culture literature.

6. The tendency with widening gaps in available economic resources is present in all OECD countries but has been particularly salient in the countries leading the finance revolution, the U.S. and the U.K. . Harvey (2005) points out that the economic inequality ratio reached its lowest point in the 1970s, being in steady decline since the 1930s, but that neoliberalism served to "restore class power" in terms of concentrating economic resources in the hands of the few. The richest percent of households today control about 40 percent of the economic resources (see Duménil and Lévy, 2004, fig. 15.6, p. 139), a return to the level of the late 1930s. In terms of the distribution of financial resources, Dore (2008: 1107) reports that "the top 1% [of the population] own 38% of total wealth; the top 10% owns 85% of all publically traded stocks." Today, "[t]he richest 1 percent of Americans spend as much as the poorest 60 million," Davis and Monk (2007: x) claim. Also Rushkoff reports a redistribution of wealth in America:

[T]he average CEO's salary [rose to] 179 times the average worker's pay in 2005, up from a multiple of 90 in 1994. Adjusted for inflation, the average worker's pay rose by only 8 percent from 1996 to 2005; median pay for chief executives rose 150 percent. The top tenth of 1 percent of earners in America today make about four times what they did in 1980. In contrast, the median wage in America (adjusted for inflation) was lower in 2008 than it was in 1980. The number of 'severely poor Americans'—defined as a family of four earning less than $9,903 per year—grew 26 percent between 2000 and 2005. (Rushkoff, 2009: 181)

This accumulation of wealth in a smaller number of groups has particularly accentuated in countries with large financial sectors and where the financial sector accounts for a large share of the total economy (the "public traded equity" accounted for 159 percent of the GDP in U.K. and 150 percent in the U.S. while only 50 percent in Germany in 2005, Dore [2008: 1106] notes). In the period of unprecedented economic growth in the world economy, since the late 1970s, the International Labour Organization (ILO) estimates that "in 2005, 84 percent of workers in South Asia, 58 percent in South-East Asia, 47 percent in East Asia . . . did not earn enough to lift themselves and their families above the U.S.$2 a day per person poverty line" (Kalleberg, 2009: 15). In addition, the internal distribution within OECD countries has changed:

A recent British report (Institute of Fiscal Studies) found that for the top 0.1 percent of taxpayers (average income £478.00 = €600,000), 80 percent of their income was labour income—as bankers, fund managers, accountants, lawyers, etc. On top of such annual incomes, they had already accumulated enough to get capital incomes four to five times the average annual salary. The accumulation of wealth at the top is increasingly a function of growing inequality of 'labour' incomes rather than inherited money. (Dore, 2008: 1107)

For instance, in the U.S. finance industry the economic compensations are substantial. In 2007, before the 2008–2009 financial crisis and economic recession, the U.S. finance industry earned $53 billion in total compensation. Goldman Sachs alone, the top of the five leading finance firms, accounted for $20 billion of that total, i.e., more than $661,000 was paid to each employee on average. The Goldman Sachs CEO, Lloyd Blankfein, made a fair share of the total compensation and took home no less than $68 million (Sorkin, 2009: 4). In January 2008, when the financial crisis was on the move, Wall Street bonuses added up to $32 billion, only a slightly lower amount than the year before (Harvey, 2010). Also Duménil and Lévy (2004) emphasize the pervasive changes taking place from the 1980s onward, influencing all sectors of society:

[T]hese developments in the 1980s led to a stark increase in social inequalities: a multifaceted process affecting incomes, holdings, status (particularly in relation to work), health, knowledge, culture . . . No one will . . . be surprised to observe that neoliberalism, which reinforces many capitalist features at the center and the peripheral countries, added even more of [the] propensity to reproduce and widen inequalities and injustice. (Duménil and Lévy, 2004: 137)

Neoliberalism has thus left its mark on both the accumulation and distribution of wealth and economic power. Wacquant (2009) examines what he calls the "penal state," the neoliberal state no longer capable of or willing to take care of its poor who therefore are poverty penalized: "Here penalization serves as a technique for the individualization of the social 'problems' that the state, as the bureaucratic level of collective will, no longer can or cares to treat at its roots. And the prison operates as a juridical garbage disposal into which the human refuse of the market society is thrown" (Wacquant, 2009: xxii. Emphasis in the original). The United States serves as the exemplary case penal state, Wacquant (2009) says, reporting that the U.S. with its 648 convicts per 100,000 residents in 1997 has between seven times as high an incarceration rate as Germany, the U.K., and France, and up to ten times as high a rate as Sweden, Denmark, and Ireland. The U.S. is thus shifting its focus from the socialization of the poor to medicalization, and, finally, to the penalization of poverty. If all U.S. prisoners were co-located in one single city, it would be the forth largest metropolitan area in the country, having 1,931,850 residents (in 1998), slightly larger than Houston. Wacquant (2009) also shows that the period from the 1950s until the mid-1970s had a relatively stable amount of prisoners (around 110 convicts per 100,000 residents); in the latter half of the 1970s and in the early 1980s, the incarceration rate rose sharply (Wacquant, 2009: 117, fig. 1). Only in the period of 1991–1995, Texas increased its incarceration rate 156 percent (Wacquant, 2009: 118, table 7). Many of these prisoners are, around 60 percent, Wacquant (2009: 132–133) argues, far from the image of "vicious predators" popularized in the media and political discourses, "disorganized offenders," committers of petty crimes such as car theft and shoplifting, lacking the skills or discipline to commit more violent acts. These offenders have often failed to find a "stable and durable occupational footing" and find no other way to support themselves but to commit "petty and pathetic" crimes. Similar to Willse's (2010) analysis of the social issue of homelessness, the penalization practice per se becomes part of the neoliberal economy, and consequently penal institutions are established as an industry in their own right, further reinforcing the tendency to commodify various institutions of the traditional welfare state, i.e., a privatization of historically state-governed activities.

7. Zweiger's (2001) book, *Transducing the Genome*, a somewhat outmoded text, is a fine illustration to McAfee's critique. "Biology is now becoming an information science, a progeny of the information age," Zweiger (2001: xi) states. "As information scientists, biologists concern themselves with the messages that sustain life, such as the intricate series of signals that tell a fertilized egg to develop into a full-grown organism, or the orchestrated response the immune system makes to an invading pathogen." In Zweiger's (2001: 15) view, the gene may be compared with a photon, because "like a photon of light teetering between being matter and energy, a gene teeters between matter and information." In Zweiger's (2001) view, the gene is matter, but it is above all information that is coded into RNA and proteins. This view is consistent with Jacques Monod's view of the organism as being nothing but "a cybernetic system governing and controlling the chemical activity at numerous points" (Jacques Monod, *Chance and Necessity*, 1970, cited in Kay, 2000: 17).

8. The case of Merck's cardio-vascular medicine Vioxx, associated with an estimated 27.000–60,000 deaths of patients taking the medicine before its withdrawal from the market, is one salient case of what may happen when scientific norms and regulatory frameworks are compromised. Lyon's (2007: 381) analysis of the market communication strategies reveals that Merck executives "[n]eutralized information about Vioxx's potential risks by favourably framing the data, omitting unfavorable data from published literature, and constructing a market-friendly warning label." The Merck sales representatives were told to avoid critical issues and to follow the provided scripts for the sales pitch and not to add or omit any information. Finally, when academic researchers articulated criticism regarding Vioxx, they were disqualified as being "anti-Merck" in the scientific community in no less than eight research universities. Lyon summarizes his argument:

> Almost immediately after the drug's FDA approval in 1999, serious cardio-vascular safety questions about Vioxx surfaced. Still, Merck tenaciously defended . . . the drug safety, denied any risks, and vigorously campaigned for Vioxx. This medication quickly became one of Merck's most lucrative drugs. Over 20 million patients took Vioxx, and annual revenue for the drug 'reached $2.5 billion' in 2003 . . . Merck finally withdrew Vioxx from the market on September 30, 2004, amid continuous pressure

from the scientific community. Executives acknowledge that Merck's most recent data showed an increased cardio-vascular risk, but insisted that no previous data had revealed this problem. The company stated that it disclosed all that it knew about Vioxx safety and rejected responsibility for patients' health complications. Unfortunately, an estimated 27,000–60,000 died while taking the drug before its withdrawal from the market . . . Deceased patients' families have since filed numerous lawsuits against Merck. (Lyon, 2007: 381)

Lyon (2007: 3949) concludes that the case calls for "[a] separation between pharmaceutical companies' economic interest and the production and reporting of scientific research on these companies' medicines. In the case of Merck, the blurry line between business and science led to the manipulation of results in order to produce a market-friendly portrayal of Vioxx data."

9. In a classic paper published in *Journal of Finance* in May 1970, Eugen Fama (1970: 383) advanced what has been called "the efficient market hypothesis": "A market in which processes always 'fully reflect' available information is called efficient . . . We shall conclude that, with but a few exceptions, the efficient-markets model stands up well."

NOTES TO CHAPTER 4

1. Sanal (2011) shows that cultural differences play a role when transplantation surgery is instituted. For instance, the ratio of brain-dead donors per million ranges between 15 and 30 in the European Union, with Spain scoring highest at 50. In contrast, in Turkey, a Muslim country, the same ratio is less than 2.4 and consequently, Sanal (2011: 50) says, cultural belief "[d]etermines the inner workings of the transplant economy."

2. Mitchell and Waldby (2001: 339) define clinical labour accordingly: "We use the term 'clinical labor' to refer to processes in which subjects give clinics and commercial biomedical institutions access to their in vivo and in vitro biology, the biological productivity of living tissues within and outside of their bodies."

3. This emphasis on the "gift-relationship" seems to be widely present in the entire bioeconomy (Tober, 2001). In their study of national biobanks, Mitchell and Waldby (2001: 340) found that such euphemisms were used to obscure the economic value generated by access to biological tissues: "Biobank planners and managers naturally have been reluctant to describe the activities of biobanking as a kind of labor, preferring instead to describe these activities as 'gifts' or modes of 'sharing,' while at the same time stressing that intellectual property rights in the tissues and data belong to the bank alone."

4. The critique of the metaphor of DNA as the script or master code underlying actual biological phenotypes is substantial in the literature. For instance, Rostoff (2010: 230) says: "The entire idea of a single gene for complex traits is a serious scientific error and leads directly to simplistic assumptions about therapeutic applications as well as more sinister social applications for this 'knowledge.'" Geneticizing is thus obscuring rather than clarifying many human disorders and health conditions. Phenyketonuria (PKU), a disorder discovered in the 1930s and causing mental retardation, was for instance initially regarded as a "simple disease" caused by a defective gene and the proteins/enzyme being produced, and it was thought that this could be treated by removing phenylalanine from the diet. As research has been conducted on the disorder, PKU is no longer treated as one single phenotype

and derives from far more complex conditions than one single defective gene. Rosoff (2010: 232) summarizes: "Those scientists who want to explain the complexities of mammalian—and especially human—behavior and socially significant traits, using the tools of modern molecular biology too often fall victim to the precision of these methods, assuming that molecularizing or geneticizing subjective phenomena by objective analysis will transform them into something more tangible and ultimately more malleable." The idea of the DNA as the "book of life," popular at the turn of the century, is thus slowly slipping away from the public mindset as more complex models of hereditary material are enacted. At the same time, the malleability of the concept of the gene, its status as an epistemic object in Rheinberger's (1997, 2010) parlance, is part of the explanation for the viability of the concept of the gene. "Imprecise epistemic objects and concepts work because they are malleable and can be integrated into different contexts in accordance with changing needs," Rheinberger (2010: 157) argues. Imprecise terms are thus not excluded from the sciences but on the contrary play a key role in coordinating actions. "As the complexity of a system increases, our ability to make precise and yet-not trivial assertions about its behaviour diminishes," Lofti Zadeh (1987, cited in Rheinberger, 2010: 169) asserts, pointing at the value of polysemic scientific concepts.

5. Smith (2009) clarifies that stem calls include a whole class of different cells collected and produced through laboratory procedures. This class includes embryonic stem cells, fetal stem cells, umbilical cord blood stem cells, adult stem cells, 'cybrid' stem cells (combining human and animal cell components), and induced pluripotent stem cells.

6. Brooks (2004: 227) calls attention to the fact that popular magazines such as *Harper's Bazaar* and *People* write appreciatively about various cosmetic surgery technologies such as Perlane and LipoDissolve, which are not clinically tested and approved by the FDA. The magazine articles reviewed by Brooks do not inform their readers about the potential risks but rather portray the use of non-FDA approved and untested cosmetic technologies "as exciting, cheerful, and fun." Apparently the regulatory control exerted in other domains of life-science innovation is not effectively transferred to the domain of cosmetic surgery.

7. The price paid for what Brooks (2004: 225) calls "aesthetic conformity" in terms of bearing pain during the healing period is substantial and, perhaps not too surprisingly, widely ignored in the popular accounts of cosmetic surgery. In addition, there are many risks involved that are potentially underrated by cosmetic surgery patients. Gimlin (2000: 79) accounts for some of these risks: "Cosmetic surgery is undeniably painful and risky and each operation involves its own potential complications. For instance, pain, numbness, bruising, discoloration and depigmentation frequently follow a liposuction, often lingering up to six months after the operation. Similarly, face-lifts can damage nerves, leaving the patient's face permanently numb. More serious disabilities include fat embolism, blood clots, fluid depletion, and in some cases, death. Indeed, health experts estimate that the risk of serious side effects from breast augmentation is between 30% and 50%. The least dramatic and most common of these include decreased sensitivity in the nipples, painful swelling or congestion of the breasts, and hardening of the breasts that makes it difficult to lie down comfortably or to raise the arms without the implants shifting." Also after successful cosmetic surgery, patients may experience that, e.g., face lifts lead to what has been called a "zombie-look," a loss of the capacity to engage some of the 15.000 expressive responses (or muscular movements) that the "non-altered face" is capable of

performing, leaving the patient with a face that "looks like marble" (*Vogue*, 2002, November: 494. Cited in Brooks, 2004: 229)—perhaps beautiful but with a reduced capacity to express emotions and thus more "non-human."

NOTES TO CHAPTER 5

1. On the body in social theory more broadly, see Shilling (1993) and Turner (1992, 1996).
2. The issue of social class is of central importance when examining practices of surrogacy. Goslinga-Roy (2000: 133) suggests that surrogates in the U.S. are "[t]ypically working-class women who, by receiving remuneration for what are essentially devalued homemaking skills in American culture, elevate their gender status by becoming professional homemakers" In this role as "professional homemakers," Goslinga–Roy (2000) continues, these working-class women "receive the attentions of wealthier middle-to upper-class couples and are celebrated at their surrogate centers as commendable altruists." Surrogacy needs to be understood within an intersectionality framework (Crenshaw, 1994), wherein gender, class, sexuality, race, and ethnicity are examined as interrelated analytical categories, in various ways structuring the field and its practices.
3. Roach (2003) offers an intriguing overview of how human cadavers serve a number of roles and functions in contemporary society. In all cases, the human bodies are treated with respect, even veneration, suggesting that that the human body is treated both as a bundle of resources or capacities and a sacred thing in Western culture, constituting an assemblage of sacred and profane elements.

Bibliography

Abbott, Andrew (1988), *The system of professions: An essay on the division of expert labor*, Chicago & London: Chicago University Press.

Abraham, John, (1995), *Science, politics, and the pharmaceutical industry*, London. UCL Press.

Abraham, John, (2010), Pharmaceuticalization of society in context: Theoretical, empirical, and health dimensions, *Sociology*, 44(4): 603–622.

Abraham, John & Davis, Courtney, (2009), Drug evaluation and the permissive principle: Continuities and contradictions between standards and practice in antidepressant regulation, *Social Studies of Science*, 39(4): 569–598.

Abraham, John & Reed, Tim, (2002), Progress, innovation and regulatory science in drug development: The politics of international standard-setting, *Social Studies of Science*, 32(3): 337–369.

Abraham, John and Sheppard, Julie, (1999), Complacent and conflicting scientific expertise in British and American drug regulation: Clinical risk assessment of Triozolam, *Social Studies of Science*, 29(6): 804–843.

Agamben, Giorgio, (1998), *Homo Sacer: Sovereign power and bare life*, Trans. by Daniel Heller-Roazen, Stanford: Stanford University Press.

Agamben, Georgio, (2009), *What is an apparatus? and other essays*, trans. by David Kishik and Stefan Pedatella, Stanford: Stanford University Press.

Almeling, Renee, (2007), Selling genes, selling gender: Egg agencies, sperm banks, and the medical market in genetic material, *American Sociological Review*, 73(3): 319–340.

Anderson, G. (2008), Mapping academic resistance in the managerial university, *Organization*, 15(2), 251–270.

Anderson, Warwick & Adams, Vicanne, (2008), Pramoedya's chicken: Postcolonial studies of technoscience, in Hackett, Edward J., Amsterdamska, Olga, Lynch, Michael & Wajcman, Judy, eds., (2008), *Handbook of science and technology studies*, 3rd. ed., Cambridge & London: MIT Press, pp.181–204.

Andrews, Lori & Nelkin, Dorothy, (2001), *Human bazaar: The market for human tissue in the biotechnology age*, New York: Crown.

Angell, Marcia, (2004). *The Truth about the Drug Companies*. New York: Random House.

Aristotle, (1986), *De Anima*, London: Penguin.

Aristotle, (1998), *Politics*, Indianapolis and Cambridge: Hackett.

Armitage, John, (1999), From modernism to hypermodernism and beyond: An interview with Paul Virilio, *Theory, Culture & Society*, 16(5–6): 25–55.

Arnoldi, Jakob, (2006), Frames and screens: The reduction of uncertainty in electronic derivatives trading, *Economy & Society*, 35(3): 381–399.

Åsberg, Cecilia and Johnson, Ericka, (2009), Viagra selfhood: Pharmaceutical advertising and the visual formation of Swedish masculinity, *Health Care Analysis*, 17(2): 144–159.

Ashcroft, Bill, Griffiths, Gareth & Tiffin, Helen, Eds., (1995), *The post-colonial studies reader*, London & New York: Routledge.

Atlan, H., (1974), On a formal definition of organization, *Journal of Theoretical Biology*, 45: 295–304.

Atkinson, Paul, Glasner, Peter & Lock, Margaret, (2009), Genetics and society: Perspectives from the twenty-first century, in Atkinson, Paul, Glasner, Peter & Lock, Margaret, eds., (2009), *Handbook of genetics and society: Mapping the new genomics era*, London & New York: Routledge, pp. 1–14.

Babkin, Michael & Mirskaya, Eelena Z., (2003), Science and totalitarianism: Lessons for the twenty-first century, in Walker, Mark, ed., (2003), *Science and ideology: A comparative history*, London & New York: Routledge, pp. 17–34.

Banerjee, Subhabrata Bobby, (2008), Necrocapitalism, *Organization Studies*, 29(12): 1541–1563.

Banerjee, Subhabrata Bobby & Linstead, Stephen, (2004), Masking subversion: Neocolonial embeddedness in anthropological accounts of indigenous management, *Human Relations*, 57(2): 221–247.

Barad, Karen, (2003), Posthumanist performativity: Towards an understanding of how matter comes to matter, *Signs: Journal of Women in Culture and Society*, 28(3): 801–831.

Barad, Karen, (2007), *Meeting the universe halfway; Quantum physics and the entanglement of matter and meaning*, Durham & London: Duke University Press.

Baradwaj, Aditja & Glasner, Peter, (2009*)*, *Local cells, global science: The rise of embryonic stem cell research in India*, London & New York. Routledge.

Barley, Steven R. & Bechky, Beth, (1994), In the backroom of science: The work of technicians in science labs, *Work and Occupations*, 21(1): 85–126.

Barry, Andrew, (2005), Pharmaceutical matters: The invention of informed materials, *Theory, Culture & Society*, 22(1): 51–69.

Beck, Melinda, (2008), Ova Time: Women Line Up to Donate Eggs––for Money. *Wall Street Journal*, Dec. 9, 2008.

Beck, Stefan, (2007), Medicalizing culture(s) or culturalizing medicine(s), in Burri, Regula Valérie & Dumit, Joseph, eds., (2007), *Biomedicine as culture: Instrumental practices, technoscientific knowledge, and new modes of life*, New York & London. Routledge, pp. 15–33.

Beijsterveld, Karin & Schulp, Marten, (2004), Breaking into a world of perfection: Innovation in today's classical musical instruments, *Social Studies of Science*, 34(5): 649–674.

Belfiore, Eleaonora, (2002), Art as a means of alleviating social exclusion: Does it really work? A critique of instrumental policies and social impact studies in the UK, *International Journal of Cultural Policy*, 8(1): 91–106.

Bennett, Jane, (2010), *Vibrant matter: A political ecology of things*, Durham & London: Duke University Press.

Bennis, W.G. and O'Toole, J., (2005), How business schools lost their way, *Harvard Business Review*, 83(5): 33–53.

Bensaude-Vincent, Bernadette, (2007), Nanobots and nanotubes: Two alternative biomimetic paradigms of nanotechnology, in Riskin, Jessica, ed., (2007), *Genesis redux: Essays in the history and philosophy of artificial life*, Chicago & London: University of Chicago Press, pp. 211–236.

Bensaude-Vincent, Bernadette & Stengers, Isabelle, ([1993]1996), *A history of chemistry*, trans. by Deborah van Dam, Cambridge & London: Harvard University Press.

Bercovitz, J. & Feldman, M., (2008), Academic entrepreneurs: Organizational change at the individual level, *Organization Science*, 19(1), 69–89.

Bergson, H., (1998), *Creative evolution*, Mineola: Dover.

Berle, Adolf A. & Means, Gardiner C., (1991), *The Modern Corporation & Private Property*, 2ⁿᵈ ed., New Brunswick. Transaction Publishers.

Bernard, Claude, ([1865]1957), *An introduction to the study of experimental medicine*, Trans. by Henry Copley Greene, New York: Dover

Berube, David M., (2006), *Nano-hype: The truth behind the nanotechnology buzz*, New York: Promotheus Books.

Beunza, Daniel & Stark, David, (2004), Tools of the trade: The socio-technology of arbitrage in a Wall Street trading room, *Industrial and Corporate Change*, 13(2): 369–400.

Bhabha, Homi K., (1994), *The location of culture*, London & New York: Routledge.

Blech, Jörg (2006), *Inventing disease and pushing pills: Pharmaceutical companies and the medicalization of normal life*, Trans. by Gisela Wallor Hajjar, London & New York: Routledge.

Blum, Virginia L., (2005), *Flesh wounds: The culture of cosmetic surgery*, Berkeley: University of California Press.

Blumenberg, Hans, (1993), Light as a metaphor for truth: At the preliminary stage of philosophical concept formation, in Levin, David Michael, ed., (1993), *Modernity and the hegemony of vision*, Berkeley, Los Angeles, & London: University of California Press, pp 30–62.

Boardman, P. Craig & Corley, Elizabeth A., (2008), University research centers and the composition of research collaborations, *Research Policy*, 37: 900–913.

Boardman, Craig & Ponomariov, Branco L., (2007), Reward systems and NSF university research centers: The impact of tenure on university scientists' valuation of applied and commercially relevant research, *Journal of Higher Education*, 78(1): 51–70.

Bok, Derek, (2002), *Universities in the marketplace: The commercialization of higher education*, Princeton: Princeton University Press.

Bozeman, Barry & Boardman, Craig, (2004), The NSF engineering research centers and the university-industry research revaluation: A brief history featuring an interview with Erich Bloch, *Journal of Technology Transfer*, 29: 365–375.

Braidotti, Rosi, (1994), *Nomadic subjects: Embodiment and sexual difference in contemporary feminist theory*, New York: Columbia University Press.

Braidotti, Rosi, (2006), *Transpositions: On nomadic ethics*, Cambridge & Malden: Polity Press.

Braidotti, Rosi, (2008), In spite of the times: The postsecular turn in feminism, *Theory, Culture & Society*, 25(6): 1–24.

Braithwaite, John, (1984), *Corporate crime in pharmaceutical industry*, London: Routledge & Kegan Paul.

Brink, Johan, McKelvey, Maureen & Smith, Keith, (2004), Conceptualizing and measuring modern biotechnology, in McKelvey, Maureen, Rickne, Annika & Laage-Hellman, Jens, eds., (2004), *The economic dynamics of modern biotechnology*, Cheltenham Northampton: Edward Elgar, pp. 20–40.

Brint, Steven, (1994), *In the age of experts: The changing role of professionals in politics and public life*, Princeton; Princeton University Press.

Broadhurst, S., (1999), The (im)mediate body: A transvaluation of corporeality, *Body & Society*, 5(1): 17–29.

Brody, Howard, (2007), *Hooked: Ethics, the medical profession, and the pharmaceutical industry*, Lanham: Rowman & Littlefield.

Brooks, Abigail, (2004), 'Under the knife and proud of it': An analysis of the normalization of cosmetic surgery, *Critical Sociology*, 30(2): 207–239.

Brown, Nik & Kraft, Alison, (2006), Blood ties: Banking the stem cell promise, *Technology Analysis & Strategic Management*, 18(3): 313–327.

Bud, Robert, (1983), *The uses of life: A history of biotechnology*, Cambridge: Cambridge University Press.

Burbeck, S & Jordan, K.E., (2006), An assessment of the role of computing in systems biology, *IBM Journal of Research & Development*, 50(6): 529–543.

Busfield, Joan, (2006), Pills, power, people. Sociological understandings of the pharmaceutical industry, *Sociology*, 40(2): 297–314.

Butler, J., (1993), *Bodies that matter*, London & New York: Routledge.

Butler, Judith, (1999), *Gender trouble: Feminism and the subversion of identity*, London: Routledge

Bynum, W.E., (1994), *Science and the practice of medicine in the nineteenth century*, Cambridge: Cambridge University Press.

Calvert, Jane, (2007), Patenting genomic objects: Genes, genomes, function and information, *Science as Culture*, 16(2): 207–223.

Cambrosio, Alberto, Keating, Peter & Mogoutov, Andrei, (2004), Mapping collaborative work and innovation in bioscience: A computer-assisted analysis of antibody reagent workshops, *Social Studies of Science*, 34(3): 325364.

Cambrosio, Alberto, Keating, Peter, Schlich, Thomas and Weisz, George, (2006), Regulatory objectivity and the generation and management of evidence in medicine, *Social Science & Medicine*, 63(1): 189–199.

Campbell, Al, (2005), The birth of neoliberalism in the United States: A reorganization of capitalism, in Saad-Filho, Alfredo and Johnston, Deborah, eds., (2005), *Neoliberalism: A critical reader*, London & Ann Arbor: Pluto, pp. 187–198.

Canguilhem, Georges, (1991), *The normal and the pathological*, New York: Zone Books.

Canguilhem, Georges, (1992), Machine and organism, in Crary, Jonathan & Kwinter, Sanford, eds., (1992), *Incorporations*, New York: Zone Books, pp. 45–69.

Canguilhem, Georges, (2008), *Knowledge of life*, Trans. by Stefano Geroulanos & Daniela Ginsburg, New York: Fordham University Press.

Carlson, Robert H., (2010), *Biology is technology: The promise, peril and new business of engineering life*, Cambridge & London: Harvard University Press.

Carolan, Michael S., (2010), The mutability of biotechnology patents: From unwieldly products of nature to independent 'object/s,' *Theory, Culture & Society*, 27(1): 110–129.

Carroll, William K. & Carson, Collin, (2006), Neoliberalism, capitalist class formation and the global network of corporation and policy groups, in Plehwe, Dieter, Walpen, Bernhard & Neunhöffer, Gisela, eds., (2006), *Neoliberal hegemony: A global critique*, New York & London: Routledge, pp. 51–69.

Carruthers, Bruce G. & Stinchcombe, Arthur L., (1999), The social structure of liquidity flexibility, markets and states, *Theory and Society*, 28: 353–382.

Cartwright, Lisa, (1995), *Screening the body: Tracing medicine's visual culture*, Minneapolis & London: University of Minnesota Press.

Casper, Steven, (2000), Institutional adaptiveness, technological policy, and the diffusion of new business models: The case of German biotechnology, *Organization Studies*, 21(5): 887–914.

Castle, Gregory, Ed., (2001), *Postcolonial discourses: An anthology*, Oxford: Blackwell.

Césaire, Aimé, (1950), *Discourse on colonialism*, Trans. by Joan Pinkham, New York: Monthly Review Press.

Chandler, Alfred D., (1977), *The Visible hand: The managerial revolution in American business*, Cambridge: Harvard University Press.

Chandler, Alfred D., (2005), *Shaping the industrial century: The remarkable story of the evolution of the modern chemical and pharmaceutical industries*, Cambridge and London: Harvard University Press.

Chapkis, Wendy, (1997), *Live sex acts: Women performing erotic labor*, New York & London: Routledge.

Cherry, Mark J., (2005), *Kidney for sale by owner: Transplantation and the market*, Washington, D.C.: Georgetown University Press.

Choi, Hyungsub & Mody, Cyrus C.M., (2009), The long history of molecular electronics: Microelectronics origins of nanotechnology, *Social Studies of Science*, 39(1): 11–50.

Chorev, Nitsan and Babb, Sarah, (2009), The crisis of neoliberalism and the future of international institutions; A comparison of the IMF and the WTO, *Theory and Society*, 38: 459–484.

Chwieroth, Jeffrey M., (2010), *Capital ideas: The IMF and the rise of financial liberalization*, Princeton & Oxford: Princeton University Press.

Clarke, Adele, (1990), Controversy and the development of reproductive sciences, *Social Problems*, 37(1): 18–27.

Clarke, Adele E., (1998), *Disciplining reproduction: Modernity, American life sciences, and the problem of sex*, Berkeley: University of California Press.

Clarke, Adele E., Mamo, Laura, Fishman, Jennifer R., Shim, Janet K. & Fosket, Jennifer Ruth, (2003), Biomedicalization. Technoscientific transformations of health, illness, and U.S. biomedicine, *American Sociological Review*, 68: 161–194.

Clarke, Adele E, Shim, Janet, Shostak, Sara & Nelson, Alondra, (2009), Biomedicalizing genetic health, diseases and identities, in Atkinson, Paul, Glasner, Peter & Lock, Margaret, eds., (2009), *Handbook of genetics and society: Mapping the new genomics era*, London & New York: Routledge, pp. 21–40.

Clarke, Simon, (2005), The neoliberal theory of society, in Saad-Filho, Alfredo and Johnston, Deborah, eds., (2005), *Neoliberalism: A critical reader*, London & Ann Arbor: Pluto, pp. 50–59.

Cohen, Margot and Athavaley, Anjali, (2009), A search for a surrogate leads to India, *Wall Street Journal*, Oct. 8, 2009.

Collins, Harry & Pinch, Trevor, (2005), *Dr. Golem: How to think about medicine*, Chicago & London: University of Chicago Press.

Conrad, Peter, (2007), *The medicalization of society*: Baltimore. Johns Hopkins University Press.

Conrad, P.O. & Potter, D., (2000), From hyperactive children to ADHD adults: Observations on the expansion of medical categories, *Social Problems*, 47: 559–582.

Cooke, Bill, (2003), The denial of slavery in management studies, *Journal of Management Studies*, 40(8): 1895–1918.

Cooper, David J. & Robson, Keith, (2006), Accounting, professions, and regulations: Locating the sites of professionalization, *Accounting, Organization and Society*, 31: 415–444.

Cooper, Melinda, (2008), *Life As surplus: Biotechnology and capitalism in the neoliberal era*, Seattle & London: University of Washington Press.

Coriat, Benjamin, Orsi, Fabienne & Weinstein, Oliver, (2003), Does biotech reflect a new science-based innovation regime? *Industry and Innovation*, 10(3): 231–253.

Costea, A., Crump. N. & Amiridis, K., (2008), Managerialism, the therapeutic habitus and the self in contemporary organizing, *Human Relations*, 61(5): 661–685.

Crenshaw, Kimberle Williams, (1994), Mapping the margins: Intersectionality, identity politics, and violence against women of color. in Fineman, Martha Albertson & Mykitiuk, Rixanne, eds., (1994), *The public nature of private violence*, New York: Routledge, pp. 93–118.

Croissant, Jennifer L. & Smith-Doerr, Laurel, (2008), Organizational contexts of science: Boundaries and relationships between university and industry, in Hackett, Edward J., Amsterdamska, Olga, Lynch, Michael & Wajcman, Judy, eds., (2008), *Handbook of science and technology studies*, 3rd. ed., Cambridge & London: MIT Press, pp. 691–718.

Crozier, M., (1964), *The bureaucratic phenomena*, Chicago: University of Chicago Press.

Cussins, Charis, (1996), Ontological choreography: Agency through objectification in infertility clinics, *Social Studies of Science*, 26: 575–610.

Cussins, Charis, (1998), Reproducing reproduction: Techniques of normalization and naturalization in infertility clinics, in Franklin, Sarah & Ragoné, Helena, eds., (1998), *Reproducing reproduction: Kinship, power, and technological innovation*, Philadelphia: University of Pennsylvania Press, pp. 86–101.

Daemmrich, Arthur, (1998), The evidence does not speak for itself: Expert witnesses and the organization of DNA-typing companies, *Social Studies of Science*, 28: 741–772.

Dahlander, Linus & McKelbey, Maureen, (2005), The occurrence and spatial distribution of collaboration: Biotech firms in Gothenburg, Sweden, *Technology Analysis & Strategic Management*, 17(4): 409–431.

Dallery, Aileen B., (1989), The politics of writing (the) body: *Écriture féminine*, in Jaggar, Alison M. & Bordo Susan R., eds., (1989), *Gender/body/knowledge: Feminist reconstructions of being and knowing*, New Brunswick & London: Rutgers University Press, pp. 52–67.

Das, Veena, (2000), The practice of organ transplants: Networks, documents, translations, in Lock, Margaret, Youg, Allan & Cambrosio, Alberto, eds., (2000), *Living and working with new medical technologies: Intersections of inquiry,* Cambridge: Cambridge University Press, pp. 263–287.

Daston, Loraine & Galison, Peter, (2007), *Objectivity*, New York: Zone Books.

Davis, Gerald F., (2009a), The rise and fall of finance and the end of the society of organizations, *Academy of Management Perspectives*, 23(3): 27–44.

Davis, Gerald, (2009b), *Managed by the markets: How finance reshaped America*, New York & Oxford: Oxford University Press.

Davis, Mike and Monk, Daniel Bertrand (2007), Introduction, in Davis, Mike and Monk, Daniel Bertrand, eds., (2007), *Evil paradises: Dreamworlds of neoliberalism*, New York & London: New Press, pp. ix–xvi.

Deetz, S.A., (1992), *Democracy in an age of corporate colonialization*, Albany: State University of New York Press.

DeGrandpre, Richard, (2006), *The Cult of pharmacology: How America became the world's most troubled drug culture*, Durham: Duke University Press.

Der Derian, James, Ed., (1998), *The Virilio reader*, Oxford: Blackwell.

Desrosière, Alain, (1998), *The politics of large numbers: A history of statistical reasoning*, Trans. by Camille Naish, Boston & London: Harvard University Press.

Dickenson, Donna, (2008), *Body shopping: The economy fuelled by flesh and blood*, Oxford: Oneworld.

Dore, Ronald, (2008), Financialization of the global economy, *Industrial and Corporate Change*, 17(6); 1097–1112.

Dougherty, Deborah, (2007), Trapped in the 20th century? Why models of organizational learning, knowledge and capabilities do not fit bio-pharmaceuticals, and what to do about that, *Management Learning*, 38(3): 265–270.

Drennan, Katherine, (2002), Patient recruitment: The costly and growing bottleneck in drug development, *Drug Discovery Today*, 7(3): 167–170.

Drews, Jürgen, (2000), Drug discovery: A historical perspective, *Science*, 287: 1960–1964.

Duhem, Pierre, (1996), *Essays in the history and philosophy of science*, Translated and edited by Roger Ariew & Peter Barker, Indianapolis & Cambridge: Hackett Publishing.

Duménil, Gérard & Lévy, Dominique (2004), *Capital resurgent: Roots of the neoliberal revolution*, Trans. by Derek Jeffer, Cambridge: Harvard University Press.

Dumit, Joseph, (2004), *Picturing personhood: Brain scans and biomedical identity*, Princeton: Princeton University Press.

Dumochel, Paul, (1995), Gilbert Simondon's plea for a philosophy of technology, in Feenberg, Andrew & Hannay, Alastair, eds., (1995), *The politics of knowledge*, Bloomington & Indianapolis: Indiana University Press, pp. 255–271.

Dunn, Mary R. & Jones, Candace, (2010), Institutional logics and institutional pluralism: The contestation of care and science logics in medical education, 1967–2005, *Administrative Science Quarterly*, 55: 114–149.

Durand, Rudolphe, Bruyaka, Olga & Mangematin, Vincent, (2008), Do science and money go together? The case of the French biotech industry, *Strategic Management Journal*, 29: 1281–1299.

Ellul, Jacques, (1964), *The technological society*, New York: Vintage.

Engelen, E., (2002), Corporate governance property and democracy: A conceptual critique of shareholder ideology, *Economy & Society*, 31(3): 391–413.

Enriques, J. & Goldberg, R.A., (2000), Transforming life, transforming business: The life-science revolution, *Harvard Business Review*, 78(2): 94–104.

Epstein, Steven, (1996), *Impure science: AIDS, activism, and the politics of science*, Berkeley: University of California Press.

Ericson, Richard, Barry, Dean & Doyle, Aaron, (2000), The moral hazard of neoliberalism: Lessons from the private insurance industry, *Economy & Society*, 29(4): 532–558.

Esposito, Roberto, (2008), *Bíos: Biopolitics and philosophy*, Trans. by Timothy Campbell, Minneapolis & London: University of Minnesota Press.

Etzkowitz, H., (1998), The norms of entrepreneurial science: Cognitive effects of the new industry-university linkages, *Research Policy*, 27: 823–833.

Etzkowitz, H., (2003), Research groups as 'quasi-firms': The invention of the entrepreneurial university, *Research Policy*, 32: 109–121.

Ezzamel, Mahmoud, Willmott, Hugh & Worthington, Frank, (2008), Manufacturing shareholder value: The role of accounting in organizational transformation, *Accounting, Organizations and Society*, 33: 107–140.

Fama, Eugen F., (1970), Efficient capital markets: A review of theory and empirical work, *Journal of Finance*, 25(2): 383–417.

Fang, Tony, (2010), Asian management research needs more self-confidence. Reflections on Hofstede (2007) and beyond, *Asia Pacific Journal of Management*, 27(1): 155–170.

Fanon, Frantz, (1963), *The wretched of the earth*, London: Penguin.

Fanon, F., (1986), *Black skin, white masks*, London: Pluto Press.

Figueroa, Robert & Harding, Sandra, Eds., (2003), *Science and other cultures. Issues in philosophies of sciences and technology*, London & New York: Routledge.

Fischer, Claude S., (1992), *America calling: A social history of the telephone to 1940*, Berkeley and Los Angeles: University of California Press.

Fischer, Jill, (2009), *Medical research for hire: The political economy of pharmaceutical clinical trials*, New Brunswick: Rutgers University Press.

Fishman, Jennifer R., (2004), Manufacturing desire. The commodification of female sexual dysfunction, *Social Studies of Science*, 34(2): 187–218.

Fligstein, Neil, (2001), *The architecture of markets*, Princeton: Princeton University Press.

Fligstein, Neil & Dauter, Luke, (2007), The sociology of markets, *Annual Review of Sociology*, 33: 105–128.

Foucault, Michel, (1972), *An archaeology of knowledge*, London: Routledge.

Foucault, M., (1973), *The birth of the clinic*, Routledge, London.

Foucault, Michel, (1977), *Discipline and punish*, New York: Pantheon.

Foucault, M., (1990), *The history of sexuality, Vol. 3: The care of the self*, London: Penguin.

Foucault, Michel, (2003), *Society must be defended: Lectures at the Colllège de France, 1975–1976*, ed. by Mauro Bertaini and Allessandro Fonatana, trans. by David Macey, London: Penguin.

Foucault, Michel, (2007), *Security, territory, population: Lectures at the Colleège de France, 1977–1978*, Trans. by Graham Burchill, Basingstoke & New York: Palgrave.

Fourcade, Marion, (2006), The construction of a global profession: The transnationalization of economics, *American Journal of Sociology*, 112: 145–194.

Fourcade, Marion, (2009), *Economists and societies: Discipline and profession in the United States, Britain, and France, 1890s to 1990s*, Princeton & London: Princeton University Press.

Frandsen, A.-C., (2009), From psoriasis to a number and back, *Information and Organization*, 19(2): 103–128.

Frank, Thomas, (2008), Rent-a-womb is where market logic leads, *Wall Street Journal*, Dec. 10, 2008.

Franklin, Sarah, (1998), Making miracles: Scientific progress and the facts of life, in Franklin, Sarah & Ragoné, Helena, eds., (1998), *Reproducing reproduction: Kinship, power, and technological innovation*, Philadelphia: University of Pennsylvania Press, pp. 102–117.

Franklin, Sarah, (2001), Culturing biology: Cell lines for the second millennium, *Health*, 5(3): 335–354.

Franklin, Sarah, (2005), Stem cells R us: Emergent life forms and the global biological, In Ong, Aihwa & Collier, Stephen J., eds., (2008), *Global assemblages: Technology, politics, and ethics as anthropological problems*, Malden & Oxford: Blackwell, pp. 59–78.

Franklin Sarah, (2007), *Dolly mixtures: The remaking of genealogy*, Durham: Duke University Press.

Franklin, Sarah & Lock, Margaret, (2001), Animation and cessation: the remaking of life and death, in Franklin, Sarah & Lock, Margaret (eds), (2003), *Remaking Life and Death: Towards an Anthropology of the Biosciences*, Santa Fe: School of American Research Press, pp. 3–22

Franklin, Sarah & Roberts, Celia, (2006), *Born and made: An ethnography of preimplantation genetic diagnosis*, Princeton & London: Princeton University Press.

Fraser, Miriam, Kember, Sarah & Lury, Celia, (2005), Inventive life. Approaches to a new vitalism, *Theory, Culture & Society*, 22(1): 1–14.

Fraser, Suzanne, (2003), *Cosmetic surgery: Gender and culture*, New York: Palgrave.

Freese, Jeremy, (2009), Genetics and the social science explanation of individual outcomes, *American Journal of Sociology*, 114(S): S1-S35.

Freidson, E., (2001), *Professionalism: The third logic*, Chicago: University of Chicago Press.

Friedman, Milton, ([1962]2002), *Capitalism and freedom*, 4th ed., Chicago & London: University of Chicago Press.

Fuchs, Stephan, (1992), *The professional quest for truth: A social theory of science and knowledge*, Albany: State University of New York Press.

Fujimura, Joan H., (1996), *Crafting science: A sociohistory of the quest for the genetics of cancer*, Cambridge: Harvard University Press.

Fujimura, Joan H., (2005), Postgenomic futures: Translating across the machine-nature border in systems biology, *New Genetics and Society*, 24(2): 195–225.

Galambos, L. and Sturchio, J., (1998), Pharmaceutical firms and the transition to biotechnology: A study in strategic innovation, *Business History Review*, 72(summer): 250–278.

Gammon, Earl, (2010), Nature as adversary: The rise of the modern economic conception of nature, *Economy & Society*, 39(2): 218–246.

Ganuza, Juan-José, Llobet, Gerard & Domínguez, Beatriz, (2009), R&D in the pharmaceutical industry: A world of small innovations, *Management Science*, 55(4): 539–551.

García, Baetriz, (2004), Urban regeneration, arts programming, and major events: Glasgow 1990, Sydney 2000, and Barcelona 2004, *International Journal of Cultural Policy*, 10(1): 103–118.

Garcia-Parapet, Marie-France, (2007), The social construction of a perfect match: The strawberry auction at Fontaines-en-Sologne, in Mackenzie, Donald A., Muniesa, Fabio & Siu, Lucia., eds., (2007), *Do economists make markets? On the performativity of economics*, Princeton & Oxford: Princeton University Press, pp. 20–53.

Garnier, J.-B., (2008), Rebuilding the R&D engine in big pharma, *Harvard Business Review*, 86: 68–76.

Gatens, Moira, (1996), *Imaginary bodies: Ethics, power, and corporeality*, London and New York: Routledge.

Gay, Peter, (1984), *The bourgeois experience: Victoria to Freud: Vol. 1: Education of the senses*, New York & Oxford: Oxford University Press.

Gilman, Sander L., (1999), *Making the body beautiful: A cultural history of aesthetic surgery*, Princeton: Princeton University Press.

Gimlin, Debra, (2000), Cosmetic surgery: beauty as commodity, *Qualitative Sociology*, 28(1): 77–98.

Gimlin, Debra, (2010), Imaging the Other in cosmetic surgery, *Body & Society*, 16: (4): 57–75.

Gitelman, Lisa, (1999), *Scripts, grooves, and writing machines. Representing technology in the Edison era*, Stanford: Stanford University Press.

Golan, Tal, (2004), The emergence of the silent witness: The legal and medical reception of X-ray in the USA, *Social Studies of Science*, 34: 469–499.

Goldman, Michael & Shurman, Rachel A., (2000), Closing the €great divide': New social theory on society and nature, *Annual Review of Sociology*, 26: 563–583.

Goldstein, Kurt, ([1934]1995), *The organism: A holistic approach to biology derived from pathological data in man*, New York: Zone Books.

Goslinga-Roy, Gillian, (2000), Body boundaries, fiction of the female self: An ethnography of power, feminism and the reproductive technologies, *Feminist Studies*, 26(1): 113–140.

Gottinger, Hans-Werner & Umali, Celia L. (2008), The evolution of the pharmaceutical-biotechnology industry, *Business History*, 50(5): 583–601.

Granovetter, M., (1985), Economic action and social structure, *American Journal of Sociology*, 91(3): 481–510.

Greene, Jeremy, (2004), Attention to details: Medicine, marketing, and the emergence of the pharmaceutical representative, *Social Studies of Science*, 34: 271–292.

Greene, Jeremy, (2007), *Prescribing by numbers: Drugs and the definition of disease*, Baltimore: Johns Hopkins University Press.

Griffin, Penny, (2009), *Gendering the World Bank: Neoliberalism and the gendered foundation of global governance*, New York: Palgrave.

Griffith, Paul E., (2001), Genetic information: A metaphor in search of a theory, *Philosophy of Science*, 68(3): 394–412.

Grosz, Elizabeth, (1994), *Volatile bodies: Toward a corporeal feminism*, Bloomington & Indianapolis: Indiana University Press.

Grosz, Elizabeth, (2004), *The nick of time: Politics, evolution and the untimely*, Durham: Duke University Press.

Grosz, Elizabeth, (2005), *Time travels: Feminism, nature, power*, Durham: Duke University Press.

Gunning, Tom, (1995), Tracing the individual body: Photography, detectives, and early cinema, in Carney, Leo & Schwartz, Vanessa R., eds., (1995), *Cinema and the invention of modern life*, Berkeley: University of California Press, pp. 15–45.

Habermas, J., (2003), *The future of human nature*, Cambridge: Polity Press.

Hacking I. (1990) *The taming of chance*, Cambridge: Cambridge University Press.

Hacking, Ian, (1998), Canguilhem amid the cyborgs, *Economy & Society*, 27(2&3): 202–216.

Hacking, Ian, (2002), *Historical ontology*, Cambridge: Harvard University Press.

Hacking, Ian (2006), Genetics, biosocial groups, and the future of identity, *Daedalus* (Fall): 81–96.

Hacking, Ian, (2007), Our neo-cartesian bodies in parts, *Critical Inquiry*, 34(autumn): 78–104.

Haigh, Elizabeth, (1984), *Xavier Bichat and the medical theory of the eighteenth century*, London: Wellcome Institute for the History of Medicine.

Halpern, Sydney A. (1992), Dynamics of professional control: Internal coalitions and crossprofessional boundaries, *American Journal of Sociology*, 97: 994–1021.

Hansen, Mark B.N, (2007), *Bodies in code: Interfaces with digital media*, Cambridge & London: MIT Press.

Hara, Takuji, (2003), *Innovation in the pharmaceutical industry: The process of drug discovery development*, Cheltenham & Northampton: Edward Elgar.

Haraway, Donna, (1989), *Primate visions: Gender, race, and nature in the modern world of science*, New York & London: Routledge.

Haraway, Donna J., (1991), *Semians, cyborgs, and women: The reinvention of nature*, London: Free Association Books.

Haraway, Donna, (1997), *Modest=Witness@Second=Milennium. FemaleMan©=Meets=OncoMouse™*, London: Routledge.

Harris, Henry, (1999), *The birth of the cell*, New Haven: Yale University Press.

Harvey, David, (2005), *A brief history of neoliberalism*, New York: Oxford University Press.

Harvey, David, (2010), *The enigma of capital and the crisis of capitalism*, London: Profile Books.

Harvey, Olivia, Popowski, Tamara & Sullivan, Carol, (2008), Individuation and feminism: A commentary on Gilbert Simondon's €The genesis of the individual,' *Australian Feminist Studies*, 23(55): 101–112.

Hayek, F.A., (1944), *The road to serfdom*, Chicago: University of Chicago Press.

Hayles, N. Katherine, (1999), *How we became posthuman: Virtual bodies in cybernetics, literature, and informatics*, Chicago & London: University of Chicago Press.

Hayles, N. Katherine, (2006), Unfinished work: From cyborg to cognisphere, *Theory, Culture and Society*, 23(7–8): 159–166.

Healy, David, (2004), Shaping the intimate: Influencing on the experience of everyday nerves, *Social Studies of Science*, 34: 219–245.

Healy, David, (2006), The new medical oikumene, in Petryna, Adriana, Lakoff, Andrew & Kleinman, Arthur, eds., (2006), *Global pharmaceuticals: Ethics, markets, practices*, Durham & London: Duke University Press, pp. 61–84.

Hedgecoe, Adam, (2006), Pharmacogenetics as alien science: Alzheimer's disease, core sets and expectations, *Social Studies of Science*, 36(5): 723–752.

Hedgecoe, Adam & Martin, Paul, (2003), The drug don't work: Expectations and the shaping of pharmacogenetics, *Social Studies of Science*, 33(3): 327–364.

Helmreich, Stefan, (2008), Species of biocapital, *Science as Culture*. 17(4): 463–478.

Heyes, Cressida J., (2009), Diagnosing culture: Body dysmorphic disorder and cosmetic surgery, *Body & Society*, 15(4): 73–93.

Hilgartner, S., (2000), *Science on stage*, Stanford: Stanford University Press.

Hindess, B., (1996), *The discourse on power: From Hobbes to Foucault*, Oxford: Blackwell.

Hirschauer, Stefan, (1991), The manufacture of human bodies in surgery, *Social Studies of Science*, 21(2): 279–319.

Hirschman, A.O., (1977), *The passions and the interests*, Princeton: Princeton University Press.

Ho, Karen, (2009), *Liquidated. An ethnography of Wall Street*, Durham & London: Duke University Press.

Hoeyer, Klaus, Nexoe, Sniff, Hartlev, Mette & Koch, Lene, (2009), Embryonic entitlements: Stem cell patenting and the co-production of commodities and personhood, *Body & Society*, 15(1): 1–24.

Hogle, Linda, (1995), Standardization across non-standard domains: The case of organ procurement, *Science, Technology & Human Values*, 20(4): 480–500.

Hogle, Linda F., (2005), Enhancement technologies of the body, *Annual Review of Anthropology*, 34: 695–716.

Hogle, Linda F., (2009), Pragmatic objectivity and the standardization of engineered tissues, *Social Studies of Science*, 39: 717–742.

Holmqvist, M., (2009), Corporate social responsibility as corporate social control. The case of work-site health promotion, *Scandinavian Journal of Management*, 25: 68–72.

Hopkins, Michael M., Martin, Paul A., Nightingale, Paul, Kraft, Alison & Mahdi, Surya, (2007), The myth of a biotech revolution: An assessment of technological, clinical and organizational change, *Research Policy*, 36(4): 566–589.

Hughes, Thomas P., (1983), *Networks of power: Electrification in Western society, 1880–1930*, Baltimore: Johns Hopkins University Press.

Hughes, Thomas P., (1999), The evolution of large technological systems, in Biagioli, Mario, ed., (1999), *The science studies reader*, London & New York: Routledge, pp. 202–223.

Hull, Richard, (2006), The great lie: Markets, freedom and knowledge, in Plehwe, Dieter, Walpen, Bernhard & Neunhöffer, Gisela, eds., (2006), *Neoliberal hegemony: A global critique*, New York & London: Routledge, pp. 141–155.

Hummel, R.P., (2006), The triumph of numbers: Knowledges and the mismeasurement of management, *Administration and Society*, 38(1): 58–78.

Ikemoto, Lisa C., (2009), Eggs as capital: Human egg procurement in the fertility industry and the stem cell research enterprise, *Signs*, 34(4):763–781.

Ingold, Tim, (1986), *Evolution and social life*, Cambridge: Cambridge University Press.

Israel, Paul, (1992), *From machine shop to industrial laboratory: Telegraphy and the changing context of American innovation, 1830–1920*, Baltimore & London: Johns Hopkins University Press.

Janssens, Maddy & Zanoni, Patrizia, (2005), Many diversities for many services. Theorizing diversity (management) in service companies, *Human Relations*, 58(3): 311–340.

Jasanoff, Sheila, Ed., (2004), Science and ideology, London & New York: Routledge.

Jasanoff, Sheila, (2005), The idiom of co-production, in Jasanoff, Sheila, ed., (2005), *States of knowledge: The co-production of science and social order*, London & New York: Routledge, pp. 1–12.

Jeacle, Ingrid, (2003), Accounting and the construction of the standard body, *Accounting, Organization and Society*, 28: 357–377.

Jones, Meredith, (2008), *Skintight: An anatomy of cosmetic surgery*, Oxford & New York: Berg.

Jones, Richard A.L., (2004), *Soft machines: Nanotechnology and life*, Oxford & New York: Oxford University Press.

Jong, Simcha, (2006), How organizational structures in science shape spin-off firms: The biochemistry departments of Berkeley, Stanford, and UCSF an the birth of biotech industry, *Industrial and Corporate Change*, 15(2): 251–283.

Jonvallen, Petra, (2006), *Testing pills, enacting obesity: The work of localizing tools in a clinical trial*, Ph.D., thesis, Department of Technical and Social Change, Linköping University.

Jordanova, Ludmilla, (1989), *Sexual visions: Images of gender in science and medicine between the eighteenth and twentieth centuries*, London: Harvester Wheatsheaf.

Kahn, Jonathan, (2008), Exploiting race in new drug development; BiDil's interm model of pharmacogenomics, *Social Studies of Science*,38(5): 737–758.

Kalleberg, Arne L., (2009), Precarious work, insecure workers: Employment realtions in transtion, *American Sociological Review*, 74: 1–22.

Kant, I., ([1790]2005), *Critique of judgment*, Trans. by J.H. Bernard, Mineola: Dover.

Kaplan, Edward H., Hershlag, Ayner & DeChercerney, Alan H., (1992), To be or not to be? *That* is conceptions! Managing in vitro fertilization programs, *Management Science*, 38(9): 1217–1229.

Kaufert, Patricia A., (2000), Screening the body: The pap smear and the mammogram, in Lock, Margaret, Youg, Allan & Cambrosio, Alberto, eds., (2000), *Living and working with new medical technologies: Intersections of inquiry*, Cambridge: Cambridge University Press, pp. 165–183.

Kay, Lily E., (2000), *Who wrote the book of life? A history of the genetic code*, Stanford & London: Stanford University Press.

Keller, Evelyn Fox, (1983), *A feeling for the organism: The life and work of Barbara McClintock*, New York & San Francisco: W.H. Freeman.

Keller, Evelyn Fox., (2000), *The century of the gene*, Cambridge & London: Harvard University Press.

Kent, Julie, Faulkner, Alex, Geesink, Ingrid & Fitzpatrick, David, (2006), Culturing cells, reproducing and regulating the self, *Body & Society*, 12(2): 1–23.

Kevles, Bettyann, (1997), *Naked to the bone: Medical imaging in the twentieth century*, New Brunswick: Rutgers University Press.

Kevles, Daniel J., (2002), Of mice and money: The story of the world's first animal patent, *Daedalus*, 131(2): 78–88.

Khurana, Rakesh, (2007), *From higher aims to hired hands: The social transformation of American business schools and the unfulfilled promise of management as a profession*, Princeton: Princeton University Press.

Knorr Cetina, Karin D., (1981), *The manufacture of knowledge: An essay on the constructivist and contextual nature of science*, Oxford: Pergamon Press.

Kohler, Robert, (1994), *Lords of the fly: Drosophila genetics and experience of life*, Chicago & London: University of Chicago Press.

Kollmeyer, Christopher, (2009), Explaining deindustrialization: How affluence, productivity growth, and globalization diminish manufacturing employment, *American Journal of Sociology*, 114(6): 1644–1674.

Konrad, Alison M., Prasad, Pushkala & Pringle, Judith K., eds., (2006), *Handbook of workplace diversity*, Thousand Oaks, CA, London & New Delhi: Sage.

Konrad, Monica, (2004), *Narrating the new predictive genetics: Ethics, ethnography and science*, Cambridge & New York: Cambridge University Press.

Koolhaas, Rem, (2002), Junkspace, *October*, 175–190.

Koyré, Alexandre, (1959), *From the closed world to the infinite universe*, New York: Harper Torchbooks.

Koyré, Alexandre, (1968/1992), *Metaphysics and measurement*, Reading: Gordon and Breach Science Publishers.

Kramer, Lawrence, (1995), *Classical music and postmodern knowledge*, Berkeley, Los Angeles & London: University of California Press.

Kuhn, Timothy, (2009), Positioning lawyers: Discursive resources, professional ethics and identification, *Organization*, 16(5): 681–704.

Lakoff, Andrew, (2006), *Pharmaceutical reason: Knowledge and value in global psychiatry*, Cambridge: Cambridge University Press.

Lakoff, Andrew, (2008), The right patients for the drug: Pharmaceutical circuits and the codification of illness, in Hackett, Edward J., Amsterdamska, Olga, Lynch, Michael & Wajcman, Judy, eds., (2008), *Handbook of science and technology studies*, 3rd. ed., Cambridge & London: MIT Press, pp. 741–760.

Lampland, Martha and Star, Susan Leigh, eds., (2009), *Standards and their stories: How quantifying, classifying, and formalizing practices shape everyday life*, Ithaca & London: Cornell University Press

Landecker, Hannah, (2007), *Culturing life: How cells became technologies*, Cambridge: Harvard University Press.

Lash, Scott, (2006), Life (vitalism), *Theory, Culture & Society*, 23(2–3): 323–329.

Latour, Bruno, (1988), *The pasteurization of France*, Trans. by Alan Sheridan & John Law, Cambridge & London: Harvard University Press.

LeBreton, David, (2004), Genetic fundamentalism and the cult of the gene, *Body & Society*, 10(4): 1–20.

Leicht, Kevin T. & Fennell, Mary L., (2001), *Professional work: A sociological approach*, Malden & Oxford: Blackwell.

Lemke, Thomas, (2001), The birth of biopolitics; Michel Foucault's lecture at the Collège de France: On neo-liberal governmentality, *Economy & Society*, 30(2): 190–207.

Lemke, Thomas, (2011), *Biopolitics: An advanced introduction*, New York: New York University Press.

Lenoir, Timothy, (2007), Techno-humanism: Requiem for the cyborg, in Riskin, Jessica, ed., (2007), *Genesis redux: Essays in the history and philosophy of artificial life*, Chicago & London: University of Chicago Press, pp. 196–220.

Lépinay, Vincent-Antonin, (2007), Decoding finance: Articulation and liquidity around a trading room, in Mackenzie, Donald A., Muniesa, Fabio & Siu, Lucia., eds., (2007), *Do economists make markets? On the performativity of economics*, Princeton & Oxford: Princeton University Press, pp. 87–127.

Leroi-Gourhan, André, (1983/1989), *The hunters of prehistory*, Trans. by Claire Jacobson, New York: Atheneum.

Leslie, Myles, (2001), Quality assured science: Managerialism in forensic biology, *Science, Technology & Human Values*, 35(2): 283–306.

Lewontin, Richard, (2000), *The triple helix: Genes, organism, environment*. Cambridge: Harvard University Press.

Lexchin, Joel, (2006), The pharmaceutical industry and the pursuit of profit, in Cohen, Jillian Clare, Illingworth, Patricia & Schüklenk, Udo, eds., (2006), *The power of pill: Social, ethical and legal issues in drugs development, marketing, pricing,* London & Ann Arbor: Pluto, pp.11–24.

Liker, Jeffrey K. (2004), *The Toyota way: 14 management principles from the world's greatest manufacturer,* Cambridge: Harvard Business School Press.

Lock, Margaret, (2001), The alienation of body tissues and the biopolitics of immortalized cell lines, *Body & Society,* 7(2–3): 63–91.

Lock, Margaret, (2002), *Twice dead: Organ transplants and the reinvention of death,* Berkeley, Los Angeles & London: University of California Press.

Lock, Margaret, (2007), The future is now. Locating biomarkers for dementia, in Burri, Regula Valérie & Dumit, Joseph, eds., (2007), *Biomedicine as culture: Instrumental practices, technoscientific knowledge, and new modes of life,* New York & London. Routledge, pp. 61–85.

Longino, Helen E., (1992), Knowledge, bodies, and values: Reproductive technologies and their strategic context, Inquiry 35(3/4): 323–340.

Louis, K.S., Blumenthal, D., Gluck, M.E. & Stoto, M.A., (1989), Entrepreneurs in academe: An exploration of behaviour among life scientists, *Administrative Science Quarterly,* 34(1), 110–131.

Lounsbury, M., (2001), Institutional sources of practice variation: Staffing university and college recycling programs, *Administrative Science Quarterly,* 46: 29–56.

Löwy, Ilana, (2011), Historiography of biomedicine: €Bio,' €medicine' and in between, *Isis,* 102(1): 116–122.

Lynch, Michael, (1988), The externalised retina: Selection and mathematization in the visual documentation of objects in the life sciences, in Lynch, Michael & Woolgar, Steve, eds., (1990), *Representation in scientific practice,* Cambridge & London: MIT Press, pp. 153–186.

Lyon, Alexander, (2007), Putting patients first: Systematically distorted communication and Merck's marketing of Vioxx, *Journal of Applied Communication Research,* 35: 376–398.

Lyotard, J.-F. (1988), *The differend,* Minneapolis: University of Minnesota Press.

Lucretius, (2001), *On the nature of things,* Indianapolis: Hackett.

MacKenzie, Donald, (2006), *An engine, not a camera: How financial models shape markets,* Cambridge & London: MIT Press.

MacKenzie, Donald (2009), *Material markets: How economic agents are constructed,* Oxford & New York: Oxford University Press.

MacKenzie, Donald. & Millo, Yuval, (2003), Constructing a market: Performing a theory: A historical sociology of a financial market derivatives exchange, *American Journal of Sociology,* 109(1): 107–145.

MacKenzie, Donald A., Muniesa, Fabio & Siu, Lucia, eds., (2007), *Do economists make markets? On the performativity of economics,* Princeton & Oxford: Princeton University Press.

Mamo, Laura & Fishman, Jennifer R., (2001), Potency in all the right places: Viagra as a technology of the gendered body, *Body & Society,* 7(4): 13–37.

Manning, Erin, (2010), Always more than one: The collectivity of a life, *Body & Society,* 16(1): 117–127.

Manovich, Lev (2001), *The language of new media,* Cambridge & London: MIT Press.

Markens, Susan, (2007), *Surrogate motherhood and the politics of reproduction,* Berkeley, Los Angeles & London: University of California Press.

Marks, John, (2006), Biopolitics, *Theory, Culture and Society,* 23(2–3): 333–335.

Marshall, Barbara L, (2009), Sexual medicine, sexual bodies and the pharmaceutical imagination, *Science as Culture.* 18(2): 133–149.

Matthews, J. Rosser, (1995), *Quantification and the quest for medical certainty*, Princeton: Princeton University Press.

Mauss, M., (1954), *The Gift: Forms and Functions of Exchanges in Archaic Societies*, Routledge and Kegan Paul, London.

Mazzucati, Mariana & Dose, Giovanni, eds., *Knowledge accumulation and industry evolution: The case of pharma-biotech*, Cambridge: Cambridge University Press, pp. 73–111.

McAfee, Kathleen, (2003), Neoliberalisms on the molecular scale. Economic and genetic reductionism in the biotechnology battles, *Geoforum*, 34(2): 203–219.

McClary, Susan, (1987), Talking politics during the Bach year, in Leppert, Richard & McClary, Susan, eds., (1987), *Music and society: The politics of composition, performance and reception*, Cambridge; Cambridge University Press, pp. 13–62.

McCloskey, D.N., (1986), *The rhetorics of economics*, Brighton: Wheatsheaf.

McNair, Brian, (2002) *Striptease culture,* London & New York: Routledge.

McNay, Lois, (2009), Self as enterprise: Dilemmas of control and resistance in Foucault's 'The birth of biopolitics,' *Theory, Culture & Society*, 26(6): 55–77.

Megill, Allan, (1994), Introduction: Four senses of objectivity, in Megill, Allan, ed., (1994), *Rethinking objectivity*, Durham: Duke University Press, pp. 1–20.

Merton, Robert K., (1973), *The sociology of science: Theoretical and empirical investigations*, ed. by Norman W. Storer, Chicago: University of Chicago Press.

Micale, Mark S., (1993), On the disappearance of hysteria: A study in the clinical deconstruction of a diagnosis, *Isis*, 84(3): 496–526.

Milburn, Colin, (2008), *Nanovision: Engineering the future*, Durham & London, Duke University Press.

Miller, Peter, (2001), Governing by numbers: Why calculative practices matter, *Social Research*, 68(2): 379–395.

Mir, Raza, Mir, Ali & Wong, Diana J., (2006), Diversity. The cultural logic of global capital? in Konrad, Alison M., Prasad, Pushkala & Pringle, Judith K., eds., (2006), *Handbook of workplace diversity*, Thousand Oaks, CA, London & New Delhi: Sage, pp. 167–188.

Mirowski, Philip & Van Horn, Robert, (2005), The contract research organization and the commercialization of scientific research, *Social Studies of Science*, 35(4): 503–548.

Mirowski, Philip and van Horn, Rob, (2009), The rise of the Chicago School of economics and the birth of neoliberalism, in Mirowski, Philip & Plehwe, Dieter, eds., (2009), *The road from Mont Pèlerin: The making of a the neoliberal thought collective*, Boston & London: Harvard University Press.

Mises, Ludwig von, (1944/1969), *Bureaucracy*, 2nd. ed., New Rochelle: Arlington House.

Mitchell, Robert and Waldby, Catherine, (2001), National biobanks: Clinical labor, risk production and the creation of biovalue, *Science, Technology & Human Values*, 35(2): 330–355.

Mol, Annemarie, (2002), *The body multiple: Ontology in medical practice*, Durham: Duke University Press.

Mol, Annemaire & Law, John, (2007), Embodied action, enacted bodies: The example of hypoglycaemia, in Burri, Regula Valérie & Dumit, Joseph, eds., (2007), *Biomedicine as culture: Instrumental practices, technoscientific knowledge, and new modes of life*, New York & London. Routledge, pp. 87–107.Monaghan, Lee F. Hollands, Robert & Pritchard, Gary, (2010), Obesity epidemic entrepreneurs: Types, practices and interests, *Body & Society*, 16(2): 13–71.

Mowery, D.C. & Ziedonis, A.A., (2002), Academic patent quality before and after the Bayh-Dole act in the United States, *Research Policy*, 31: 399–418.

Munck, Ronaldo, (2005), Neoliberalism and politics, and the politics of neoliberalism, in Saad-Filho, Alfredo and Johnston, Deborah, eds., (2005), *Neoliberalism: A critical reader*, London & Ann Arbor: Pluto, pp. 60–69.

Munos, Bernard, (2009), Lessons from 60 years of pharmaceutical innovation, *Nature, Nature Reviews*, 8: 959–968.

Murray, F. (2002), Innovation as co-evolution of scientific and technological networks: Exploring tissue economics, *Research Policy*, 31: 389–403.

Murray, Fiona, (2010), The oncomouse that roared: Hybrid exchanges as a source of distinction at the boundary of overlapping institutions, *American Journal of Sociology*, 116(2): 341–388.

Myles, Leslie, (2010), Quality assured science: Managerialism in forensic biology, *Science, Technology & Human Values*, 35(2): 283–306.

Myers, Natasha, (2008), Molecular embodiments and the body-work of modeling in protein crystallography, *Social Studies of Science*, 38: 163–199.

Navon, Daniel, (2011), Genomic designation: How genetics can delineate new, phenotypically diffuse medical categories, *Social Studies of Science*, 41(2): 203–226.

Negrin, Llewellyn, (2002), Cosmetic surgery and the eclipse of identity, *Body & Society*, 8(4): 21–42.

Nerkar, A. & Shane, S. (2007), Determinants of invention commercialization: An empirical examination of academically sourced inventions, *Strategic Management Journal*, 28: 1155–1166.

Newton, Tim, (2003), Crossing the great divide, *Sociology*, 37(3): 20–42.

Nightingale, Paul & Mahdi, Surya, (2006), The evolution of the pharmaceutical innovation, in Mazzucati, Mauss, M., (1954), *The gift: Forms and functions of exchanges in archaic societies*, London: Routledge and Kegan Paul.

Novas, C. & Rose, N. (2000), Genetic risk and the birth of the somatic individual, *Economy & Society*, 29: 485–513.

Oakes, L.S., Townley, B. & Cooper, D.J., (1998), Business planning as pedagogy: Language and control in a changing institutional field, *Administrative Science Quarterly*, 43: 257–292.

Oliver, Richard W., (2000), *The coming biotech age: The business of biomaterials*, New York: McGraw-Hill.

Orlikowski, Wanda J., (2007), Sociomaterial practices: Exploring technology at work, *Organization Studies*, 28(9): 1435–1448.

Orlikowski, Wanda J. (2010).The sociomateriality of organizational life: Considering technology in management research, *Cambridge Journal of Economics* (34): 125–141.

Orlikowski, Wanda J. & Scott, Susan V., (2008), Sociomateriality: Challenging the separation of technology, work, and organization, *Academy of Management Annals*, 2(1): 433–474.

Oudshoorn, Nelly, (2003), *The male pill: A biography of a technology in the making*, Durham & London: Duke University Press.

Oudshoorn, Nelly & Somers, André, (2007), Constructing the digital patient: patient organization and the development of health websites, in Burri, Regula Valérie & Dumit, Joseph, eds., (2007), *Biomedicine as culture: Instrumental practices, technoscientific knowledge, and new modes of life*, New York & London. Routledge, pp. 205–222.

Owen-Smith, Jason, (2001), Managing laboratory work through scepticism: Processes of evaluation and control, *American Sociological Review*, 66: 427–452.

Owen-Smith, Jason & Powell, Walter W., (2004), Knowledge networks as channels and conduits: The effects of spillovers in the Boston Biotechnology community, *Organization Science*, 15(1): 5–21.

Oyama, Susan, (2000), *Evolution's eye: A systems view of the biology-culture divide*, Durham: Duke University Press.

Pande, Amrita, (2009), "It may be her eggs but it's my blood": Surrogates and everyday forms of kinship in India, *Qualitative Sociology*, 32: 379–397.

Parry, Benita, (2004), *Postcolonial studies: A materialist critique*, London & New York: Routledge.

Parry, Bronwyn, (2004), *Trading the genome: Investigating the commodification of bio-information*, New York: Columbia University Press.

Peet, Richard, (2007), *Geography of power. The making of global economic policy*, London & New York: Zed Books.

Perrow, C., (1986), *Complex organizations: A critical perspective*, New York: McGraw-Hill.

Petryna, Adriana, (2006), Globalizing human subjects research, in Petryna, Adriana, Lakoff, Andrew & Kleinman, Arthur, eds., (2006), *Global pharmaceuticals: Ethics, markets, practices,* Durham & London: Duke University Press, pp. 33–60.

Petryna, Adriana, (2009), *When experiments travel: Clinical trials and the global search for human subjects*, Durham & London: Duke University Press.

Pfaffenberg, Brian, (1988), Fetishised objects and humanized nature: Towards an anthropology of technology, *Man*, 23: 236–252.

Pfaffenberg, Brian, (1992), Social anthropology of technology, *Annual Review of Anthropology*, 21: 491–516.

Pfeffer, Jeffrey, (1993), Barriers to the advance of organizational science: Paradigm development as a dependent variable, *Academy of Management Review*, 18(4): 599–620.

Pfeffer, Jeffrey & Sutton, Robert I.; (2006), *Hard facts, dangerous half-truths, and total nonsense: Profiting from evidence-based management,* Boston: Harvard Business School Press.

Pickering, Andrew, (1995), *The mangle of practice: Time, agency, and science,* Chicago & London: University of Chicago Press.

Pickering, Andrew (2010), *The cybernetic brain: Sketches of another future*, Chicago & London: University of Chicago Press.

Pickstone, John V., (2011), Sketching together the modern histories of science, technology, and medicine, *Isis*, 102(1): 123–133

Pisano, Gary O., (2006), *Science business: The promise, the reality and the future of biotech*, Boston: Harvard Business School Press.

Pitts-Taylor, Victoria, (2007), *Surgery junkies: Wellness and pathology in cosmetic culture*, New Brunswick: Rutgers University Press.

Pitts-Taylor, Victoria, (2010), The plastic brain: Neoliberalism and the neuronal self, *Health*, 14(6): 635–652.

Plehwe, Dieter & Walpen, Bernhard, (2006), Between network and complex organization: The making of neoliberal knowledge and hegemony, in Plehwe, Dieter, Walpen, Bernhard & Neunhöffer, Gisela, eds., (2006), *Neoliberal hegemony: A global critique*, New York & London: Routledge, pp. 27–50.

Porter, Theodore M., (2009), How science became technical, *Isis*, 100: 292–309.

Powell, Walter W. & Grodal, Stine, (2005), Networks of innovation, in Fagerberg, Jan, Mowery, David C. & Nelson, Richard R., eds., *The Oxford handbook of innovation*, Oxford & New York: Oxford University Press, pp. 56–85.

Powell, W.W., Koput, K.W., White, D.R. & Owen-Smith, J., (2005), Network dynamics and field evolution: The growth of interorganizational collaboration in the life sciences, *American Journal of Sociology*, 110(4): 1132–1205.

Prainsack, Barbara, Gesink, Ingrid & Franklin, Sarah, (2008), Stem cell technologies, 1998–2008: Controversies and silences, *Science as Culture*, 17(4): 351–362.

Prasad, Amit, (2009), Capitalizing disease: Biopolitics of drug trails in India, *Theory, Culture & Society*, 26(5): 1–29.

Preda, Alex, (2009), *Information, knowledge and economic life: An introduction to the sociology of markets*, Oxford & New York. Oxford University Press.

Prentice, Rachel, (2005), The anatomy of surgical simulations: The mutual articulation of bodies in and through the machine, *Social Studies of Science*, 35(6): 837–866.

Pulley, Thomas I., (2005), From Keynesianism to neoliberalism: Shifting paradigms in economics, in Saad-Filho, Alfredo & Johnston, Deborah, eds., (2005), *Neoliberalism: A critical reader*, London & Ann Arbor: Pluto, pp. 20–29.

Quéré, Michel, (2004), The post-genome era: Rupture in the organization of the life science industry, in McKelvey, Maureen, Rickne, Annika & Laage-Hellman, Jens, eds., (2004), *The economic dynamics of modern biotechnology*, Cheltenham Northampton: Edward Elgar, pp. 76–98.

Raab, Jörg & Kenis, Patrick, (2009), Heading toward a society of networks: Empirical developments and theoretical challenges, *Journal of Management Inquiry*, 18(3): 198–210.

Rabinow, Paul, (1992), Artificiality and enlightenment: From sociobiology to biosociality, in Crary, Jonathan & Kwinter, Sanford, eds., (1992), *Incorporations*, New York: Zone Books, pp.234–251.Rabinow, Paul, (1996), *Making PCR: A story of biotechnology*, Chicago & London: The University of Chicago Press.

Rabinow, Paul, (1999), *French DNA. Trouble in purgatory*, Chicago & London: University of Chicago Press.

Rabinow, Paul, Marcus, George E., Faubion, James D. & Rees, Tobias, (2008), *Designs for an anthropology of the contemporary*, Durham & London: Duke University Press.

Rader, Karen Ann, (2004), *Making mice: Standardizing animals for American biomedical research*, Princeton: Princeton University Press.

Rafferty, M. (2008), The Bayh-Dole act and university research and development, *Research Policy*, 37: 29–40.

Raman, Sujatha & Tutton, Richard, (2010), Life, science, and biopower, *Science, Technology & Human Values*, 35(5): 711–734.

Ramirez, Paulina & Tylecore, Andrew, (2004), Hybrid corporate governance and its effects on innovation. A case study of AstraZeneca, *Technology Analysis & Strategic Management*, 16(1): 97–119.

Reay, T. & Hinings, C.R., (2009), Managing the rivalry of competing institutional logics. *Organization Studies*, 30(6): 629–652.

Rheinberger, Hans-Jörg, (1997), *Toward a history of epistemic things: Synthesizing proteins in the test tube*, Stanford: Stanford University Press.

Rheinberger, Hans-Jörg, (2010), *The epistemology of the concrete: Twentieth-century histories of life*, Durham & London: Duke University Press.

Rifkin, Jeremy, (1998), *The biotech century: Harnessing the gene and remaking the world*, New York: Penguin Putnam.

Roach, Mary, (2003), *Stiff: The curious lives of human cadavers*, New York: W.W. Norton & Company.

Roberts, Celia, (2007), *Messengers of sex: Hormones, biomedicine and feminism*, Cambridge: Cambridge University Press.

Rose, Nikolas , (2007a), *The politics of life itself: Biomedicine, power and subjectivity in the twenty-first century*, Princeton & Oxford: Princeton University Press.

Rose, Nikolas, (2007b), Genomic susceptibility as an emergent form of life? Genetic testing, identity, and the remit of medicine, in Burri, Regula Valérie & Dumit, Joseph, eds., (2007), *Biomedicine as culture: Instrumental practices, technoscientific knowledge, and new modes of life*, New York & London. Routledge, pp. 141–150.

Rosenberg, Charles & Golden, Janet, eds., (1997), *Framing disease: Studies in cultural history*, Brunswick: Rutgers University Press.

Rosoff, Philip, (2010), In search of the mommy gene: Truth and consequences in behavioral genetics, *Science, Technology & Human Values*, 35(2): 200–243.

Rothaermel, F.T., Agung, S.D & Jiang, L. (2007), University entrepreneurship: A taxonomy of the literature, *Industrial and Corporate Change*, 16(4): 691–791.

Rothaermel, Frank T. & Thursby, Marie, (2007), The nanotech versus the biotech revolution: Sources of productivity in incumbent firm research, *Research Policy*, 36(6): 832–849.

Rubin, Beatrix P., (2008), Therapeutic promise in the discourse of human embryonic stem cell research, *Science as Culture*, 17(1): 13–27.

Rushkoff, Douglas, (2009), *Life, inc.: How the world became a corporation and how to take it back*, London: Vintage.

Saad-Filho, Alfredo & Johnston, Deborah, (2005), Introduction, in Saad-Filho, Alfredo and Johnston, Deborah, eds., (2005), *Neoliberalism: A critical reader*, London & Ann Arbor: Pluto, pp. 3–6.

Said, Edward W., (1979), *Orientalism*, New York: Vintage Books.

Salter, Brian & Salter, Charlotte, (2007), Bioethics and the global moral economy: The cultural politics of human embryonic stem cell science, *Science, Technology & Human Values*, 32(5): 554–581.

Samuel. Sajay & Dirsmith, MarkW., McElroy, Barbara, (2005), Monetized medicine: From the physical to the fiscal, *Accounting, Organization and Society* 30: 249–278.

Sanal, Aslihan, (2011), *New organs within us: Transplant and the moral economy*, Durham & London: Duke University Press.

Sauder, Michael, & Espeland, Wendy Nelson, (2009), The discipline of rankings: Tight coupling and organization change, *American Sociological Review*, 74: 63–82.

Scheper-Hughes, Nancy, (2000), The global traffic in human organs, *Current Anthropology*, 41: 191–211.

Schickore, Jutta, (2007), *The microscope and the eye: A history reflection, 1740–1870*, Chicago & London: University of Chicago Press.

Schmittlein, David C. & Morrison, Donald G., (2003), A live baby or your money back: The marketing of in vitro fertilization procedures, *Management Science*, 49(12): 1617–1835.

Schrödinger, Erwin, (1946), *What is life? Physical aspects of the living cell*, Cambridge: Cambridge University Press.

Schrödinger, Erwin, (1958), *Mind and matter*, Cambridge: Cambridge University Press.

Schultz, Majken, Hatch, Mary Jo & Larsen, Mogens Holten, eds., (2000), *The expressive organization: Linking identity, reputation, and the corporate brand*, Oxford: Oxford University Press.

Scott, Richard W. (2004), Reflections on a half-century of organizational sociology, *Annual Review of Sociology*, 30: 1–21.

Selin, Cynthia, (2007), Expectations and the emergence of nanotechnology, *Science, Technology & Human Values*, 32(2): 196–220.

Serres, Michel, Ed., (1995), *A history of scientific thought*, Oxford: Blackwell.

Shah, Sonia, (2006), *The body hunters: Testing new drugs on the world's poorest patients*, London & New York: New Press.

Shapin, Steven, (1994), *A social history of truth: Civility and science in seventeenth-century England*, Chicago & London: Chicago of University Press.

Shapin, Steven, (2008), *The scientific life: A moral history of a late modern vocation*, Chicago: University of Chicago Press.

Sharp, Lesley, (2000), The commodification of the body and its parts, *Annual Review of Anthropology*, 29: 287–328.

Sharp, Lesley A. (2003), *Strange harvest: Organ transplants, denatured bodies, and the transformed self*, Berkeley, Los Angeles & London: University of California Press.

Sharp. Lesley A., (2011), The invisible woman: The bioaesthetics of engineered bodies, *Body & Society*, 17(1): 1–30.

Shaviro, Steven, (2010), Interstitial life: Remarks on causality and purpose in biology, in Gaffney, Peter, ed., (2010), *The force of the virtual: Deleuze, science, and philosophy*, Minneapolis & London: University of Minnesota Press, pp. 133–146.

Shilling, Chris, (1993), *The body and social theory*, London, Thousand Oaks, CA & New Delhi: Sage.

Shostak, Sara, (2009), The emergence of toxiocogenomics. A case study of molecularization, *Social Studies of Science* 13: 539–562.

Shostak, Sara & Conrad, Peter, (2008), Sequencing and its consequences: Path dependence and the relationships between genetics and medicalization, *American Journal of Sociology*, 114: S287-S316 (special issue on biomedicalization).

Simmel, Georg, ([1916]2005), *Rembrandt: An essay in the philosophy of art*, trans. by Alan Scott & Helmut Straubmann, London & New York: Routledge.

Simondon, Gilbert, (1964/1992), The genesis of the individual, in Crary, Jonathan & Kwinter, Sanford, eds., (1992), *Incorporations*. New York: Zone Books, pp.297–319.

Simondon, Gilbert, ([1958]1980), *On the mode of existence of technical objects*, Trans. by Ninian Mallahphy, London: University of Western Ontario.

Simonds, Wendy, (1996), *Abortion at work: Ideology and practice in a feminist clinic*, New Brunswick: Rutgers University Press.

Sklair, Leslie, (2002), *The transnational capitalist class*, London & New York: Routledge.

Skloot, Rebecka, (2010), *The immortal life of Henrietta Lacks*, New York: Crown Publishers.

Smith, Helen, (2009), Umbilical cord blood banks: Modern day alchemy, *Journal of Commercial Biotechnology*, 15(3): 236–244.

Smith, H.L. & Bagni-sen, S., (2006), University-industry interactions: The case of UK biotechnology, *Industry & Innovation*, 13(4), 371–392.

Smith Hughes, Sally, (2001), Making dollars out of DNA: The first major patent in biotechnology and the commercialization of molecular biology, 1974–1980, *Isis*, 92(3): 541–575.

Solanas, Valerie, (1996), *SCUM manifesto*, Edinburgh & San Francisco: AK Press.

Sorkin, Andrew Ross, (2009), *Too big to fail: The insider story of how Wall Street and Washington fought to save the financial system—and themselves*, New York: Viking.

Spar, Deborah L., (2006), *The baby business: How money, science, and politics drive the commerce of conception*, Boston: Harvard Business School Press.

Spinoza, Baruch, (1994), *Ethics*, London: Penguin.

Spivak, Gayatri Chakravorti, (1987), *In other worlds: Essays in cultural politics*, New York & London: Methuen.

Spivak, Gayatri Chakravorty, (1990), *The post-colonial critique: Interviews, strategies, dialogues*, Ed. by Sarah Harasym, London & New York: Routledge.

Squire, Susan Merrill, (2004), *Liminal lives: Imaging the human at the frontiers of biomedicine*, Durham & London: Duke University Press.

Star, Susan Leigh, (1999), The ethnography of infrastructure, *American Behavioral Scientist*, 43(3): 377–391

Starbuck, William H., (2003), Shouldn´t organization theory emerge from adolescence? *Organization*, 10(3): 439–452.

Standage, Tom, (1998), *The Victorian internet: The remarkable story of the telegraph and the nineteenth century's online pioneers*, London: Weidenfeld & Nicolson.

Sternitzke, Christian, (2010), Knowledge sources, patent protection, and commercialization of pharmaceutical innovation, *Research Policy*, 39: 810–821.

Stiglitz, Joseph E., (2010), *Freefall: America, free markets, and the sinking of the world economy*, New York & London: W.W. Norton.

Stinchcombe, Arthur L., (1995), *Sugar island slavery in the age of enlightenment: The political economy of the Caribbean world*, Princeton & London: Princeton University Press.

Stuart, Toby E. & Ding, Waverly W., (2006), When do scientists become entrepreneurs? The social structural antecedents of commercial activity in the academic life sciences, *American Journal of Sociology*, 112(1): 97–114.

Suchman, L.A., (2007), *Human-machine reconfigurations: Plans and situated actions*, Cambridge: Cambridge University Press.

Suddaby, R. & Greenwood, R., (2005), Rhetorical strategies of legitimacy, *Administrative Science Quarterly*, 50: 35–67.

Sunder Rajan, Kaushik, (2006), *Biocapital: The constitution of postgenomic life*, Durham: Duke University Press.

Swann, John P., (1988), *Academic scientists and the pharmaceutical industry*, Baltimore & London: Johns Hopkins University Press.

Taylor, Janelle S., (2005), Surfacing the body's interior, *Annual Review of Anthropology*, 34: 741–756.

Terranova, Tiziana, (2004), *Network culture*, London: Pluto.

Thacker, Eugene, (1999), Performing the technoscientific body: Real video surgery and the anatomy theatre, *Body & Society*, 5(2–3): 117–136.

Thacker, Eugene, (2003), Data made flesh: Biotechnology and the discourse of the posthuman, *Cultural Critique* 53 (special issue on posthumanism, winter 2003).

Thacker, Eugene, (2004), *Biomedia*, Minneapolis & London.: University of Minnesota Press.

Thacker, Eugene, (2006), *The global genome: Biotechnology, politics and culture*, Cambridge & London: MIT Press.

Thacker, Eugene, (2010), *After life*, Chicago & London: University of Chicago Press.

Thomas, David, (1995), Feedback and cybernetics: Reimaging the body in the age of the cyborg, in Featherstone, Mike & Burrows, Roger, eds., (1995),*Cyberspace/cyberbodies/cyberpunk: Cultures of technological representations*, London: Sage.

Thompson, Charis, (2005), *Making parents: The ontological choreography of reproductive technologies*, Cambridge: MIT Press.

Thornton, Patricia H. & Ocasio, William, (2008), Institutional logics, in Greenwood, Royston, Oliver, Christine, Sahlin, Kerstin & Suddaby, Roy, eds., (2008), *The Sage handbook of organizational institutionalism*, London, Thousand Oaks, CA & New Delhi: Sage, pp. 99–129.

Throsby, Karen, (2009), The war on obesity as a moral project: Weight loss drugs, obesity surgery and negotiating failure, *Science as Culture*. 18(2): 210–216.

Timmermans, Stefan, (2008), Professions and their work: Do market shelters protect professional interests? *Work and Occupations*, 35(2): 164–188.

Timmermans, Stefan & Berg, Marc, (1997), Standardization in action: Achieving local universality through medical protocols, *Social Studies of Science*, 27(2): 273–305.

Titmuss, Richard M., (1970), *The gift relationship: From human blood to social policy*, London: George Allen & Unwin.

Tober, Diane M., (2001), Semen as gift, semen as good: Reproductive workers and the market in altruism, *Body & Society*, 7(2–3): 137–160.

Torgersen, Helge, (2009), Fuzzy genes: Epistemic tensions in genomics, *Science as Culture*. 18(1):65–87.

Turner, Barry S., (1992), *Regulating bodies: Essays in medical sociology*, London: Routledge.

Turner, Barry S., (1996), *The body and society*, London, Thousand Oaks, CA & New Delhi: Sage.

Twine, France Winddance, (2011), *Outsourcing the womb: Race, class and gestational surrogacy in a global market*, London & New York: Routledge.

Vemuri, Goutham & Nielsen, Jens, (2008), Systems biology: Is the hope worth the hype? *SIM News*, Sept.–Oct., 58(5): 177–188.

Vestergaard, J., (2007), The entrepreneurial university revisited: Conflicts and the importance of role separation, *Social Epistemology*, 21(1), 41–54.

Vrecko, Scott, (2008), Capital ventures into biology: Biosocial dynamics in the industry and science of gambling, *Economy & Society*, 37(2): 50–67.

Vrecko, Scott, (2010), Global and everyday matters of consumption: On the productive assemblage of pharmaceuticals and obesity, *Theory & Society*, 39: 555–573.

Wacquant, Loïc J. D., (2009), *Punishing the poor: The neoliberal government of social insecurity*, Durham & London: Duke University Press.

Waldby, Catherine, (2000), *The visible human project: Informatics bodies and posthuman medicine*, London & New York; Routledge.

Waldby, Catherine, (2002), Stem cells, tissue cultures, and the production of bio-value, *Health*, 6(3): 305–322.

Waldby, Cathy & Cooper, Melinda, (2007), The biopolitics of reproduction: Post-fordist biotechnology and women's clinical labour, *Australian Feminist Studies*, 23(55): 57–73.

Waldby, Cathy, & Mitchell, Robert, (2006), *Tissue economies: Blood, organs, and cell lines in late capitalism*, Durham & London. Duke University Press.

Walkenhauer, Olaf, (2001), Systems biology: The reincarnation of systems theory applied in biology? *Briefings in Bioinformatics*, 2(2): 258–270.

Warwick, Andrew, (2005), X-ray as evidence in German orthopedic surgery, 1985–1900, *Isis*, 96: 1–24.

Washburn, Jennifer, (2005), *University Inc.: The corruption of higher education*, New York: Basic Books.

Watkins, Elizabeth S., (2001), *On the pill: A social history of oral contraceptives, 1950–1970*, Baltimore & London: Johns Hopkins University Press.

Weeks, John, (2004), *Unpopular culture: The rituals of complaints in a British bank*, Chicago: University of Chicago Press.

Wiener, Norbert (1948), *Cybernetics, or control and communication in the animal machine*, New York: John Wiley.

Wiener, Norbert, (1950), *The human use of human beings*, London: Eyre & Spottiswoode.

Wilkinson, Stephen, (2006), *Bodies for sale: Ethics and exploitation in the human body trade*, London & New York: Routledge.

Willse, Craig, (2010), Neo-liberal biopolitics and the invention of chronic homelessness, *Economy & Society*, 39(2): 144–184.

Witz, Anne, (2000), Whose body matters? Feminist sociology and the corporeal turn in sociology and feminism, *Body & Society*, 6(2): 1–24.

Yakubovich, Valery, Granovetter, Mark & McGuire, Patrick, (2005), Electric charges: The social construction of rate systems, *Theory & Society*, 34: 579–612.

Young, Robert Y.C., (2001), *Postcolonialism: An historical introduction*, Oxford & Malden: Blackwell.

Youtie, J., Libaers, D. & Bozeman, B, (2006), Institutionalization of university research centers: The case of the national cooperative program in infertility research. *Technovation*, 26(9): 1055–1063.

Zajac, E.J. and Westphal, J.D., (2004), The social construction of stock market value: Institutionalization and learning perspectives on stock market reactions, *American Sociological Review*, 69: 433–457.

Zald, Meyer N. and Lounsbury, Michael, (2010), The wizards of Oz: Towards an institutional approach to elites, expertise, and command posts, *Organization Studies*, 31(7): 963–996.

Zaloom, C., (2006), *Out of the pits: Trading and technology from Chicago to London*, Durham & London: Duke University Press.

Zelizer, Vivianne, (2005), *The purchase of intimacy*, Princeton: Princeton University Press.

Zelizer, Viviana, (2007), Pasts and futures of economic sociology, *American Behavioral Scientist*, 50(8): 1056–1069.

Žižek, Slavoj, (2009), *First as tragedy, then as farce,* New York & London: Verso.

Zucker, L.G, Darby, M.R. & Armstrong, J.S., (2002), Commercializing knowledge: University science, knowledge capture, and firm performance in biotechnology, *Management Science*, 48(1), 138–153.

Zweiger, G., (2001), *Transducing the genome: Information, anarchy and revolution in the biomedical sciences*, New York: McGraw-Hill.

Index

Printed and bound by CPI Group (UK) Ltd, Croydon, CR0 4YY

18/10/2024

01776245-0003